Executive Defense

Executive Defense

Shareholder Power
and Corporate Reorganization

Michael Useem

Harvard University Press
Cambridge, Massachusetts
London, England
1993

Library of Congress Cataloging-in-Publication Data

Useem, Michael.
  Executive defense: shareholder power and corporate reorganization
/ Michael Useem.
      p.   cm.
  Includes bibliographical references and index.
  ISBN 0-674-27398-2 (alk. paper)
    1. Corporate governance—United States—Case studies.
2. Corporations—United States—Investor relations—Case studies.
3. Stockholders' voting—United States—Case studies. 4. Stock
ownership—United States—Case studies. 5. Directors of
corporations—United States—Case studies. 6. Organizational
change—United States—Case studies. 7. Industrial management—
United States—Case studies. I. Title.
HD2785.U848   1993
658.4'063—dc20   92-36914
                                                               CIP

Acknowledgments

This account had its origins in a research project sponsored by the National Planning Association (NPA), a project that studied change and restructuring in the American workforce. Edward Masters, then president of NPA, Phillip Ray, a vice-president, and an NPA working committee had opened the doors of several large corporations for a research team headed by economist Peter Doeringer, making it possible for this team to examine how companies were responding to an unusually large number of workforce problems. In the course of completing this study (later published as *Turbulence in the American Workplace* by Oxford University Press), I had occasion to talk with a number of managers at several large firms. One company was in the throes of dismissing several thousand employees; another had just redeployed several thousand. The recent leveraged buyout of RJR Nabisco and the escalating bids of hostile raiders seemed much on the minds of many managers, and not simply out of idle curiosity.

Following discussions with Masters, Ray, and Doeringer, I developed a proposal for an inside look at the impact of restructuring on senior management and company organization at a select set of firms. The National Planning Association provided funding for the project, and then helped me gain access to those companies. Such inside access was essential: without direct discussions with people at the center of events, I felt, the events could not be pieced together. Tireless efforts by Edward Masters, early groundwork by Phillip Ray, and facilitating actions by firms associated with NPA enabled me to gain access to the highest levels of six major corporations.

A seventh corporation was later added through the offices of another individual, whose assistance was indispensable. On entering the companies, I received generous support from a number of managers. Though I cannot identify them here because of guarantees of confidentiality, I thank them all for their willingness to share their time and experience and thus to provide the essential foundation for the study's completion.

Two other initiatives supplied informative backdrops for the present inquiry. The Sloan School of Management of the Massachusetts Institute of Technology, where I had served as a visiting scholar and faculty member in 1989–1990, brought together a group of researchers and managers for a cross-disciplinary assessment of the motors of organizational change. The dialogue that transpired during two Sloan-sponsored conferences and preparation of an edited book (*Transforming Organizations,* also published by Oxford University Press) pointed to the value of examining systemic corporate change. A number of Sloan colleagues and book contributors were helpful here; I extend particular thanks to Thomas Kochan, Paul Osterman, and Robert Thomas.

At about the same time, I also had the good fortune to be associated with the Institutional Investor Project of the Center for Law and Economic Studies, Columbia University. Though the research I did at that time is the subject of a forthcoming study, my travels in connection with the project enabled me to gather background information for the present study. I had very useful discussions with a number of people affiliated with the project, especially Bernard Black, Carolyn Kay Brancato, John M. Conley, Louis Lowenstein, Ira M. Millstein, and William M. O'Barr.

In addition, I am grateful to a number of other individuals who provided research suggestions, comments on the manuscript, or other forms of assistance. These people include Howard Aldrich, University of North Carolina, Chapel Hill; James Auerbach and Malcolm R. Lovell, Jr., National Planning Association; Lance Berger, LBA Consulting Group; Fred Block and John Roemer, University of California, Davis; Val Burris, University of Oregon; Dan Clawson, University of Massachusetts, Amherst; Gerald F. Davis, Paul Hirsch, and Arthur S. Stinchcombe, Northwestern University; Paul DiMaggio and Paul Starr, Princeton University; Russell Epker, Berkshire Partners; Amitai Etzioni, George Washington University; Sandra D. Ford and Stephen E. Gross, Hay Management Consultants; Martin Gottlieb, Hewlett-Packard; Mark Granovetter and Michael Schwartz, State University of New York, Stony Brook; Edwin S. Harwood, Boston University; David Jacobs, University of Oregon; Donald Lessard, Robert McKersie, William Pound, and Edgar Schein, Massachusetts Institute of Technology; William F. Mahoney and Louis M. Thompson, Jr., National Investor Relations Institute; Donald McCabe, Fariborz Damanpour, and Nancy DiTomaso, Rutgers University; Mark Mizruchi and Mayer Zald, University of Michigan; Alan Neustadtl, University of Maryland, College Park; Peg O'Hara, Investor Responsibility Research Center; Michael Powers, Hewitt Associates; Maurice Punch, Nijenrode University, Netherlands Business School; David Riesman, Harvard University; Joseph Rosenbloom, WGBH, Boston; Stephanie Rosenfelt, Korn/ Ferry International; Richard H. Swedberg, Stockholm University; Eric Wanner, Russell Sage Foundation; and Harrison White, Columbia University.

I also received valuable suggestions from participants in the Economic Sociology Seminar, 1990–1992, sponsored by the Russell Sage Foundation; a conference entitled "Efficiency and Ownership: The Future of the Corporation," 1992, sponsored by the Program on Economy, Justice and Society, University of California, Davis; a Public Policy Seminar of the U.S. Office of Educational Improvement and Research, 1991, sponsored by the National Center on the Educational Quality of the Workforce; and several university seminars and colloquia.

Enormously helpful, as well, were my many discussions with colleagues and associates at the University of Pennsylvania, including Ivar Berg, Edward H. Bowman, Marlene E. Burkhardt, Peter Cappelli, William Evan, Constance Gager, Joseph W. Harder, Robert House, Jerry Jacobs, John Kimberly, Stephen Kobrin, Bruce Kogut, Robin Leidner, John Paul Mac-Duffie, Marshall Meyer, Tina Nemetz, Johannes M. Pennings, Samuel Preston, Peter Sherer, Harbir Singh, Jitendra Singh, Vicki Smith, Saskia Subramanian, Ross A. Webber, and Robert Zemsky. Michael Aronson of Harvard University Press provided guidance throughout the process of transforming thought to expression. His many suggestions and those of three reviewers have also been of great value.

Contents

1. THE RESTRUCTURING OF AMERICAN BUSINESS   1

    Learning about Restructuring and Alignment 3
    Organizational Alignment 5
    Defining Shareholder Value 10
    Corporate Stakeholders 11
    Issues in Organizational Alignment 14
    Rethinking Corporate Organization 16

2. THE RISE OF SHAREHOLDER POWER   19

    Turnover in Corporate Ownership 22
    The Rise of Institutional Shareholding 28
    Mobilization of Shareholder Pressure 33
    Shareholder Proposals 43
    Corporate Defenses 48
    Impact of Owner Challenges on Company Policies 51
    Conclusion 55

3. ORGANIZATIONAL ALIGNMENT   57

    Devolution of Authority 58
    Decentralized Planning and Business Development 62
    When Devolution Is Incomplete 65
    When Devolution Backfires 70
    Creating a Culture of Self-Reliance 71
    Measuring Decisions and Results 75
    Contraction of Central Management 79
    Conclusion 85

4. INTENSIFIED MANAGEMENT OF MANAGERS   89
  Knowledge of Management and Managerial Positions   90
  Managerial Investment in Managing Managers   94
  Managerial Misappointment   98
  Incentives in Management Compensation   101
  Spreading Contingent Compensation   102
  Linking Contingent Compensation to Shareholder Value   106
  The Problems of Asymmetry and Measurement in
     Linkage   111
  In the Minds of Managers   116
  Transforming Managers into Owners   119
  From Social Similarity to Managerial Performance   121
  Balkanization of Managerial Careers   124
  Conclusion   126

5. ALIGNING SHAREHOLDERS   129
  The Rise of Investor Relations   131
  Shareholder Communications   133
  Recruiting, Retaining, and Changing Investors   136
  Investors' Impatient Message   141
  Educating Unmotivated Learners   144
  Mobilizing Shareholder Support   146
  Preserving a Shareholder Rights Plan   149
  Conclusion   155

6. RESTRUCTURED AGENDAS FOR POLITICAL
   ACTION   158
  Contracted Corporate Action   159
  Political Action for Shareholder Value   164
  Fine-Tuning the Networks   168
  Political Action for State Protection   170
  Legislating State Protection   173
  Opting Out of State Protection   177
  The Accidental Element   180
  Weakened Classwide Political Action   181
  Conclusion   190

7. MOVING ALIGNMENT UP   191
  Directors' Compliance   192
  Representation of Shareholder Interests   195

Aligning the Board   200
Moving Alignment Out   210
Conclusion   214

8. THE PARADOXES OF MANAGEMENT AND
   OWNERSHIP   216
   The Paradox of Executive Power   217
   The Paradox of Preemptive Executive Action   219
   The Paradox of Internal Ownership   221
   Ideology for Action   223
   Managerial Action and Short-Term Gain   227
   Systemic Alignment   232
   Investor Capitalism   234
   Counterpoints   238
   Conclusion   243

   Appendix 1: A Note on Compiling Information   247

   *Appendix 2: Tables Related to the Rise of Shareholder
      Power   255*

   References   260

   Index   279

Executive Defense

The Restructuring of American Business

This book develops a single thesis. A managerial revolution early in the twentieth century moved control of many large corporations from owners to professional managers. Companies built organizational forms well suited to pursuing the managerial agenda. During the late 1980s and early 1990s, however, that revolution was challenged. Large shareholders rebelled, pressing companies to build organizational forms more suited to their purposes. As owners exercised new-found muscle, corporate structure was transformed. A driving principle behind this transformation was that the organization's architecture should be aligned more closely around what shareholders sought from their ownership stake.

The organizational change ramified into many reaches of corporate life. Headquarters staffs contracted, authority devolved into operating units, and compensation became more contingent upon performance. Change extended up to corporate governance. Managers sought formal safeguards against takeovers, and board terms were staggered. The effects of the organizational change also spilled outside the firm, reshaping the texture of American life. The new ownership alignment focused more company attention on shareholders, less on other stakeholders. Corporate political agendas shifted from fighting government regulation to resisting shareholder intrusion. Frequent redeployments and "rightsizings" left hundreds of thousands of employees numbed, and sometimes jobless.

Corporate realignment around ownership-defined objectives became an enduring axis of corporate reorganization during the late 1980s and early 1990s, and the consequences were enormous. For many people, even the casual science of personal observation confirmed the pervasive impact of restructuring. It seemed that nearly everybody had been touched by corporate restructuring, or knew somebody who had.

Here is one personal illustration. In 1987, while working on a project with a business-supported organization concerned with the future of college education, I visited New York for a meeting. The organization's office was on the twenty-second floor of a building known (because of its dark marble exterior) as the "black rock," located on Fifty-seventh Street, in the heart of a headquarters area favored by Fortune 500 companies, including McGraw-Hill, ITT, and Exxon. Getting off the elevator at the twenty-second floor, I expected to find the usual blend of busy receptionists and company bustle. Before me was, instead, a virtual corporate ghost town. The offices suggested former life. Desks were cluttered with unfinished work; filing cabinets bulged; personal mementos could be seen here and there. While artifacts abounded for the curious archaeologist to infer the past, no natives were available to corroborate the findings.

The building was the headquarters of CBS Incorporated, and the ghostly atmosphere was the result of a fateful board meeting just several months earlier. In an effort to reverse its sagging fortunes and stave off a wave of unwanted takeover threats (from Ivan F. Boesky, Ted Turner, and, earlier, an organization associated with conservative North Carolina senator Jesse Helms), CBS's chief executive Thomas Wyman went into the September 1986 board meeting seeking authorization to explore a purchase by Coca-Cola, a kind of "white-knight" defense. Instead, he came out of the meeting without his job, and the board handed control of the company to a hitherto unwanted suitor, Laurence A. Tisch, the major external shareholder (he held almost a quarter of its stock). In his capacity as CEO, Tisch could directly impose policies that he could not have implemented as a nonmanaging owner and director. He sold CBS's magazine and publishing divisions, dismissed executives, and cut employment by half. A single action in March 1987 eliminated 200 of 1,200 employees from CBS News, several prominent correspondents among them, in what became known as "the slaughter on 57th Street" (Boyer, 1988; Slater, 1988).

So swift was the downsizing that the twenty-second floor appeared to have been the victim of some radioactive flux, which decimated living creatures but left inanimate objects unscathed. The fallout had drifted up to the next floor, the location of CBS's personnel department. Here was the action that was missing one floor below: the office was flooded with paperwork relating to the overnight dismissals. Severance, pension, and health benefits for thousands of employees were being processed. But company resizing had reached this floor, too: the personnel staff had been cut from 120 to fifty. "We are down to just keeping our heads above water," said the vice-president for personnel. Later, our project group went out for a working lunch at a midtown restaurant. The maître d' warmly greeted one of our party, who was herself a casualty of the takeover. As we were seated, she whispered that the maître d' had been a colleague just several months back, one of CBS's more senior program managers.

Many readers will recall their own encounters with the results or residues of restructuring. The people affected came from all walks of life. They ranged from the high school graduate who attended a reunion and found his classmates obsessed with the ravages of company downsizing on their careers, to the division manager who had somehow survived four purchases and resellings of his operation in four years. As with home purchases and delayed airplane flights, almost everybody had a personal story to offer. The accounts frequently centered on the extraordinary human stress and personal costs involved. The *Wall Street Journal,* for instance, offered a graphic account of the toll that a leveraged buyout of Safeway Stores had taken on the firm's employees, 63,000 of whom lost their jobs (Faludi, 1990). Yet in many instances the restructuring improved the quality of worklife for those who remained. Survivors often reported having more authority to get their job done, being better rewarded for doing it well, and facing fewer bureaucratic pitfalls along the way. The events of the era displayed many edges.

In what follows, we will lift one central organizational thread from the variegated fabric of those reported experiences. Our focus will be on the organizational change induced by or structured around shareholder interests. Corporate restructuring affected other areas of corporate behavior. Impact on the employment environment and management of human resources, for example, was extensive (Buono and Bowditch, 1989; Doeringer et al., 1991; Napier, 1989; Smith, 1990). So, too, were the effects on financial performance, though the precise impact remains a subject of dispute (Auerbach, 1988; Coffee, Lowenstein, and Rose-Ackerman, 1988; Garrison, 1990; Weston, Chung, and Hoag, 1990; Lowenstein, 1991; Yago, 1991). Although these and other consequences of the restructuring process are not central to our account, aspects will appear as they bear on the shareholder-value alignment issues that are at the core of this book.

Learning about Restructuring and Alignment

I have based my arguments here on information from several sources, as no single source could generate enough of the picture. I interviewed an array of informed observers, attended seminars for company officials, and consulted company surveys and other research studies. To examine the organizational consequences first-hand, I also gathered information on the experiences of seven large corporations.

The seven companies had each undertaken significant restructuring during the late 1980s and early 1990s. In no instance had their ownership changed hands, but in every case they had experienced intensified shareholder pressures. I focused on this comparatively small set of companies to characterize the organizational change within. Given the complexity of these settings, which together employed nearly half a million people, a concentrated assessment was essential for capturing the thrust of the change.

The seven corporations would rank in the upper rungs of any size chart. The smallest company employed more than 10,000 people, and two firms more than 100,000 each. On the traditional *Fortune* magazine barometer, the four manufacturing companies I selected numbered among the Fortune 200, and the three service companies were among the top ten of their respective rankings. In terms of market value, all seven stood among the nation's largest 300 corporations. Institutional investors, a primary source of shareholder pressure, held more than half of the shares of all seven. By design, the companies' major product areas represented diverse sectors of the economy, as can be seen in Table 1.1.

Table 1.1. Characteristics of seven large corporations, 1989.[a]

Major product area	1989 revenue (in billions of dollars)	Employees (in thousands)	Percent of shares held by institutional investors	Market value rank[b]
Pharmaceuticals	2–5	20–50	60–70	Top 100
Special machinery	2–5	10–20	60–70	Top 300
Transportation	2–5	20–50	60–70	Top 100
Chemical products	5–10	20–50	50–60	Top 200
Retail services	5–10	>100	50–60	Top 100
Electrical products	>10	>100	50–60	Top 100
Financial services	>10[c]	50–100	60–70	Top 100

Sources: Company reports and records; Standard and Poor's *Stock Reports.*
a. Ranges rather than exact figures are provided to preserve company confidentiality.
b. Based on the number of outstanding shares times the share price on March 16, 1990.
c. Represents the company's assets.

I completed interviews with an array of senior managers at the seven firms. Among the interviewed executives were those responsible for operations, finance, human resources, industrial relations, strategic planning, public affairs, communications, legal affairs, acquisitions and divestitures, and investor relations. Interviews were also conducted with executives carrying general corporate responsibilities, including chief operating officers and presidents of major business units. The study's information is thus drawn from top staff members, heads of operating units, and general managers, cross-sections of the senior ranks common to most large companies (Donaldson and Lorsch, 1983). Many of those interviewed consented to requests for extensive follow-up discussions and reviews of company documents and files. All interviews and visits were completed in 1989–1991. (Further details on these and related sources of information are provided in Appendix 1.)

Because of the selective focus on a limited set of firms, the arguments that follow cannot be generalized with any certainty to other companies. Yet the recurrence of the alignment patterns in seven unrelated firms operating in divergent markets suggests that the forces giving rise to the alignment were shared or faced by many. Major organizational changes announced by General Motors, IBM, Xerox, Du Pont, and other companies during the early 1990s display striking parallels with the changes reported by these seven firms.

Organizational Alignment

Intensified focus on shareholder value during the late 1980s and early 1990s led to a stress on consistent, integrated linkages among major elements of company organization. Some firms tightened their focus on core businesses. Others disposed of office perquisites, extolling the virtues of a lean operation. Still others pushed more authority into the hands of those responsible for key operations. While the specific strategies for restructuring varied from firm to firm, an underlying objective was the enhancement of the company's worth to its owners.

The optimal strategy for enhancing shareholder value was far from certain, leading to varied courses of action. Yet out of the diverse actions emerged similar lines of organizational change, change that ramified into the ways that the companies organized their managerial systems. These lines of change are grouped together here under the concept of "alignment.'' Driving the alignment was an ownership-disciplined organizational logic. The logic stressed consistent, integrated linkages among the major elements of company organization, ranging from the distribution of authority and power to the structure of management development and succession. The logic guided organizational design, decision making, and performance assessment in comprehensive and consistent ways.

Many of the organizational changes described on the following pages received impetus from a host of factors. The catalog of sources for corporate change is long, from international competition and takeover threats to new information systems and executive turnover. Few organizational phenomena can be traced to as many independent sources as change in a company's basic design and decision-making procedures (Kanter, 1983; Kimberly and Quinn, 1984; Fligstein and Dauber, 1989; Campbell and Lindberg, 1991; Pettigrew and Whipp, 1991; Thomas, 1993).

By virtue of size alone, the seven companies chosen for study felt the touch of most such sources of change. Managers acknowledged responding to the sources, taking it for granted that much of an executive's job was to identify and respond to the changing internal and external environments. There were no surprises here. What was not expected, however, was the incessant operational reference back to shareholders as a benchmark for judging change. A reading of traditional works on managing change would have offered little forewarning. Thomas Peters and Robert Waterman's book *In Search of Excellence* (1982) offered extensive guidance on corporate innovation. Almost all of their exemplary companies were publicly traded, but company stockholders were not on stage. Only implicitly were ''America's best-run companies'' run best for their owners. One of the few early warnings had come from Peter Drucker, who in his book *The Unseen Revolution* (1976) had written of the rising power of pension funds. But most accounts made passing reference if any to owners as a source of corporate change. If senior management's mandate was to preemptively anticipate the major drivers of change, stockholders were not deemed to be among them.

Little wonder that shareholders so rarely appeared in such accounts, for the managerial revolution had long ago afforded executives the privilege of ignoring them if they so chose. Most did. Ritual obeisance to hallowed principles obligated due reference, of course. But such allusions carried little operational weight. Episodic assertions that the company was working for the shareholders without further reference to how it did so became one of the arts of public affairs.

What was strikingly evident among the seven companies was a cultural ambience in which the references were neither occasional nor a gloss. Daily movements in stock price, proxy challenges, analysts' reports, and investor complaints had etched an enduring presence. They were now a factor in management calculus, an impetus for change if not always a valued one. Many managers privately denigrated shareholder activists and their passive allies. Frequently repeated rhetorical questions carried the message: What did shareholders know about the daily process of producing wealth? Wasn't the fixation with short-term profit taking a sure path to corporate ruin? Despite the private derision, a normal by-product of any conflict, most managers had come to respect the activists' will and the latent powers of the still-silent majority.

In reading this investor challenge more seriously than in the past, management also did what it had not done in the past: it translated rhetoric into action. Rarely was the shift sharply demarcated. Instead, investor interests gradually acquired greater salience, as internal teeth were added to lofty principle. A new vocabulary evolved, most generally captured under the rubric "shareholder value." The vocabulary was increasingly applied to specific company decisions, ranging from the choice of new managers and development of strategic directions to performance review and executive compensation. Other sources of change continued to intrude or even dominate. Unabated were management concerns with globalization, customer service, and product quality. But to this list was added investor challenge.

A host of organizational features followed. Though seemingly disparate, they came from much the same cloth, and I draw them together here under the umbrella of alignment. The organizational logic of this ownership-disciplined alignment is related to the concepts of congruence, coherence, and kindred formulations that stress consistent fits among major organizational components (Nadler, 1977; Nadler and Tushman, 1988; Pettigrew and Whipp, 1991; Powell, 1992). It is also akin to Richard Cyert and James March's emphasis on an "aligning" of the goals of an organization's many components. Individuals and units, they argued, tend to pursue a range of personal and local goals, goals often at odds with organizational objectives (Cyert and March, 1963). A central task of any organization, then, is to make these individual and unit goals consistent with its overarching objectives.

The special stress on ownership discipline, however, meant that acceptable forms of alignment were explicitly defined and evaluated according to the criteria of shareholder value. This organizational logic was distinct from the configuration that had long prevailed in many firms, that of manager-controlled alignment. The latter was the organizational system that had come to dominate under the protective shroud of the managerial revolution.

The concept of organizational logic here implies that organizational designs, decisions, and evaluations are repeatedly tested against their contribution to shareholder value. It does not mean that there is a single preferred practice, or that the optimal course of action can be readily identified. Nor does it signify that the best or even just better actions are taken. Competing organizational logics often dictate other courses. And the usual array of organizational uncertainties and information limitations ensure that the results of the ownership-disciplined alignment are frequently far from what might be ideally prescribed or expected. Still, the concept does imply that the rise of shareholder power made investor wealth more salient in the actions of the companies studied here. Managers differed in how this principle should be applied, and they varied in the weight placed on it against competing claims. But they shared some agreement on the principle, and when they compared alternative courses of action, it became clear that shareholder value had acquired more importance than in the past.

These elements together constituted what Ann Swidler (1986) might term a management's new "cultural repertoire" or "strategy of action." Executives acquired a fresh cognitive and interpretive frame for making and evaluating major decisions. Ownership-disciplined alignment did not contain explicit guidance on specific decisions, but it did furnish a template for judging and specifying such actions. It offered what David Cohen and Michael Garet (1975, p. 21) have called a "grand story": a "large and loose set of ideas" about how a company works, "why it goes wrong and how it can be set right." The story placed daily evidence and experience in a context of general ideas, presumptions, and judgments about a company's present condition and future direction.

The concepts of organizational logic and alignment also display parallels with organizational concepts developed by other analysts. One group of analysts, for example, advanced a concept akin to organizational logic to explain enduring cross-national variations in business systems. A second group developed a concept akin to alignment to explain why some companies had successfully revitalized while others attempting to do so had failed.

In seeking to characterize the systems of business in several East Asian nations, Marco Orru, Nicole Biggart, and Gary Hamilton identified three distinctive models, each with its own driving logic (Orru, Biggart, and Hamilton, 1991; Biggart, 1991). The three models were based on separate "principles that provide coherent logic for competitive economic action" and "shape organizational behavior and structure." Japanese firms, these analysts argued, followed a "communitarian logic," Korean firms a "patrimonial logic," and Taiwanese firms a "patrilineal logic." The differing logics led to distinctive workplace designs, contracts among firms, investment strategies, and a host of other managerial decisions. None dictated a particular course of action, but each provided a template for preferred directions. So deeply were the principles embedded in management cultures and organizational patterns that, although socially constructed, they were taken to be natural and necessary guides to management actions in their respective national settings.

In seeking to explain why some companies had successfully revitalized their cultures and operations, Michael Beer, Russell Eisenstat, and Bert Spector found that a key component was what they called "task alignment" (Beer et al., 1990). They compared companies that had achieved "corporate renewal" with a matched set of companies that had not. The differing courses could not be explained, these analysts found, by the initiation of quality circles, management education, and other stock changes that would have been expected to make a difference. Both the revitalized companies and the comparison group had implemented many such efforts. What was found to distinguish the two sets, instead, was whether the firms practiced what these analysts termed "task alignment." This entailed a sharpening of employee understanding of company objectives, a focusing on company resources around these objectives, and a tightening of organizational support, such as linking performance appraisal and compensation systems more explicitly to the objectives. The successfully revitalized firms had reconfigured work responsibilities and job designs to focus work tasks more precisely on achieving the objectives of the business unit and company. They were also better able on a company-wide basis to build on local innovations within their various business units.

The organizational logic of ownership-disciplined alignment observed in the seven corporations studied here carried its own distinctive blend of elements. The emergent company organization could hardly be characterized as communitarian or patrimonial. And the specific objectives were formulated with reference to shareholder value, not revitalization for its own sake. Yet the generic similarities are evident, suggesting that organizational logic and internal alignment can be useful concepts for understanding business systems and corporate change in a range of settings.

Defining Shareholder Value

In the logic of ownership-disciplined alignment, shareholder value becomes the central yardstick of organizational life. It is both a driver and measure of decisions and designs, and its specific definition thus has fundamental bearing on the thrust of organizational change. In its simplest form, a company's shareholder value can be defined as the worth of the firm as judged by the stockholders. In its complex reality, shareholder value became a blend of diverse stockholder preferences and managerial constructions of them.

Management specification of shareholder value exhibits parallels with an elected official's articulation of the public interest. Political leaders represent diverse constituencies with varying concerns and capacities for mobilizing their interests. Though relying upon polls, the media, and personal contact for reading constituency concerns, elected officials nonetheless exercise considerable discretion in deciding what policies best serve the general good.

Leaders of the seven companies studied represented constituencies with great diversity as well. Public pensions, mutual funds, and insurance companies shared some common ground as investors. But they also differed on such investment objectives as yield, growth, and voice. This is partly a matter of legal constraints, partly a matter of investment policy. Private pension fund managers are required by the federal Employee Retirement Income Security Act of 1974 to optimize financial benefits for fund participants; managers of public pensions, bank trusts, and investment houses carry fiduciary responsibilities defined by other federal and state statutes (Sommer, 1991).

Within these differing legal environments, investment styles further varied in their stress on short- and long-term holdings, low- and high-risk investments, and actively managed versus indexed funds. The diversity of the shareholder constituency gave company managers, like political leaders, latitude for interpreting what the constituency as a whole most valued.

The final interpretation acquired greater salience in the case of business than it did in the case of politics because there was to be a single output for the entire constituency—company performance—and little or no opportunity for allotting special benefits or favors to subgroups of shareholders.

Managers of the companies observed in this study generally chose to define shareholder value as a combination of stock dividends and share appreciation, accumulated over a period of years. Equally important, it was understood that it was distinct from traditional accounting measures of corporate achievement such as revenue growth or return on equity. Furthermore, the firms had each sought to make the concept operational, an essential first step for using it to make decisions and assess results.

At the electrical-products firm, for instance, a broad array of decisions had come to be judged by a central measure of shareholder value: growth in the company's stock price and its dividends over a period of several years. Similar definitions were shared by the other firms, though they differed on specific elements: the period for judging growth, minimum acceptable rates of growth, whether current growth rates were satisfactory to investors, and the extent to which faster growth could be achieved. However specified, each of the firms had defined some measure of shareholder value for operating purposes.

Corporate Stakeholders

Shareholders were but one of several constituencies seeking to shape a company's organizational logic. Government agencies imposed a range of regulations and reporting requirements; community leaders pressed for increased support of local nonprofit activities; and organized labor sought improved working conditions. A network of senior managers and directors of large corporations placed its own demands on companies, at times to promote general business aims not always shared by the individual companies. Still other corporate "stakeholders" sometimes expressed their voices. Among them were the company's creditors, unrepresented employees, customers, and suppliers (Freeman and Reed, 1983; Kreiner and Bhambir, 1991).

The interests of these constituencies in the outcomes of many decisions were similar to and sometimes identical to shareholder interests. But not always; and when they diverged, the organizational logic of ownership-disciplined alignment introduced systematic bias in favor of stockholders. Since the forces pressing for enhanced shareholder value were relatively new, competing organizational logics—above all that of management-controlled alignment—continued to dominate many companies. But the organizational logic of ownership-disciplined alignment had become more important in the seven firms studied.

Organizational logics other than those of management and shareholders receive little explicit attention here. This is because, in contrast to managerial and shareholder interests, they made only passing appearance in the discussions and information sources compiled during direct study of the seven corporations. I had entered the companies expecting considerable diversity in constituency pressures. Contrary to expectations, it became clear that company attention was riveted on the interests of a single external constituency.

This was evident, for instance, in the contrasting lack of attention paid to another external stakeholder, the company's major creditors. Financial institutions have long sought to influence and sometimes control the companies they finance (Kotz, 1978; Mintz and Schwartz, 1985; Stearns and Mizruchi, 1992). Commercial banks have furnished short-term loans, insurance companies have provided long-term financing, and investment banks have opened access to the bond and securities markets. All have held a stake in decisions by the borrower, and because of their pivotal role in financing growth and averting bankruptcy at critical junctures, they have been able to exert substantial influence on the borrower. In return for financing expansion, companies have placed bank and insurance officers on their boards; to avoid bankruptcy, firms have ceded powers to banking and insurance representatives (Glasberg, 1989). Investment banks played a powerful role in the formation and rise of large corporations in the early part of the century, and in helping smaller firms in recent years to obtain high-risk financing (Chandler, 1977; Yago, 1991).

Yet, in the seven companies studied, what might be termed the organizational logic of bank-disciplined alignment did not have nearly the presence of ownership-disciplined alignment. This was evident, for example, in the criteria that central management used in evaluating strategic plans and acquisition proposals from its business units. As discussed below, shareholder value was an explicit criterion at all seven of the companies. A broad array of the companies' senior managers justified their organizational design, decisions, and assessments with this criterion. By contrast, few cited relations with the lending side of banks or other creditors. The chief financial officer and chief executive focused on the company's banking relations, but such concerns found little echo in the concerns of others. Commercial bank trust departments, investment banks, and insurance companies were among the leading institutional investors for all of the companies, and their interests as shareholders did attract general management attention. Their interests as lenders, however, drew less. To the extent that financial institutions' lending sides did exercise influence on the internal organization and decisions of companies, the evidence here indicates that their voice, actual or imputed, was less audible than that of shareholder interests, at least in the areas examined in this study.

Still other organizational logics could be identified, but their salience during the late 1980s and early 1990s was found to be relatively muted as well. The logic of ownership-disciplined alignment was thus among the more pervasive and powerful of the organizational drivers evident, and it ramified into an array of company practices. The kinds of organizational changes described here have been observed in many firms, and components have been derived from financial, market, and managerial sources (Napier, 1989; Easterwood, Seth, and Singer, 1989). They acquired a distinctive cast during the late 1980s and early 1990s, however, as a result of the resurgence of shareholder power and the consequent emphasis on shareholder value. The cast was more systemic, more pervasive, and more precisely tied to shareholder value than in the past.

The impetus for change was often external, coming from aggrieved shareholders pressing for greater value from their investments. Sometimes the impetus was more internal, with alignment initiated long before the shareholder revolt had generated momentum. Whatever the source, the similar experiences evident among the seven diverse companies suggest that the organizational changes chronicled here were—or will be—on the agendas of other corporations as well.

Corporate decision making and change should not be overinterpreted with this framework, however. Decision-making criteria and sources of change are of course numerous, and many company actions were entirely unrelated to any logic of ownership-disciplined alignment. Some observed actions even ran counter to shareholder value, and others, as we shall see, were clearly intended to counter shareholder power. The organizational logic identified here should be seen as shaping and not determining company behavior. Moreover, it is a logic that at times led companies to challenge, not accede to, investor pressures. Sometimes companies applied the new principles; at other times they resisted shareholder entreaties; and at still others they rejected all proffered advice. Like any relations among mutually dependent organizations, company relations with shareholders were fraught with conflict, cooperation, and cooptation (Pfeffer and Salancik, 1978).

Issues in Organizational Alignment

My account begins with a brief chronicle of the rise of ownership power during the late 1980s and early 1990s, and the attendant emphasis on shareholder value. Set against the theory of the managerial revolution, Chapter 2 shows that turnover in the market for corporate control became more vigorous, that company ownership became concentrated among a small set of institutional investors, and that new means were created for the exercise of ownership influence on company management.

The organizational alignment resulting from this owners' challenge is the subject of Chapter 3. Here I shall focus on several primary components. First, authority to succeed and fail was pushed lower in the organization, giving managers and operating units greater autonomy. Second, measures of success and failure were altered to emphasize the value of actions for creating company value. Third, headquarters managerial and professional staffs were scaled back as administrative control yielded to financial oversight. Features of these components had made their appearance in a number of firms as a result of other developments. They acquired a distinct cast, however, as a result of the resurgence of ownership power. There was a cautionary tale here also, as the devolution of authority could backfire when those selected to exercise it fell short of the task.

Organizational alignment placed a premium on performance. Chapter 4 assesses the consequences of this emphasis for the management of managers. If individuals and units acquired more autonomy to perform, their independent actions had greater impact on the fortunes of the firm. Their actions could also do more grievous damage. The development and selection of managers thus became a more demanding activity. Compensation incentives linked to creating shareholder value became more important as well.

Company alignment efforts were not limited to redesigning the inside of the company. As shown in Chapter 5, such efforts were also directed at deflecting and diverting the source of the pressure for change. One avenue for resisting investor demands was reeducation, with initiatives undertaken to move shareholders from short-term petulance to longer-term patience. Failing that, efforts were made to reconstitute the shareholder base itself, replacing high-demand investors with more loyal, and more passive, stockholders. Organizations could be better configured to meet shareholder interests, but shareholders could also be better configured to meet management interests.

The intensified struggle between owners and managers for the soul of the firm extended into corporate political action. Public policy became an arena of active company action, and Chapter 6 focuses on the ways in which companies sought to alter their political environment. Already adept at managing their political worlds from years of lobbying in Washington and state capitals, companies readily adapted the strategies of managing for political advantage to managing for investor advantage. Traditional forms of business outreach, especially giving by corporate political action committees to congressional candidates, and giving by company foundations to nonprofit organizations, were tightened and redirected. And in one of the more ironic consequences of the struggle for corporate control, companies sought state protection. Business had long been antagonistic toward public regulation, but when confronted with hostile raiders and fellow-traveler investors, many firms opted for legislative protection. By 1990, almost all states with major corporate headquarters had passed antitakeover laws.

Lodged between shareholders and managements, governing boards somehow serenely avoided entanglement in the emergent conflict, at least through much of the late 1980s. Chapter 7 reports that some firms experimented with enhancements of their directors' capacity to represent the stockholder constituency that they were nominally elected to serve. Otherwise, though investor activists and company managers found some common ground for governance reform, they were sharply divided on how directors should be elected, who should serve, and how they should be compensated. Organizational reform had been moved down the organization, but it had received little in the way of a boost upward. Alignment was moved outward, however, as companies pressed other organizations to restructure in ways analogous to their own. As a new conception of corporate organization emerged, the conception was readied for export. Universities, hospitals, charities, and public agencies often look to private companies for organizational models. Though few organizational forms are fully imitated, many are partially adapted. The new ownership-alignment of the private sector thus found echo, if not replication, in the nonprivate sectors.

Finally, Chapter 8 identifies one of alignment's enduring paradoxes. As shareholders sought to exercise greater voice in company affairs, senior management sought to exercise less voice in divisional affairs. Management constructed a comprehensive ideology to guide such actions, applying it to some of the remotest corners of the organization.

Rethinking Corporate Organization

Taken together, these arguments suggest that we should revise the way we think about business corporations. The implications are not certain, but the evidence is compelling enough to bring about a recasting in at least two areas: the nature of corporate restructuring and the balance of organizational power. In both areas, the following analysis implies, traditional conceptions should give way to altered models.

The Nature of Corporate Restructuring

The actions of corporate restructuring were often dramatic, the outcomes sometimes tragic. The actions ranged from abrupt dissolution of corporate empires to the quiet empowerment of divisional managers. The immediate pretexts for such actions were as varied as the phenomenon itself: the loss of a major account, the rise of a Japanese competitor, the ravages of a recession, the accession of a new chief executive. The outcomes were equally varied, from great turnarounds to near bankruptcies. Yet within this diversity were to be found several recurrent threads.

When a company announced that its operating divisions would have far more independent authority, or that it would be shedding 10 percent of its workforce, observers inside and out could invariably identify specific precipitating factors. Though the consequences of the actions might often be felt by employees as arbitrary, the reasons for the actions were rarely seen as arbitrary. Thus, when Du Pont Company initiated a massive program to reduce costs and improve efficiency in 1991, the official and interpreted rationales were entirely plausible. The firm's announced goal was to enhance pretax profits by $2 billion over five years by eliminating duplicative work and staff. Financial writers attributed the program to weak markets for Du Pont's main products: "Du Pont and many other chemical companies are retrenching," wrote the *Wall Street Journal*, "to cope with excess supplies that have forced down prices of their commodity chemicals and plastics." The recession was deemed a culprit as well:

"Economic slowdowns around the world also have hurt demand for many chemicals and plastics" (McMurray, 1991). When General Motors and IBM announced similar workforce cutbacks and internal reorganization at about the same time, the companies and the media offered similar explanations. In the words of an Associated Press summary: "Though GM and IBM both cited the economy as a reason for their scale-backs, they also blamed heightened competition, their bloated management structures and high costs of doing business" (Ziegler, 1991). Personalities were a factor as well. It was significant, said the analysts, that General Motors' relatively new chief executive had taken the reigns from a predecessor viewed as far less willing to face restructuring.

Yet behind many of the unique blends of such circumstances and biographies, I would argue, was a common cause. And underlying the particular set of changes was a common direction. The enduring changes would leave a different, not just leaner, corporate organization in place. And it would be an organization designed to meet a set of objectives long enshrined in principle but usually ignored in fact.

The Balance of Organizational Power

Perched atop the corporation and guiding the change was the executive suite. Scattered across the American landscape like the fortified castles of medieval Europe, headquarters were the source of almost unlimited authority within the realm. Here, lifelong careers were secured or shattered, shareholders' wealth productively invested or frittered away, and divisions the size of small nations bought or sold. Striking entryways, vast offices, and original art informed visitors of the powers residing there. Yet it was a power structure whose seemingly timeless qualities were proving timebound.

In the story that follows, we will see that the balance of power was shifted, probably for at least a decade. Shareholders slowly but steadily acquired the means for shaping their stake, for giving more direction to those entrusted with enhancing their wealth. If top managers had long been the unchallenged lords of the realm, their actions would no longer be considered quite so sacrosanct. The scales were tipped, albeit still modestly and not without pitched struggle, away from headquarters management.

The tipping could not be deemed a counterrevolution. As we will see, many of the changes were readily embraced by senior management, at times well in advance of shareholder demands. Moreover, the challengers were rarely the original owners. Many founding families had long since diversified their holdings, retaining little more than residual presence in the ownership structure that their forefathers had created. The challengers were, rather, a new breed of "money managers." These individuals were charged with overseeing and increasing the pension, endowment, and personal assets of thousands of organizations and investors. Many were career investment counselors. Few had been present at the creation.

If less unconstrained power remained in the hands of the executives, more was obtained by both outside money managers and inside line managers. As a result, company strategy would be less the free prerogative of top management and more a negotiated product of newly empowered constituencies. As managements evolved new organizational designs to master these altered realities, they hit upon appealing and logically interconnected forms of systemic change. In the period studied, the systemic change was most extensively applied to the higher managerial ranks of the corporation. But so appealing were the new forms that, even in the absence of confirming evidence, they were viewed as eminently applicable elsewhere. This would include the top of the organizational chart, the board of directors. It would include the bottom of the organizational chart, the nonexempt employees. And it would include sectors outside the organizational chart, the thousands of other organizations with which a company does business.

The corporate changes chronicled in the pages that follow may thus serve to reshape organizational life far beyond the confines of the offices in which they were conceived. Company alignment could affect American life in ways never intended by those company managers who had originally sought little more than to improve their firm's worth to its shareholders.

The Rise of
Shareholder Power

Much of the corporate restructuring that occurred during the late 1980s and early 1990s could be traced to a more open contest for control of large business firms. The intensified struggle derived from a weakening of the long-standing dominance of professional managers over the fate of many major corporations. In decades past, there had been a gradual but seemingly inexorable shift of control of large corporations from founding owners and shareholders to nonowning professional managers. This was the "managerial revolution" identified by Adolph Berle and Gardiner Means in their 1932 landmark study of corporate organization and governance. A company's board of directors was in principle the instrument for shareholder sovereignty over management, but in practice the board had often instead evolved into an instrument of management. Unable to change an unresponsive board, unhappy shareholders were left with the sole alternative of exiting. The "Wall Street Rule" of disinvesting, rather than challenging management, became a norm of necessity.

Later analyses confirmed that by the 1970s, ownership control of the corporation had been replaced with managerial control in a substantial proportion of the nation's largest firms. One of the major studies reported that 82 percent of the country's 200 largest nonfinancial corporations had come under management control by 1974, up from 40 percent in 1929. Of the 40 largest companies in 1900, just 22 percent were management controlled (Berle and Means, 1967; Herman, 1981). While outside financial institutions and family groups continued to exercise considerable influence on some companies that were seemingly management dominated, inside professional management acquired active control of many other publicly traded corporations (Fligstein, 1990; Herman, 1981; Kotz, 1978; Larner, 1970; Mintz and Schwartz, 1985).

Senior managers had lost virtually all of what little ownership stake they had once had in large firms. Chief executives of the nation's 120 largest companies and their families held an average 0.30 percent of the company's shares in 1938; by 1974 this had declined to a scant 0.047 percent (Jensen and Murphy, 1990). Yet many had wrested control on the premise that they would be more effective at serving ownership interests than the owners themselves. The premise had been persuasive. The enormous scale of the new organizational forms and the task of operating them in highly complex environments placed a premium on sophisticated leadership. As Alfred Chandler characterized it in *The Visible Hand* (1977, p. 491), the founding family and favored financier had relinquished all but residual control over company decisions. "They could say no," observed Chandler, "but unless they themselves were trained managers with long experience in the same industry and even the same company, they had neither the information nor the experience to propose positive alternative courses of action." Decision making came to be viewed as a learned rather than intuitive or inherited skill, and a university education and professional management training became the norm for those who would oversee the nation's largest companies (Gordon and Howell, 1959; Levine, 1986; Pierson, 1959; Porter and McKibbin, 1988).

The solution to one set of organizational problems, however, ushered in a new set of dilemmas. While professional nonowning managers might come to be technocratic masters at solving problems, the owners found it inherently difficult to ensure that the managers did so in a way that best served shareholder interests. Once professional managements were installed as the owners' agents, the door was opened for career, power, and other motives to intrude into decision making. Likewise, the decision-making door was opened to the concerns of local communities, company employees, nonprofit organizations, and other corporate stakeholders as they prodded their companies to be more "socially responsible." Despite the institution of a host of organizational mechanisms to better link managerial and ownership interests, such as the widespread use of performance-based executive compensation schemes, the door could never be fully closed (Fama, 1980; Jensen and Meckling, 1976; Shleifer and Vishny, 1986).

When large corporations entered a prolonged period of profit decline during the 1970s, blame was at first placed on neither this "agency" problem nor other possible shortcomings of professional management. Rather, business executives tended to single out the growing role of the federal government in costly areas of social regulation—above all, environmental protection, occupational health and safety, and equal employment opportunity. Instead of suggesting internal restructuring or new business strategies to overcome the long-term problem of declining performance, many company leaders chose to target reduction of government intervention in the marketplace. Large corporations aggressively sought a rollback through Washington lobbying, political donations, and employee mobilization (Himmelstein, 1990; Silk and Vogel, 1976; Vogel, 1989).

Yet despite the reduction in state interference and the improved political climate following inauguration of the Reagan administration in 1981, performance and competitiveness for many firms were still not restored to full health. Then, in a fateful turn, the search for causes veered inward on management itself. Poor business performance came finally to be blamed on entrenched managers who, it seemed, had become unresponsive to shareholder concerns. The assessment of Michael Jensen (1989, p. 65), a leading advocate of change in top management of publicly traded corporations, is illustrative of a critique that gained wide currency during the late 1980s: the autonomy of professional management from ownership oversight, he concluded, had caused "widespread waste and inefficiency of the public corporation and its inability to adapt to changing economic circumstances." Peter Drucker (1991, p. 109) echoed the appraisal: "What made takeovers and buyouts inevitable . . . was the mediocre performance of enlightened-despot management, the management without clear definitions of performance and results and with no clear accountability to somebody."

While professional managers and their policies came to be viewed by many as the problem, the solutions proposed for improving performance depended on the proponent. Incumbent managements naturally preferred to remain so and to stimulate earnings through internal reform, such as workforce downsizing. Corporate "raiders," by contrast, placed little stock in the ability of incumbent management ever to reform itself. "We're supporting managements who produce nothing," complained Carl Icahn, one of the active practitioners of hostile corporate acquisitions, in justifying his actions: "Not only are we paying those drones to produce nothing, but we're paying them to muck up the works" (Icahn, 1988). Still other outsiders proposed to install management teams that also possessed a major ownership stake through leveraged buyouts, thereby recombining ownership and control of the corporation in the same individuals.

Corporate downsizing, acquisitions, and buyouts thus emerged, in the more active market of the 1980s, among the varied means of reasserting or gaining control of the corporation. Incumbent managements, outside raiders, and investment groups vied for the opportunity to restructure the corporation. Lining up behind those with the most promising strategy was a new set of moneyed actors, the institutional investors. Slowly, almost imperceptibly, they had gained ground as vast numbers of company shares became concentrated in their hands. At first they adopted a largely passive stance, with institutions routinely supporting incumbent management against any challengers from the outside. During the 1980s, however, the institutions moved onto more active ground, still siding with management in most cases but increasingly pressing for changes and, failing that, joining the challengers. The result was a rediscovery of "shareholder rights" and the emergence of a new conception of organizational design. This chapter focuses on the forces that fostered that new-found shareholder power.

Turnover in Corporate Ownership

Early warning of the transformation in shareholder power appeared in the sharp increase in the turnover of company ownership during the mid to late 1980s. Especially significant was the heightened activity in the market for ownership control of the publicly traded firm. Even more so was the emergence of a transaction not previously witnessed on a large scale: the conversion of publicly traded corporations to closely held private ownership. The intensity of such transactions had declined by the turn of the decade, but the underlying forces had not.

Intensification of ownership turnover can be tracked using the rates of company mergers and acquisitions, defined as the purchase of a company or company unit by a new owner. Mergers and acquisitions were not the only form of ownership change, but they constituted an area for which systematic annual information on ownership change was most extensively available.

The number of turnovers in company ownership did not increase during the 1980s, but the aggregate value of the turnovers expanded by a factor of more than five, from $44.3 billion in 1980 to $246.9 billion in 1988 (see Figure 2.1, and Table A.1 in Appendix 2). A strong contraction occurred in 1987, in part because of the sharp drop of the stock market in October of that year. Another contraction occurred in 1989 and continued into the 1990s, partly a product of the softened high-yield bond market following the bankruptcy of firms that had been at the forefront of acquisi-

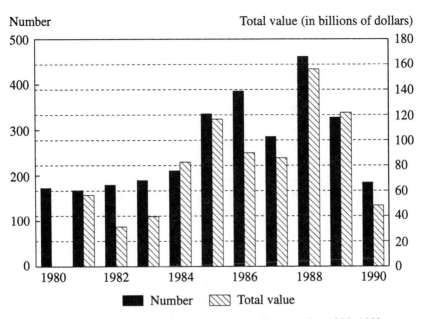

Figure 2.1. Mergers and acquisitions, publicly traded companies, 1980–1990.
(Sources: Grimm, 1989; Merrill Lynch, 1991.)

tions during the 1980s, such as Drexel Burnham Lambert and the Campeau Corporation (Yago, 1991, pp. 198–215). Turnover levels and rates returned to their early 1980s levels.

The changes in company ownership during the 1980s remained concentrated among privately held firms—and thus generally among smaller companies. The proportion of reported mergers and acquisitions involving publicly traded firms, however, steadily increased. Whereas in the early 1980s less than one in ten transactions involved a publicly traded firm, during the late 1980s the proportion nearly doubled (from an average of 8 to 14 percent; see the third column of Table A.1). The number of ownership transactions also nearly doubled, averaging 184 during the first five years of the decade but 360 during the last five years. Particularly notable was the sharp increase in the aggregate value of the annual ownership turnover among the publicly traded firms: the average annual dollar value doubled, from $57 billion in the first half of the decade to $114 billion in the second half.

Previous periods of ownership turnover, at least as measured by company mergers and acquisitions, were often relatively short-lived (Golbe and White, 1988). The most recent prior wave of ownership transactions, spurred by a surge of diversification, rose rapidly during the late 1960s, peaking at more than 6,000 acquisitions and mergers in 1969. But thereafter the transaction rate equally swiftly declined, with fewer than 3,000 companies or divisions changing hands by the mid-1970s. The national political climate was an important ingredient: one analysis of acquisitions among major manufacturers from 1953 to 1976 revealed that annual acquisition rates were significantly higher in periods when Congress and the national administration were more conservative (Yantek and Gartrell, 1988). Some of the growth in the mid to late 1980s could thus be attributed to public policies more favorable to mergers and acquisitions during the Reagan administration, rather than to any shift in the balance of power between owners and managers.

Other signs, however, pointed to the importance of a power shift as well. The most complete form of the reemergence of ownership control was the conversion of publicly traded corporations into privately held firms, usually achieved through the device of a "leveraged buyout," in which a company's shares were purchased on credit with the assets of the acquired company as collateral. Company shares were no longer publicly traded, and the firm became "private." The buyer, most commonly inside management, an outside group, or a partnership of both, came to be the firm's owner. The de facto separation of ownership and control that had developed over the years was thus abruptly ended. Managerial and ownership interests were joined in an act of organizational fusion. In some cases a division of a company rather than the entire enterprise was "taken private," but the outcome was the same: corporate resources formerly under the control of a nonowning management were placed firmly under the control of owner-managers. The management-led buyout of Borg-Warner in 1987, the largest leveraged buyout to date ($3.8 billion), illustrates the transformation. Before the transaction, management held 1.0 percent of the company's equity; afterward, it held 18.2 percent (Cook and Ward, 1991).

A substantial rise in the conversion of publicly owned corporate resources into privately held companies during the mid-1980s is evident in trend data in Figure 2.2 (and Table A.1 in Appendix 2). The total dollar value of buyout transactions involving either company divisions or entire companies rose rapidly during the first half of the decade, with a better than 60 percent annual growth rate in the total dollar volume between 1979 and 1985. Buyout activity reached almost $30 billion in 1986 and

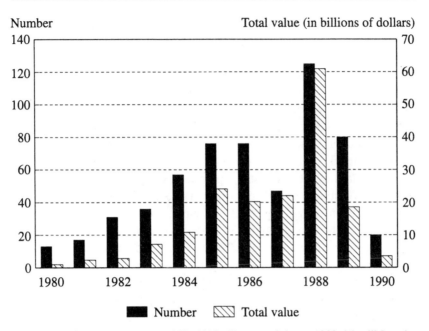

Number   Total value (in billions of dollars)

Figure 2.2. Company buyouts, 1980–1990. (Sources: Grimm, 1989; Merrill Lynch, 1991.)

1987, and it peaked the following year at nearly $70 billion, more than double the amount recorded in any previous year. Moreover, the conversion of public to private companies soared as well: in 1981, only 4 percent of the dollar value of public-firm mergers and acquisitions involved leveraged buyouts, but in 1988 it reached 39 percent (final column, Table A.2 in Appendix 2). At the end of the decade, however, the buyout intensity abruptly subsided. The dollar value of divisional and company buyouts in 1989 totaled only $22.6 billion; in 1990, it declined to $5.6 billion, the lowest level since 1982. A host of factors may have caused the drop, including a tightening of bank credit and junk bonds for such deals (Kaplan and Stein, 1992).

While most leveraged buyouts were of relatively modest-sized public firms, the upper end of the transactional distribution reached the point where virtually any publicly traded corporation could conceivably have been taken private. In 1986 and 1987 the purchase price in leveraged buyouts of companies averaged $281 million and $469 million, respectively, levels that would be of concern to few firms among the Fortune

500. Yet the largest buyouts—$3.8 billion for Borg Warner in 1987 and $5.4 billion for Beatrice Companies in 1986—were sufficient to alert many that they too could be put "into play." And although the average price was not much larger in 1988 ($488 million), the ceiling was radically raised that year: one of the nation's largest publicly owned corporations, RJR Nabisco, was acquired by a company specializing in private buyouts, Kohlberg Kravis Roberts, for $24.9 billion. Only a tiny fraction of the nation's publicly traded companies presided over assets significantly above that level.

The annual buyout totals still represented only a small proportion of the assets of publicly traded companies. The $29.1 billion buyout total in 1985, for instance, was equivalent to approximately 1.1 percent of the total value of all corporate equity; in 1988, the peak buyout year, it reached only 2.2 percent (final column in Table A.2). Yet the cumulative total of corporate assets taken private during the 1980s was considerable. The total divisional and company resources involved in buyouts from 1980 to 1990 exceeded $217 billion. The scope of the aggregate impact, at least for the earlier years, can be seen in a study of 2,519 publicly traded manufacturing firms that existed at some point between 1976 and 1985. Of the total of 704 firms that had been on the roster but were no longer public companies in 1986, 199 had been acquired by privately held companies (Hall, 1988). Thus, nearly 8 percent of all publicly traded manufacturing companies had been taken private during that period.

The conversion of publicly traded companies to privately held, owner-managed firms remained a minority phenomenon. But the threat posed by outside raiders and investors able to finance a hostile takeover of nearly any corporation brought ownership interests more centrally to the fore among corporations whose managements had successfully fended off acquisition bids or had come to worry that they, too, could become a target. The scope of the threat could be seen in one statistic. Of the Fortune 500 largest manufacturers listed in 1980, 143 were the targets of at least one takeover or buyout effort by 1990. Most of these efforts were hostile and most were ultimately successful. Over the decade, nearly a third of the country's largest industrial firms ceased to exist as independent, publicly traded companies (Davis, 1991a; Davis and Stout, 1992).

Taking actions perceived as favorable to shareholder interests was one means for fending off hostile or would-be suitors. The actions frequently consisted of lowering administrative costs, reforming governance structures, and raising stockholder dividends. Lockheed Corporation's successful resistance of several aggressive takeover bids in 1989–1991 by Harold Simmons and his NL Industries was a case in point. As part of the battle for control, Simmons and NL Industries in 1990 had fielded their own slate of directors for Lockheed, including such national figures as former U.S. senator John G. Tower and former chief of naval operations Elmo R. Zumwalt. They had also added a proposal to the proxy ballot to rescind Lockheed's "poison pill," a device intended to thwart unwanted takeovers. California and New York City pension funds had added their own dissident proxy measures that would require confidential board voting and an "opting out" of a Delaware antitakeover law.

With three antimanagement proposals and two full rosters of directors up for election to the Lockheed board, both Simmons and Lockheed vigorously courted the shareholders. Each recognized that the outcome depended in large part on how the institutional investors voted, since they held a majority of the shares (some 53 percent). Simmons and Lockheed's chief executive, Daniel Tellep, personally met with a number of the major investors. It was a process familiar to those in pursuit of elective office, each side seeking to hold its natural constituencies and woo the uncommitted. "It came down not to a contest decided by valuation," observed Lockheed's vice-president for investor relations, "but a corporate governance contest in the mold of a political campaign" (Skowronski, 1991). In the end, more than 70 percent of the share votes on the three governance measures were cast against management. But on the crucial ballot measure—election of the insurgent directors—inside management prevailed. The Simmons / NL Industries board nominees received 36 percent of the vote, considered a remarkable level of shareholder dissidence—but it left the incumbent board intact (Biersach, 1990).

By the conclusion of the hard-fought proxy struggle, however, Lockheed had cut its workforce by more than 10 percent, added four independent directors, and bolstered earnings. It also sought to portray itself as a born-again shareholders' company. National advertising in early 1991, just prior to battle's end, announced that the company had now demonstrated "greater responsiveness to shareholder concerns on corporate governance" and had "outperformed most of its industry peers in terms of shareholder returns" (Lockheed Corporation, 1991; Wartzman, 1991; Blumenthal and Wartzman, 1991; Hayes, 1991). Although the dissident shareholders had lost the critical proxy vote, by another yardstick their formal defeat had nonetheless resulted in a victory.

The Rise of Institutional Shareholding

Shareholder voting on the 1990 Lockheed proxy questions signified the potential power of the institutional investors. Their accumulating resources and prospective clout had been barely noticed during the early 1980s. Then, with scant warning, they loomed large on some company radars.

Leading the stealth attack were those institutions that were the first to shed the Wall Street Rule. Exit was no longer necessary, since they had now accumulated the power to be heard by management. Equally important, exit was no longer feasible. Few untapped domestic opportunities remained, and few international opportunities were appealing (in 1989, American investors placed only 6.2 percent of their equity in foreign stocks; French and Poterba, 1991). Almost the only buyers large enough to acquire an institution's holdings were other institutions. The College Retirement and Equities Fund (CREF), with 1990 investments of approximately $35 billion, characterized the limitation facing all funds of its size (CREF, 1990): "[CREF] is not in a position to divest itself of a company's stock when it disagrees with the action of that company's management. Furthermore, CREF's obligations to its participants preclude it from making speculative investments. Accordingly, CREF believes that it has a responsibility to use its rights as shareholder to protect shareholder values." The chief investment officer of Calpers (the California Public Employees' Retirement System), presiding over 1992 investments of $68 billion, had reached much the same conclusion (Grant, 1992, p. D2): "We realized we don't have the option of voting with our feet. The only course available is to see [that] companies are effectively run." The same course of action was foreseen by the controller of New York City, who serves as investment adviser to the New York City Employees' Retirement System (Nycers), a fund with more than $40 billion invested in 1992 (Grant, 1992, p. D2): "We are long-term investors. We can't get out of these companies. We want to break up the concentration of power at the top, create more accountability, provide checks and balances."

To understand the role of the changed ownership terrain of large companies in fostering organizational alignment, a brief mapping is provided here. The territory includes pension funds (company and state and local government funds), mutual funds, investment trusts, insurance companies, nonpension funds managed by banks, and foundation and nonprofit endowment funds (Table 2.1).

Pension funds, both private and public, constitute the map's largest features. The ten largest private and public pension funds in 1990 reported

Table 2.1. Holdings of institutional investors, 1981 and 1988.

Institutional investor	Holdings (in billions of dollars)		Annual growth 1981–1988 (in percent)
	1981	1988	
Pension funds	891.2	2,266.8	14.3
Private trusteed	486.7	1,139.9	12.9
Private insured	180.3	516.8	16.2
State/local government	224.2	610.1	15.3
Investment companies	248.3	816.0	18.5
Open-end/mutual funds	241.4	777.8	18.2
Closed-end/invest trusts	6.9	38.7	27.9
Insurance companies	599.0	1,258.8	12.3
Life insurance	347.0	781.8	12.3
Property/casualty	212.0	476.9	12.3
Bank trusts (Nonpension)	334.9	774.6	12.7
Foundation and endowments	56.0	133.0	13.2
Total	2,099.4	5,249.2	14.0

Source: Brancato and Gaughan (1990).

more than $500 billion in assets (Table A.3 in Appendix 2). The single largest fund, Calpers, then presided over more than $57 billion. In 1990 it was increasing its holdings by some $20 million per day, requiring a staff of some 800 to run the empire. Indicative of pension funds' inability or unwillingness to churn their funds, Calpers held its average investment for eight years.

Shareholding by institutional investors had steadily increased during the postwar period. Estimates of the specific levels of institutional shareholding vary somewhat with the specific definitions and data sources employed, but the trends all point in the same upward direction. According to one time series, the market value of institutional holdings of shares on the New York Stock Exchange (NYSE) rose from $31 billion in 1955 to $440 billion in 1980 (Table A.4 in Appendix 2). Institutional holding in 1955 represented 15 percent of the outstanding NYSE shares; by 1980 the fraction stood at 35 percent. Trend data also indicate that the 1980s were marked by even more rapid concentration of institutional ownership. From 1970 to 1980, the proportion of stock in the hands of institutional investors rose, according to one time series, from 31 to 33 percent, but during the next six years it jumped another 10 points. According to a second time series, the proportion rose during the 1970s from 21 to 29 percent, and during the next decade it added 16 points (see Figures 2.3 and 2.4).

Institutional investors also became a more potent force on the stock exchanges during the 1980s by almost any measure. It could be seen, for instance, in the rise of large block trading, defined by the New York Stock Exchange (NYSE) as trades of 10,000 or more shares. In 1965, only 3 percent of the shares traded on NYSE were exchanged in blocks of 10,000 or more. In 1980, the proportion had reached 29 percent. By the middle part of the decade, it had soared to some 50 percent (Figure 2.5).

Many companies found that a majority of their shares were in the hands of the institutions. By decade's end, for instance, institutional investors held 52 percent of General Electric, 59 percent of Johnson and Johnson, 71 percent of Digital Equipment, 83 percent of Intel, and 84 percent of Dayton Hudson (Standard and Poor's *Stock Reports,* 1991). Of the 1,000 largest publicly traded firms in 1990, the average institutional shareholding stood at 50 percent, up from 44 percent five years earlier (Table 2.2). The concentration within the concentration was considerable as well, with a

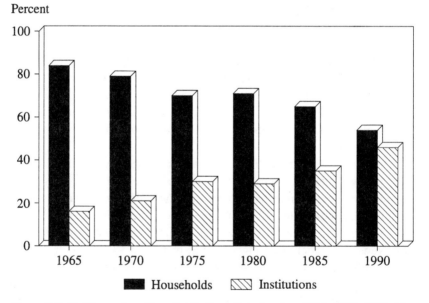

Percent

Figure 2.3. Holdings of equities, distribution of stock value, 1965–1990. 1990 data are for end of third quarter. (Source: Securities Industry Association, 1990.)

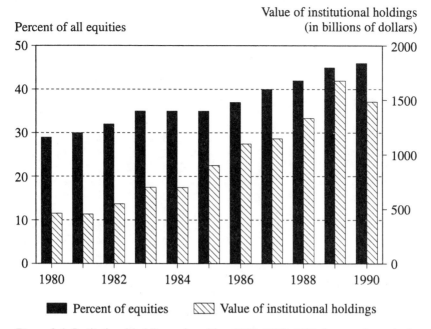

Figure 2.4. Institutional holdings of equities, 1980–1990. 1990 data are for end of third quarter. (Source: Securities Industry Association, 1990.)

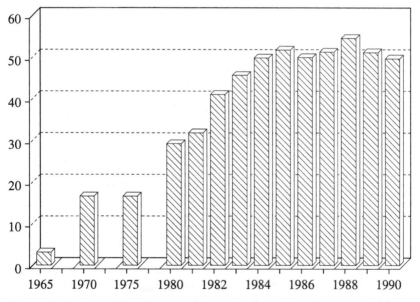

Figure 2.5. Percent of New York Stock Exchange shares traded in large blocks (10,000+ shares), 1965–1990. (Source: New York Stock Exchange, 1991.)

Table 2.2. Percent of stock of large corporations held by institutions, 1983–1990.[a]

Company	1983	1984	1985	1986	1987	1988	1989	1990
1,000 largest companies	n.a.	n.a.	43	44	47	49	48	50
IBM	50	51	51	50	50	49	49	51
Exxon	31	32	33	35	25	34	35	38
General Electric	48	49	49	51	47	47	51	52
AT&T	n.a.	17	17	18	22	23	26	24
Philip Morris	61	64	59	60	60	64	65	65
General Motors	39	40	38	40	42	42	43	41
Merck	61	61	63	64	58	55	55	56
Bristol-Myers	54	57	56	56	53	56	n.a.	61
Amoco	n.a.	n.a.	36	40	42	46	45	46
Du Pont	35	34	38	40	39	40	40	40
Wal-Mart Stores	36	38	41	36	34	31	32	31
BellSouth	n.a.	n.a.	24	28	28	26	29	27
Mobil	37	38	38	41	45	47	49	51
Chevron	43	44	47	39	41	39	39	43
Coca-Cola	50	53	56	52	51	53	56	55
Ford Motor	58	60	53	63	60	55	54	53
Procter & Gamble	42	44	46	48	44	42	43	46
GTE	42	46	50	52	53	52	56	56
Atlantic Richfield	52	54	56	52	55	54	56	56
Johnson & Johnson	57	56	60	66	64	63	62	59

Source: Business Week (1991 and earlier years).

a. Companies are ranked by market value in 1988, defined as the share price in March multiplied by the latest available number of outstanding shares. Institutional holdings are the shares held by pension funds, investment companies, insurance companies, banks, and colleges, as compiled by Vickers Stock Research Corporation.

small set of the largest institutional investors responsible for a large portion of the holdings. One study, for example, examined the holdings in 1990 of a random sample of twenty-five companies from the Standard and Poor's 500, the 500 largest companies ranked by market capitalization. Most companies among the largest 500 had at least several hundred institutional investors, but the twenty largest investors accounted on average for more than a third (34.1 percent) of the outstanding shares. "Only an ostrich," observed analyst Louis Lowenstein, "would ignore twenty stockholders who collectively own 34 percent of his company" (Lowenstein, 1991, pp. 210–211).

As always, however, aggregate trends masked significant individual variants. The diversity of experience within even the same industry can

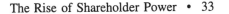

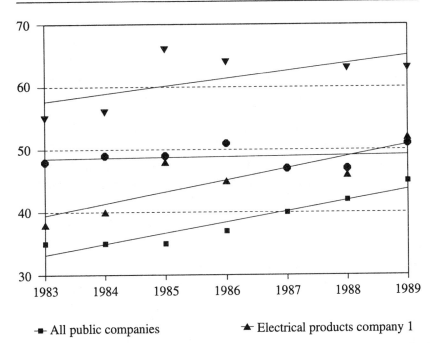

Figure 2.6. Percent of shares in three large electrical-products companies held by institutional investors, 1983–1989. (Sources: Securities Industry Association, 1990; *Business Week,* 1990 and earlier years.)

be seen in Figure 2.6, which shows the shareholding of three electrical products manufacturers, including the electrical products company intensively studied here. Institutional holdings in two of the firms consistently tracked the rising proportions for all publicly traded firms, while institutional holdings in a third firm were relatively flat during the 1980s.

Mobilization of Shareholder Pressure

The increased rates of turnover in corporate ownership, buyouts of public companies, and concentration of institutional ownership placed more power to shape company enterprise in the hands of owners, less in the hands of top managers. Some firms experienced abrupt restructuring, as fresh ownership groups radically redesigned their new possessions. Power had gone to the takeover engineers. Other firms experienced nothing at all, as incumbent managements continued to enjoy full control of their boards and shareholders. For them, the umbrella of Berle and Means's managerial revolution was not leaking and seemed unlikely ever to do so. These were the extremes, however, and most major firms found themselves somewhere in between. Still free from ownership control, they could no longer afford to ignore it.

Firms experienced several kinds of pressures to be more responsive to shareholder interests and demands. The distinctive forms reflected well-known alternatives for the exercise of power (Etzioni, 1968). Some firms came under direct ownership control; others became more responsive as they developed mutually dependent relations with major investors; and still others were the target of concerted shareholder actions.

Direct Control through Organizational Fusion

Direct control was achieved as companies and units previously insulated from ownership pressures were placed under the oversight of owners and managers-*cum*-owners. Led by leveraged buyouts, this wholesale transformation in corporate control attracted public attention out of proportion to the actual number of firms affected. As already noted, buyouts reached but a tiny fraction of publicly traded firms during the 1980s. Their special salience lay in the completeness with which ownership control was reimposed, an appealing model to advocates of reform. In the opinion of one proponent, they even heralded the "eclipse of the public corporation" (Jensen, 1989).

The leveraged buyout of RJR Nabisco by Kohlberg Kravis Roberts (KKR) was illustrative. R. J. Reynolds Industries, the larger of the two entities that had merged to form RJR Nabisco in 1985, had been solidly controlled by professional management in the 1970s, the period of the most recent assessment of control among major manufacturers (Herman, 1981, p. 318). In purchasing all stock in 1989 for nearly $25 billion, KKR completely transformed the control structure. As a firm of little more than a dozen professionals, KKR could not hope to exercise day-to-day control over this and its more than a dozen other companies, whose aggregate value was near $60 billion (Kohlberg Kravis Roberts, 1989; Bartlett, 1991a). Nor did the past owners aspire to do so. But the new owners did exercise tight financial control, which the previous owners could not, even if they had so aspired. When a company was acquired, observed two journalists who chronicled the RJR Nabisco buyout, Kohlberg Kravis

Roberts "kept a close watch on its budgets, but otherwise gave its management more or less free reign to streamline and meets its mountainous debt." But KKR's financial power remained absolute. There "is no mistaking who calls the shots," concluded the journalists, for the principals "approve every budget, and retain power to remove senior executives at their whim" (Burrough and Helyar, 1990, p. 166).

When a buyout fell short of its targets, as in the case of KKR's second purchase, an oil-field services firm, intervention was swift. Incumbent management was ousted, new management swiftly installed (Burrough and Helyar, pp. 139–140). When buyouts did not fall short, the leash was long, its only tug toward strategic thinking. Duracell, the maker of alkaline batteries, was one of KKR's later successes (1988). Its chief executive, who with other managers owned some 13 percent of the company (the rest was held by KKR), had free reign to make money for both sets of owners. "When I talk with Henry Kravis at lunch," he said, "we don't spend time talking about cost reductions. We talk about how we're increasing the strategic value of the company" (Kidder, 1990, pp. 8–9).

Unlike the organizations described by Meyer and Zucker (1989) in their account of permanent underperformance, this situation would leave no room for failing enterprise. Thousands of independent shareholders in the past had looked to their elected board to police management, a policing function that the managerial revolution had effectively thwarted. Now, the owners themselves were both on the board and in the management. The resulting organizational fusion ensured that all primary agents remained closely wedded to ownership principles.

Mutual Dependency through Shareholding

Organizational theorists have long argued that resource dependency is a critical lever of power: the greater the reliance of organization A on resources of organization B, the greater the power of B over A (Aldrich and Pfeffer, 1976; Pfeffer and Salancik, 1978; Aldrich, 1979; Burt, 1983). When shareholding was widely dispersed, there were so many Bs that A was dependent on none in particular. Companies enjoyed, in the framing of Henry Mintzberg (1983, pp. 32–37), a diffuse environment characterized by a "dispersed and detached ownership." With shareholding far more concentrated by the late 1980s, however, they now faced instead a "concentrated and involved ownership," with a corresponding loss of autonomy. The fewer Bs could rightfully demand far more of A's attention.

Other constituencies, such as suppliers, political agencies, and employees vied for attention as well, and their resources, too, had concentrated in some instances. Yet theorists also remind us that other constituencies' cases were inherently weaker: their resources were important but still less essential to the firm than investors' capital (Jacobs, 1974). Equity sources came first; other providers followed.

The exercise of mutual influence between company *A* and its now more limited set of investor *B*s was based on the presumption that they knew one another. The identity of a company's shareholders has sometimes remained partially obscured, but in this case the presumption was largely correct. Under U.S. law, investors with portfolios of at least $100 million in securities are required to file quarterly "13(f)" reports to the U.S. Securities and Exchange Commission. The reports identify the number of shares held in each of the investor's portfolio companies. Several business services consolidate the investor reports into a single data base and then create company reports listing all of a firm's institutional investors. Because of technical problems with 13(f) reporting, the reconstituted lists are not entirely precise pictures of a company's investor environment, but they are close approximations (Wines, 1990). Most large firms subscribe to one or more of the reporting services (for example, CDA Investment Technologies or Technimetrics) to track their major investors and the turnover in their portfolios. Companies also typically learn through informal channels of any major transaction among their largest holders well before the quarterly reports reach their offices (Vickers Stock Research Corporation, 1991).

The resulting picture that a company has of its investor field is well illustrated by the profiles available to the special-machinery and retail-services companies (the top ten investors for each appear in Table A.5 in Appendix 2). Nearly two-thirds of the special-machinery firm's shares in 1990 were owned by 192 institutional investors, and the top ten held more than a fifth. The senior vice-president who included investor relations among his responsibilities closely followed movement in these shares and maintained frequent contact with those responsible for managing the funds (a process taken up in Chapter 5). He and the other senior managers who were responsible for investor relations had long maintained personalized relations with what is termed the "sell side" of corporate investing. The sell side consists largely of Wall Street analysts and brokers who research the company, make investment recommendations, and facilitate transactions but usually do not themselves make investment decisions. In addition, in recent years they had cultivated ties with the "buy side," the institutional investors themselves. It had been a good quarter for the special-machinery company: the top ten investors had increased their aggregate stake in the company by more than 200,000 shares, some 2.7 percent. Overall, the 192 investors had enlarged their holdings by 1.5 percent. Though there were still many *B*s, the director of investor relations concentrated his attention on the several dozen largest, which together owned more than half of the firm. A relatively similar investor profile characterized the retail-services company, though it was slightly less concentrated and included several public pension funds among the top ten investors.

Contrary to some conventional wisdom, institutional investors tend to take long-term positions in many of their companies. But this should not be surprising, since their holdings are so large that high turnover would be costly if not impractical. The turnover observed among top shareholders of the electrical-products company is typical of many major firms (see Table A.6 in Appendix 2). Three investors ranked among the top ten every year during this period, and eight ranked among the top ten for at least two years. Though several of the major investors abruptly altered their holdings, changes in investor stakes were generally incremental. At least 400 institutions held stock in this company in each of the seven years, but only twenty-seven investors ranked among the ten largest in one or more of those years.

Though companies saw increasingly concentrated institutional holdings, large investors rarely placed more than one or two percent of their own equity holdings in a given company. The relative holdings of several investors in the pharmaceutical company illustrate the range (Table 2.3). While the public pension fund held 1 percent of the firm's shares in 1990,

Table 2.3. Selected institutional shareholdings in a pharmaceutical corporation, 1990.

Institutional investor	Shares as percent of	
	Company shares	Investor equity
Public pension fund	1.0	0.4
Commercial bank trust	0.8	0.9
Insurance company	0.1	2.4

Source: Company records (1990).

the fund had invested less than 0.5 percent of its total equity in this way. A reverse skew can be seen in the case of the insurance company, which held only 0.1 percent of the pharmaceutical's stock. That amount, however, constituted 2.4 percent of the insurer's investments. Stakes of this size or greater, however, were the exception. Of the nearly 700 investors in the electrical-products company in 1989, only one in ten had placed more than 1 percent of its holdings in the corporation, and only a single investor had put more than 4 percent of its equity in the firm.

These investor profiles indicate that neither specific companies nor particular institutions were vitally dependent upon one another. The relative stake of each side in the other rarely exceeded several percent of total value. Most companies were beholden to no single shareholder, and most institutional investors were reliant on no one firm. The steady aggregation of holdings among the institutional investors during the 1980s had made each side more important to the other. But the symbiotic dependency was still built on networks involving many players. No single institution could expect to exercise major influence, at least by virtue of its holdings alone.

Promoting Shareholder Interests through Concerted Action

Until the 1980s, few conventions in the financial world had seemed so like bedrock as the "Wall Street Rule." The concentration of shareholding changed that. Dissident voices emerged from the high end of institutional investing, particularly large public pension funds. They pressed companies for reform in a variety of areas, ranging from governance structures to executive succession, lines of business, and managerial compensation. Illustrative of the actions are those of Calpers, one of the half-dozen most active. Displeased with the financial performance of General Motors Corporation in 1990, and mindful of GM's planned replacement of the chief executive, the top officer of Calpers, Dale Hanson, wrote to each of GM's directors. He asked about their standards for managerial performance and about the "kinds . . . of policies and structure . . . you contemplate for an on-going relationship with your shareholders" (Hanson in Sommer, 1991, p. 374). The directors' response was largely noncommittal but the company invited Hanson for an informal visit to headquarters. Subsequently he wrote the chief executives of other companies, complaining of their financial performance and notifying them that a proxy resolution was being submitted for shareholder vote. In a letter to J. Peter Grace, chief executive of W. R. Grace and Company, Hanson stated that the company is "one of our poorest performing holdings" of the 1,300 companies in Calpers' portfolio (it held 644,300 shares in W. R. Grace). An accompanying analysis noted that despite the poor performance, Mr. Grace's "compensation had risen significantly" and in 1989 was "82% over market, after taking into account the Company's size, performance and other factors." The shareholder resolution would amend the firm's bylaws to create a board compensation committee comprised of "independent directors" with access to outside advisers (Hanson, 1990). Rather than face an embarrassing proxy defeat, the company voluntarily accepted Calpers proposal and the measure was dropped before going to shareholder vote.

As is common in political mobilization in general and corporate political action in particular, the largest players optimized their interests by pursuing both individual and collective strategies (Vogel, 1989). The smaller players of necessity sought strength through numbers. Finding common cause by the mid-1980s, both large and small institutional investors coalesced in several collective initiatives. Even individual shareholders discovered that there could be strength in numbers. The formation of collective action organizations for the advancement of shareholder interests was less surprising than their historical absence.

The primary vehicle for collective voice among the pension funds was the *Council of Institutional Investors*. Created in 1985 as an association of large public and private pension funds, the council included more than sixty members by 1990 whose combined assets exceeded $300 billion. The council had been formed on the premise that "the enormity of pension fund holdings limits their ability to sell stock and move money into other companies," and thus "pension funds' interests are truly inseparable from those of the country's economy" (Council of Institutional Investors, 1990). The association's services concentrated on timely circulation of information among its members, promoting public policies serving pension interests, and fostering reform in corporate governance to increase responsiveness to shareholders. In a move that is indicative of the implicit political alliances created to advance their joint interests, several of the largest buyout and takeover groups such as Kohlberg Kravis Roberts and Fortsmann Little annually provided $7,500 as sustaining members of the council.

The small shareholder found collective voice in the *United Shareholders Association* (abbreviated USA). Founded in 1986 by one of the prominent hostile takeover specialists, T. Boone Pickens, USA claimed more 64,000 members in 1991. The barriers to entry were small: the $50 annual membership fee brought full association services. USA offered an annual rating of the 1,000 largest publicly traded companies on their "responsiveness to shareholders," combining measures of financial performance, governance policies (under the rubric "shareholder rights"), and executive compensation (United Shareholders Association, 1991a). It also published an annual evaluation of the compensation received by the chief executives of the same 1,000 companies (United Shareholders Association, 1991b). Among USA's leading tactics was the submission of shareholder proposals for governance changes at fifty companies per year rated as among the worst performers (its "Target 50" program).

A range of other players, some nonprofit, others for-profit, furnished additional services and political clout for groups of shareholders (see Table 2.4). The *Analysis Group* (formed in 1981) compiled detailed financial information on company performance and policies for institutional investors, and its data were used by those waging campaigns to pass shareholder resolutions or unseat incumbent management (as during the campaign by Harold Simmons and NL Industries to replace the Lockheed board of directors). *Institutional Shareholder Services* (established in 1985) provided money managers, public pension funds, bank trusts, and other clients with an array of information on proxy and corporate governance questions (e.g., it issued a "Proxy Alert" in January 1991 recommending that its clients holding NCR shares vote for a special shareholders meeting requested by AT&T in its battle to acquire NCR). *Institutional Shareholder Partners* (founded in 1990) offered consulting services to clients concerned with enhancing shareholder power. *Investor Responsibility Re-*

Table 2.4. Major associations and information services for shareholders.

Organization	Founding year	Services
Institutional Shareholder Partners	1990	Consulting services for investor action
United Shareholders Association	1986	Information, shareholder resolutions
Council of Institutional Investors	1985	Information, lobbying
Institutional Shareholder Services	1985	Information for investor action
Analysis Group	1981	Information for investor action
Investor Responsibility Research Center	1972	Information for investors and companies

Sources: The associations and services.

search Center (established in 1972), the largest of the information services, offered extensive data on a broad range of issues around corporate governance and shareholder concerns. Its reporting also included such questions as company investments in South Africa and Northern Ireland and an array of social issues confronting companies that the other firms did not ordinarily track.

A host of commercial services also developed during the 1980s to facilitate distribution of company information to institutional investors. *First Call Corporate Release,* for instance, provided immediate delivery of the complete text of all company news releases to some 500 institutional investors subscribing to the network. Though generally facilitating information flow, the fast communication technologies did not always make a positive contribution to communication. Witness the experience of a senior vice-president for investor relations and communications of a large California savings and loan bank. The bank's financial report at the end of one of the 1990 quarters contained little to boast about: $96 million had been set aside in a reserve for mounting real estate losses, and a dividend cut was announced. The news was passed to the wire services, newspapers, and investment managers through one of the investor network services. A week later Standard and Poor's called the service to obtain another copy of the bank report, having misplaced the original. In response, the service again sent the report across the entire network, with only a single additional word at the top: "Repeat." Missing the warning, a number of institutional investors mistakenly believed it was a new report. The oversight was not surprising given the work load borne by some institutions. One investment manager, for example, was in the middle of evaluating sixty-five other bank reports when he saw the California bank news come across the network. As the adverse news was digested seemingly anew by some of the investors, the bank's stock price dropped again, this time more than it had following the original release of the report.

Such experiences, however, were the exception. The new technologies of computer networks and faxes ensured that major company communications were in the hands of large shareholders almost instantly. With common information and common cause, the conditions were fertile for collective action. Grievances were shared. Investors knew one another. And they knew what should be targeted.

The legal environment, however, inhibited collective mobilization. Rules of the U.S. Securities and Exchange Commission (SEC) created significant barriers to joint action. Holders of more than 5 percent of a company's stock who join together for the purpose of voting their securities are required to follow several onerous procedures. If just the top three institutional shareholders of the special machinery or retail service companies were to have joined forces in 1990, their aggregate holdings of 8.6 and 6.1 percent, respectively, would have required such steps (see Table A.5 in Appendix 2). They would have had to file a document (Schedule 13d) with the SEC reporting substantial information about their group and the purpose of their shareholding. Even if not formally constituted as a group, if the three institutional investors had communicated with one another about the two companies, such action could have been construed as the formation of a group that would fall under the special reporting provisions. The institutional investors would then have been required to give advance notification to the Justice Department and the Federal Trade Commission (under the Hart-Scott-Rodino Act) if they and the target met certain size standards and if the purchase was for any purpose other than purely passive financial investment. Most major institutional investors and the target firms would meet the size requirement. And the FTC had chosen to regard the solicitation of proxies or other means of acquiring shareholder support as nonpassive investment—and thus grounds for prior reporting (Sommer, 1991; Black, 1992a).

Despite such constraints, both the associations and individual institutional investors increased their pressure on companies during the late 1980s. While avoiding formal and even informal alliance, de facto the institutions often acted in concert. With access to the same information and sharing similar concerns, they took parallel actions whose aggregate impact was virtually the same as if formally coordinated.

One avenue for doing so was through placement of investments in takeover and buyout funds of Kohlberg Kravis Roberts and like organizations (Bartlett, 1991a, pp. 119–134; idem, 1991b). Buyout fund managers were typically free to draw on the funds as they found undervalued opportunities. Companies attracting their interest knew that the bulk of such funds had been supplied by major institutional investors. The buyout fund device circumvented any legal constraints on collective action, since the owners were not technically acting in concert.

A second avenue was opened by proxy contests and stock solicitations initiated during hostile takeover bids. This could be seen in an effort by AT&T in 1991 to acquire NCR. After NCR had turned down a tender offer by AT&T, AT&T sought the votes of shareholders and called a special meeting of the shareholders to replace four members of the board who were up for reelection, a group that included the chief executive. Some 64 percent of NCR's stock in mid-1990 was in the hands of institutions, and AT&T's bid necessarily required strong support from them if it was to be successful. NCR vigorously resisted: "Do you really want to entrust your NCR investment to AT&T's handpicked nominees?" it asked in full-page advertising directed to the investment community. "Don't hand over your investment in NCR for less than its full value . . . Act in your own best interest. Keep NCR's board intact" (NCR, 1991). Both NCR and AT&T also sought the support of the institutions by direct contact with their managers. Though the institutions' response could not be formally orchestrated, for most the answer was much the same: the AT&T offer was too good to pass up.

Still, legal constraints prevented more overt forms of collective action (though the SEC loosened some constraints in 1992). And with the waning of buyout funds and hostile takeovers at the end of the 1980s, major shareholders sought new vehicles for exercising their voice. After experimental fits and starts, one of the preferred vehicles became the shareholder proposal.

Shareholder Proposals

Shareholder proposals are resolutions on company proxy statements inviting shareholders to vote for change in company governance structures. Shareholder proposals are also directed at company policies in such areas as South African investments, environmental policies, and affirmative action, but such measures are not of direct interest here (they rarely garnered more than 5 to 10 percent of the stockholder vote). The proposed governance changes are intended to favor investor interests, and they are almost universally opposed by management. During the late 1980s and early 1990s, such proposals attracted increasing shareholder support, a trend indicative of intensifying investor resolution and power.

The five leading areas of shareholder governance proposals near the turn of the decade were (1) rescinding a poison pill, a financial device intended to make an unfriendly takeover prohibitive; (2) instituting confidential voting, a provision that insulates shareholders from company pressure to vote with management; (3) repealing classification of directors, a policy that prevents wholesale replacement of the board by a hostile suitor;

(4) implementing cumulative voting, a procedure that permits shareholders to cast all of their proxy votes for a single director candidate, thereby heightening the chance of electing dissident directors; and (5) requiring minimum stock ownership for directors, a provision that presumably more closely links their interests with those of shareholders. Other areas of shareholder governance proposals included creation of shareholder advisory committees, opting out of antitakeover laws in Delaware and other states, fuller disclosure of executive compensation, reinstitution of cumulative voting, and elimination of golden parachutes (see Krasnow, 1989; Black, 1990). Drawing on a number of data summaries compiled by the Investor Responsibility Research Center, Table 2.5 provides a sample of shareholder resolutions voted in 1990, and Figure 2.7 shows that the total number of shareholder resolutions and the number of companies targeted rose sharply from 1985 to 1990 (shareholder resolutions are counted in the year in which they are voted).

It should be kept in mind that a relatively small number of institutions and individual shareholders were responsible for the bulk of the institutionally sponsored proposals. Of the 358 proposals pending or voted during

Table 2.5. Illustrative shareholder resolutions voted in 1990.

Corporation	Area of governance	Main sponsor[a]	Percent of vote for resolutions
May Department Stores	Rescind or vote on poison pill	Cref	25.1
Lockheed	Confidential voting	Nycers	61.2
Chase Manhattan Bank	Repeal classified board	E. Davis	35.1
PepsiCo	Cumulative voting	Gilberts	16.6
Pacific Gas & Electric	Minimum stock for directors	E. Rossi	18.7
Avon Products	Establish shareholder advisory committee	Calpers	45.5
Boeing	Opt out of Delaware antitakeover law	Nycers	23.4
Champion International	Ban golden parachutes	R. Gulde for USA	22.0

Source: Investor Responsibility Research Center, *Corporate Governance Bulletin* (May–June 1990), pp. 79–88.

a. Cref = College Retirement Equities Fund; Nycers = New York City Employees' Retirement System; Calpers = California Public Employees' Retirement System; USA = United Shareholders Association.

Number

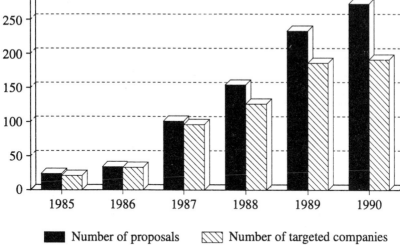

■ Number of proposals   ☒ Number of targeted companies

Figure 2.7. Shareholder proposals voted on corporate governance, 1985–1990.
(Source: Investor Responsibility Research Center, 1990.)

the first six months of 1990, for instance, fifteen institutional investors accounted for almost all of the institutional sponsorships. Their proposals and those of the United Shareholders Associations constituted nearly a third of all shareholder resolutions (see Table A.7 in Appendix 2). The only kinds of institutional investors taking a leadership role in this area were the major public and union pension funds.

Whatever the origin of the shareholder proposals, some attracted large segments of the vote. Few of the proposed reforms drew sufficient favorable votes to pass, but the number that were approved increased at the turn of the decade. During the first half of 1990, for example, at least sixteen of the 358 shareholder proposals had passed, more than during the same period in 1989. Moreover, the average vote in nearly all areas of shareholder initiative was higher in 1990 than 1989, as shown in Table 2.6.

Proxy contests increased in number as well, and the challenger's rate of success expanded. Proxy contests are generally defined to include conflicts in which a challenger or dissident set of shareholders offers its

Table 2.6. Average level of voting support for shareholder governance proposals to companies, 1989–1990.

Shareholder proposal[c]	1989[a]		1990[b]		Percent change 1989–1990
	Percent in favor[d]	(N)[e]	Percent in favor[d]	(N)[e]	
Rescind poison pill	39.5	(18)	42.7	(40)	3.2
Confidential voting	27.4	(39)	33.6	(50)	5.2
Repeal classified directors	21.5	(46)	25.3	(38)	4.2
Cumulative voting	15.6	(39)	20.6	(45)	5.0
Minimum stock ownership for directors	9.0	(17)	14.4	(14)	5.4
Restore preemptive rights	9.8	(9)	11.0	(7)	1.2

Sources: Krasnow (1989); Investor Responsibility Research Center, *Corporate Governance Bulletin* (July–August 1990).

a. Figures are for the period from mid-September 1988 through mid-August 1989.

b. Figures are based on proposals voted during the first eight months of 1990.

c. Types of shareholder proposals that were brought before fewer than seven companies in 1989 or 1990 are not included.

d. Represents the percent of votes for the shareholder proposal relative to the number of shares voted.

e. Represents the number of proposals upon which the voting percent was averaged.

own slate of nominees for the board. The effort by Harold Simmons and NL Industries to take control of the Lockheed board was one such example. Proxy contests are also considered to include situations in which the challenger or dissident shareholders stand in opposition to management on a governance proposal, and both sides actively solicit shareholder votes through the distribution of competing proxy materials. The three governance proposals on the Lockheed proxy in 1990 are also illustrative.

Drawing upon a data series compiled by Georgeson and Company, a proxy solicitation and investor relations consulting firm, Table 2.7 reveals modest and somewhat uneven growth in the number of proxy challenges during the late 1980s. The success of management in fully defeating the challenges, about half of which were for full or partial control of the board of directors, averaged 45 percent from 1985 to 1988, but dropped to 39 percent in 1989–1990.

Though the outcomes of the proxy challenges indicate a substantial rates of dissident success, the observed rates could underestimate the

Table 2.7. Proxy contests on corporate governance and control, 1985–1990.

	1985	1986	1987	1988	1989	1990[a]
Number of proxy contests	31	28	21	36	41	(31)
Proxy contests for control or partial control of a company	17	16	14	14	23	(20)
Percent of proxy contests won by management[b]	46	43	44	48	41	38

Source: Wines (1991).

a. Figures are for the first nine months only.

b. Management wins do not include settlements with challengers.

potential power of future proxy challenges by shareholders. One study of 100 proxy contests in the 1981–1985 period revealed that the practical costs of proxy vote solicitation gave management the advantage (Pound, 1988). As a result of the apparent bias, shareholder pressures on company governance and federal regulation to "level the playing field" mounted significantly during the late 1980s and early 1990s. Several large institutional investors and shareholder action groups pressed companies to introduce confidential voting (reducing the ability of management to lobby large investors to alter their vote on shareholder proposals). They also pressed for new proxy regulations by the Securities and Exchange Commission. In late 1989 the California Public Employees' Retirement System petitioned the SEC to undertake extensive revision of the federal proxy rules, and the United Shareholders Association filed a similar petition in early 1990 (Calpers, 1989; United Shareholders Association, 1990). The proposals were comprehensive in nature (the Calpers petition included forty-eight separate points), and both requests included proposals to give challengers better vehicles for communicating with other shareholders, more open access to proxy statements, and better protection from corporate lobbying through confidential voting provisions. In a move that was indicative of the political challenge, however, the Business Roundtable and other groups associated with management (for example, the American Society of Corporate Secretaries, with a membership representing more than 2,000 corporations) rejected many or most of the recommendations. The Business Roundtable, a select association of chief executives of the nation's 200 largest corporations, offered a blunt appraisal: "All the evidence we have seen confirms that the proxy system is working very well for shareholders. While it is certainly appropriate for the S.E.C. to examine the proxy rules periodically, our preliminary analysis suggests the absence of any compelling case for major change'' (Business Roundtable, 1990a, p. 6).

Corporate Defenses

Individual companies did not remain passive during the rising takeover threat and shareholder pressure. A majority of large publicly traded firms instituted governance devices designed to thwart unwanted acquirers. Many of the measures were financial in character but political in purpose. In making hostile acquisitions more difficult, management also implicitly reduced the power of large shareholders. A range of defensive measures was available, some the mirror reverse of shareholder proposals:

Poison pill. If a board does not approve a takeover bid and the bidder nonetheless seeks to acquire the firm, a poison pill policy typically gives shareholders rights to purchase stock in the company or acquirer at a discount price once a hostile buyer accumulates a certain number of shares. Poison pills are also termed "shareholder rights plans."

Classified directors. Directors are classified into several groups, usually three, which are up for reelection at different times. Their staggered terms prevent a hostile suitor from placing an unfriendly majority on the board during a single electoral cycle.

Golden parachutes. Severance agreements for senior executives provide for generous cash and noncash benefits if they are fired or resign following a change in control of the firm. They are not an antitakeover device per se, but they may serve to discourage unwanted acquisitions by giving executives sufficient comfort to mount more vigorous resistance to takeover initiatives. (Wade, O'Reilly, and Chandratat, in their 1990 study, offer indirectly supportive evidence, reporting that chief executives who wield more influence over their boards of directors are also more likely to institute golden parachutes.)

Fair-price requirements. Bidders sometimes make two-tier offers in which an above-market price is offered for some of a company's shares, and then a lower price is offered for the remaining shares after control of the company is secured. A fair-price requirement discourages such two-tier bids in hostile takeovers.

Supermajority vote to approve merger. Going beyond state law, a supermajority provision requires that as much as 75 percent or more of a company's shareholders must approve an unfriendly merger. Since minority blocks of stock may be controlled by managers, directors, and employee stock option plans, a relatively small minority could defeat an unwanted acquisition.

Eliminate cumulative voting. Under cumulative voting for directors, shareholders can cast votes equal to the number of shares times the number of board positions up for reelection. A dissident shareholder could thus concentrate its votes on a single nominee, heightening the likelihood of electing a director friendly to shareholder interests and hostile to incumbent management.

Dual capitalization. Companies sometimes issue two classes of stock, one class having more votes per share than the other. If management purchases a large block of the higher-voting stock, it can dilute the voting power of other shareholders.

Require boards to consider nonfinancial effects of mergers. Firm charters require or permit directors to consider the impact of a change in control on groups other than shareholders. These typically include employees, local communities, and buyers and suppliers.

Antigreenmail. Company policy prohibits above-market purchase of a block of stock (sometimes acquired by a raider). The policy can help deter the accumulation of large blocks of stock that may be used to prepare a takeover effort (Rosenbaum, 1990, pp. vii–xii; Weston, Chung, and Hoag, 1990, pp. 481–529).

Three time series on company adoption of these takeover defenses confirm the heightening of resistance. Comparing three of the most common antitakeover provisions among *Fortune* magazine's 500 largest manufacturing firms in 1985 and 1986 with 1990, Figure 2.8 reveals net growth in all. Using a more limited time span but a larger set of firms, Table 2.8 shows expansion of virtually every major tactic. Of the nation's 1,500 largest publicly traded firms, by 1990 more than half had adopted poison pills and provisions for classified directors. Finally, focusing on poison pill adoptions among 452 manufacturing firms on the Fortune 500 list between 1985 and 1984 and 1989, Figure 2.9 indicates a growth from less than 1 percent in 1984 to more than 64 percent in 1989.

The value of the classified board as a takeover defense was evident in the effort by NCR to resist purchase by AT&T in 1991. After NCR management rejected AT&T's offer, AT&T sought to replace NCR's directors with those more favorable to the offer. Yet because only four of

Percent

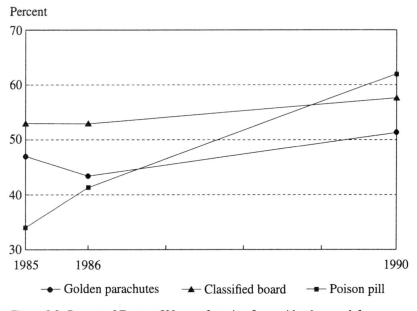

Figure 2.8. Percent of Fortune 500 manufacturing firms with takeover defenses, 1985–1990. (Source: Rosenbaum, 1989, 1990b.)

Table 2.8. Percent of 1,500 large corporations with takeover defenses, 1989–1990.

Takeover defense	1989	1990	Percent change 1989–1990
Classified directors	54.2	57.2	3.0
Poison pill	42.8	51.0	8.2
Fair-price requirement	31.6	31.9	0.3
Supermajority vote to approve merger	16.7	16.9	0.2
Eliminate cumulative voting	7.8	8.8	1.0
Dual capitalization	7.3	7.5	0.2
Require boards to consider nonfinancial effects of mergers	6.0	6.5	0.5
Antigreenmail	5.6	5.6	0
(Number of companies)	(1,440)	(1,487)	

Source: Rosenbaum (1989, 1990b).

Percent

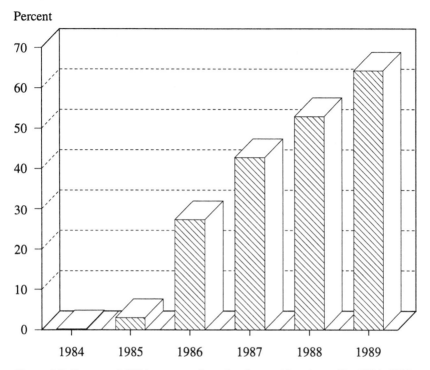

Figure 2.9. Percent of 452 large manufacturing firms with poison pills, 1984–1989. (Source: Davis, 1991a, 1991b.)

thirteen NCR members were up for reelection at its 1991 annual meeting, AT&T could not secure a majority on the board using the normal proxy process (Smith, 1991; Shapiro, 1991).

The overall impact of the corporate shift to classified boards can be seen in studies by the Conference Board. Of 851 companies surveyed in 1972, the policies of 81 percent called for one-year terms. By 1989, only 43 percent of 589 surveyed companies retained such provisions, a majority having adopted three-year staggered terms for board members (Bacon, 1990).

Impact of Owner Challenges on Company Policies

Systematic evidence on the impact of the rising shareholder pressures on company policies and practices confirms that their influence was felt, if not always in predictable or intended ways. Scattered studies permit the construction of a partial mosaic, with some areas still largely unexplored. Let us consider the areas of impact as they relate to the three major avenues for the exercise of ownership influence.

Direct control. The placement of companies and units previously insulated from ownership pressures under direct ownership control transformed a number of financial and organizational elements of the corporation. A study of large leveraged buyouts between 1979 and 1985, for example, found that under new ownership, corporate strategy was more centrally controlled while operating decisions became more decentralized (Easterwood, Seth, and Singer, 1989).

Mutually dependent influence. The mutual interdependence of large corporations and large investors created a nexus in which influence was subtly transmitted. There were few distinctive events to mark the flow, but some outcomes became notable events. Texaco, for example, announced in 1990 that it would bring onto its board a new director who was suggested by major shareholders rather than management. The action constituted a kind of quid pro quo in return for Calpers' earlier decision to support Texaco management in a successful rebuff of an unwanted takeover. Similarly, General Motors announced in 1991 that it would adopt a corporate bylaw that called for a majority of its board to be independent directors, a decision that Calpers, a major GM shareholder, had asked the company to make (White, 1991).

The concept of mutual symbiosis achieved widespread acceptance among major companies. A 1990 survey of 130 large companies, all listed on the New York Stock Exchange (the revenues of three-fifths of them exceeded $1 billion), reported that only a single responding firm viewed the current level of shareholder activism as a ''serious detrimental challenge to corporate control,'' and 38 percent saw it as a ''positive influence on corporate governance.'' Similarly, 22 percent of the companies accepted the view that ''institutional investors, because of the size of their holdings, [should] have special influence on corporate policy and/or management.'' And 58 percent asserted that the importance of ''institutional investors to the financial viability'' of the company was ''vital.'' The symbiosis, at least if one judges by such responses, was less developed among smaller firms. In a parallel survey of seventy companies whose shares were traded over the counter, the comparable figures were, respectively, 10 and 39 percent (National Investor Relations Institute, 1990a; Mahoney, 1991b).

The symbiosis between companies and institutional investors is reported to have measurable impact on certain areas of company policy, though the reports are not necessarily consistent. In the area of research and development, for instance, one study found a positive correlation between the level of institutional investment and company investment in research and development (R&D). Examining R&D spending relative to total revenue among more than 300 companies in the early 1980s, the analysis showed that firms with higher levels of institutional ownership were also those with higher levels of R&D investments (Jarrell, Brickley, and Netter, 1985). By contrast, however, a focused look at twenty-two computer-manufacturing firms from 1976 to 1985 reported a negative relationship between these two factors (Graves, 1988). A third study examined the impact of ownership concentration related to all sources, not just institutional holdings, on R&D spending per employee. Focusing on 122 large manufacturers in 1980, the investigation revealed that companies with higher concentrations of ownership were also those with higher rates of R&D investment (Hill and Snell, 1989).

Mutual dependency is also evident in an observed correlation between the level of institutional shareholding in a firm and its capital structure. One study, focusing on forty paired manufacturing firms, compared the companies with the largest and smallest levels of institutional shareholding in each of forty industries during the 1983–1985 period. The investigation found that firms with high institutional shareholding were also those with low debt-to-equity ratios (the two factors correlated 0.23; Chaganti and Damanpour, 1991). The causal ordering was not clear, but the symbiosis between low debt and high institutional shareholding was.

Concerted individual and collective action. Direct action by owners of company shares, either individually or collectively, also had measurable impact. Institutional investors, example, voted more often for shareholder proposals than did individual shareholders. This inference is based on a 1987 study of voting on thirty shareholder proposals to rescind poison pill provisions. Most of the proposals had been sponsored by just three major institutional shareholders (the College Retirement Equities Fund, the California Public Employees' Retirement System, and the California State Teachers' Retirement System). Support for the proposals averaged 28 percent. In detailed analysis of the records, the study found that about 10 percent of the votes of individual shareholders had been cast for the proposals, while approximately 30 percent of the institutional shares had been so cast (Georgeson and Company, 1987).

Reanalysis of these data for the present study shows that companies with higher proportions of their shares in institutional hands received larger antimanagement votes. The correlation between the percentage of institutional ownership and the percentage of votes for the shareholder proposal was 0.20. These results are corroborated by an investigation of shareholder voting on 288 antitakeover amendments proposed by 191 firms in 1984. This study revealed that when a company's institutional ownership was higher, the rate of voting was higher and more votes were cast against the antitakeover provision (Brickley, Lease, and Smith, 1988). Conflicting results came, however, from a study of 100 dissident proxy contests in 1981–1985 for board seats or governance changes such as antitakeover measures, proposed either by management or dissident stockholders. The challengers' voting success in these contests was higher when institutional shareholding was lower (Pound, 1988; Jensen and Warner, 1988, pp. 11–12).

As in other areas of collective conflict, the process was often one of action, reaction, and still further action among the contending parties. Companies with larger fractions of ownership in institutional hands were more likely to have adopted a poison pill in the first place (Davis, 1992). By inference, their managements felt more vulnerable to takeover threats because of the shakier loyalty of large investors, and they were thus more likely to seek security behind antitakeover defenses. But once the defenses were erected, companies with more of their shares held by large investors were also more vulnerable to shareholder votes to dismantle the defenses. Still other defensive and then offensive measures could follow in succession, a reactive spiraling until détente was reached or the defenses breached.

Most shareholder proposals still failed to win a majority, but indirect evidence indicates that even failed challenges sometimes succeeded. Failed tender offers, for example, were often followed by a set of company changes that the bidder had suggested it would have made had the offer been successful. Polaroid Corporation, for example, resisted an unwanted takeover attempt in 1988–1989 by cutting costs, reducing the workforce, reorganizing top management, and promising enhanced earnings. All were actions that the unfriendly acquirer had stated it would take if its tender had prevailed (Simon, 1988, 1990). Cross-sectional evidence confirming the importance of takeover threats in changing corporate behavior comes from a study of severance packages for top managers in the event of a threatened takeover. Comparing companies that had successfully resisted a hostile takeover attempt with companies that had not been so threatened, the analysts find that the former were significantly more likely to have implemented "golden parachute" polices for their senior managers (Singh and Harianto, 1989). Companies thus often make significant policy changes in response to direct ownership pressures even when such challenges are successfully rebuffed.

Conclusion

After a half-century of unchallenged supremacy, senior management at many corporations faced a revolt from one of the least likely of sources, the shareholders. They were, after all, the owners. But their real ownership powers had long been lost in an atomization of holdings that had left them weak and divided. The disenfranchisement seemed so irreversible that the managerial revolution appeared to be one of those fixed and perhaps eternal qualities of advanced capitalism.

The ownership challenges of the 1980s shattered such conceptions. The surge of corporate mergers and acquisitions was not just another of the shufflings that periodically sweep through American business. The surge carried unique qualities, qualities presaging the owners' revolt. Battles for corporate control ensnarled some of the country's largest enterprises. And a new type of winner appeared, as leveraged owners installed themselves at the center of the company's command and control structure.

The waning of such transactions at the close of the decade signaled more a shift in strategy than any stilling of the revolt. The capacity of shareholders to express their voice only further intensified, as atomization gave way to coherence. Stockholding became concentrated in fewer hands, and the larger of the hands became adept in tugging at corporate management through new means. Shareholder proposals and proxy fights moved to the fore, with less radical but frequently more effective strategies. The struggle for direct control through buyouts was displaced by a struggle for indirect influence through reformation of corporate governance and restoration of shareholder rights.

Managerial capitalism and its conception of control no longer prevailed unchallenged. Management's power to define the parameters of debate and decision making remained enormous. When directly challenged, some of the power was restored through antitakeover legislation and poison pills. But alongside it emerged an institutional capitalism, its conception of rightful control radically different. Shareholders, not professional managers, were to specify and evaluate a company's achievements. The board of directors was to protect outsider interests, not insider perquisites.

As institutional capitalism gained ground and occasionally even the upper hand, a new logic of assessment emerged. The logic called for a distinctive set of organizational principles, for the company was being asked to measure up to different objectives. Major companies, as a consequence, moved to restructure their operations to mollify if not always satisfy the challengers. Some even moved preemptively, before they were challenged. The internal organization of the firm was redesigned in the process, and the resulting alignment of its parts is the subject of what follows.

THREE

Organizational Alignment

In response to shareholder pressures, and at times in anticipation of them, companies moved to reshape their internal organization. Other considerations often fostered such changes simultaneously, and most cannot be uniquely traced to investor concerns, or even to management-attributed investor concerns. But improving shareholder value was an animating management concern, and the changes were frequently justified in such terms.

Whether specific changes actually enhanced the worth of the company to investors was beyond what most managers needed to know to in order to make such changes. Effectiveness could not be definitively established through the groping steps of any single company, and executives were rarely prepared to await the outcome of an exacting academic study of a cross-section of companies. With weakly based but strongly felt foundation, they simply proceeded to alter company design, decision making, and performance assessment.

This chapter identifies four primary components of the resulting change in organization: (1) authority to succeed and fail was pushed deeper in the organization, giving managers and operating units greater autonomy; (2) information was more widely distributed among managers and more focused on shareholder value; (3) managerial decisions were more explicitly judged on the basis of the anticipated value to shareholders; and (4) central managerial and professional staffs were scaled back and headquarters reduced in size. A related component, greater organizational investment in the management of managers, is the subject of Chapter 4. These components have been singled out here not from prior theoretical expectations, for most had not been expected. Rather, they were inductively identified from the many interviews and observations conducted in the company settings. These were the organizational components where ownership-related considerations were most recurrently heard and seen.

Many of these changes were prompted by other considerations as well, and most had appeared in other firms where the principles of shareholder value enjoyed little more than occasional reference. Here, however, they were explicitly and jointly fashioned around ownership concerns, at least ownership concerns as identified by top management. The outcomes were by no means assured or even positive. We will see later in this chapter that the dispersion of authority could lead to disastrous consequences when those who received this authority failed to exercise it well. But as testimony to the staying power of the new ideology, setbacks were treated as tactical problems requiring adjustment and not retreat. And we will see in later chapters that companies also devised ways of simply thwarting ownership pressures, helping to protect the discretionary latitude that they had long enjoyed and felt essential for effective oversight.

Devolution of Authority

By one line of reasoning, the reemergence of ownership power should lead not to a delegation of authority but rather to more centralized control of the firm. After all, much of the momentum behind the original managerial revolution was a forced displacement of founder-owners by nonowning professional managers. The latter had prevailed in the name of eliminating the autocratic and sometimes capricious style of the founding entrepreneur. The exercise of the professionals' superior managerial abilities required that they be well insulated from potentially meddlesome owners. They successfully created that isolation by ensuring that boards of directors, nominally responsible to the shareholders, were in fact responsive to inside management. Research has generally confirmed a picture of boards as more often the "pawns" of management than "potentates" over it (Lorsch, 1989).

As owners reasserted their power, it could be expected that they would demand that top management exercise more authoritative control over the enterprise than before. Systematic study of one set of large firms provides suggestive evidence: compared with management-dominated firms, owner-controlled companies were less divisionalized, less geographically dispersed, and more tightly overseen (Palmer et al., 1987). A study of small and middle-sized firms in the Netherlands yields similar results: as owner-dominated firms became larger, unlike firms dominated by professional managers, they did not decentralize decision making (Geeraerts, 1984).

Yet in each of the companies I studied, decision-making authority was pressed deeper into the organization. Units and managers were accorded greater discretion in making decisions, in areas ranging from product development and pricing to acquisitions and staffing. Units and managers acquired broader control over the resources required for their work. At the same time, they were held more responsible for the outcome of their work. The devolution of authority acquired distinctive features in each company, but generic elements were evident in all.

The special-machinery company had advanced the reorganization as far as any, providing a model of what could be achieved. Two of its officers expressed the company's new managerial premises. According to one senior vice-president: "Our philosophy is to let action happen where it can happen the quickest and most effectively, which on a day-to-day basis is right in the field, the field being the plant or the field sales operation . . . We have tried to keep away from any staff functions, to just keep it flat, and to give a lot of responsibility and authority to our branch and plant managers. We absolutely do not believe in the centralization of a bunch of decisions. We try as hard as we can to not allow people to push the decision up the channel, to make the decision at the point it needs to be made at." And another senior vice-president and former chief financial officer said: "On a day-to-day basis we are decentralized. A lot of the authority has to go to the local managers. We don't have the staff to have day-to-day control. Our corporate staff is less than it was ten years ago, even though we are now ten times as large . . . When you have more control you take away the entrepreneurial spirit."

The organization of corporate headquarters of the special-machinery company reflected the firm's philosophy. The culture was largely verbal, with little written communication. Several managers asserted that actions just moved too quickly to justify lengthy memos. Secretarial staffing mirrored the flow, but violated the business norm. Large corporate headquarters typically place an executive secretary outside nearly every officer's office. At this company, the entire top management relied instead on just several pooled secretaries. The firm's senior vice-president for marketing and sales shared a single secretary with a general sales manager, who himself was responsible for a $600 million operation.

Though business units reported their financial performance regularly, little other documentation, including strategic plans, was expected. Telephone conversations with—or visits by—headquarters' executives were frequent. The senior managers did not hesitate to make telephone contact across their organization. Said one senior vice-president:

> Anybody can call anybody in this company. We try very hard not to have a pyramid structure. "You can't talk to your branch manager before you talk to me first"—that just doesn't go here. [The chief operating officer] will pick up the phone and talk to anybody in the company that calls, and so will all the rest of us. The hell with this damned hierarchy stuff.
>
> If you have a problem, let's find out what it is . . . [If] a branch manager is on vacation, [his subordinates] are not afraid to pick up the phone and call us, and that's the way we want it. Don't give me a line chart that says that this guy reports to this guy who reports to this guy. Let's keep it flowing.

The top executives described themselves less as "instruction givers" and more as "objective setters" and facilitators for resolving conflicts among divisions. As a result, some 160 managers who carried significant profit-and-loss responsibilities more often sought absolution for poor decisions than clearance to make them. The chief operating officer described the decision-making style that he had helped cultivate over a decade:

> If you're used to an organization that provides you with a lot of support, group decisions, committees, and not really having to make significant decisions on your own, this is the wrong place to be. You are just not going to be comfortable in this environment. But if you want an environment with unlimited income where you can make decisions . . . you can really be turned on . . .
>
> [But we] are not going to have success all the time. We are going to have a good plan and we are going to try something, but we may go out and get killed. [So long as] we really thought about it and worked it through, there is no penalty . . . Our managers come back and ask for forgiveness, as opposed to permission.

The reassertion of centralized authority in one area occasioned by a sharp downturn in sales during the recession in late 1990 provided an exception that served to illuminate the rule. So independent had the company's divisions become that many turned to suppliers outside the firm even though other divisions within the firm produced the needed product, albeit at a slightly less competitive price. With the recession's costs mounting, the chief operating officer issued a directive limiting the divisions' autonomy in this area, requiring them to give preferential treatment to internal sources. The directive created considerable stir, in large part because it ran against a culture of divisional autonomy that had become the operating norm.

The transformation in control mechanisms accompanying devolution is also illustrated by the changing rules on "headcounts." At the chemical-products company, for instance, divisional budget requests still included a target for total divisional employment. But the lingering concern with personnel counts was now considered a relic of the past. Once used as a primary method for controlling divisional costs, headcounts had come to be seen as incidental by-products of business strategies. Decisions on how many people to place on payroll, and in what kinds of positions, were to be left to the units themselves. The rationale seemed obvious to all concerned. If the units were responsible for results, they could best balance personnel costs against other costs.

The devolution of authority was more concretely illustrated by an architectural decision of the pharmaceutical company. During the process of implementing arms-length decentralization, the main offices of the operating business units were deliberately located elsewhere when a new headquarters was constructed. The building was of modest proportions, unimposing by contemporary power standards. Given the low traffic volume, the pastoral setting attracted an array of wildlife to its perimeter. "When things are going well and businesses are hitting their objectives," observed the senior vice-president for human resources, "we stay away." But the power to intervene was not far behind the arms-length attitude. "Don't misunderstand decentralization," this official warned, "for a lack of interest, commitment, or willingness to go in . . . if things are not going well." If the financials are slipping and business is not responding, "then we do reserve the right to get more actively involved, and to become more day-to-day partners."

Architectural representation of the altered authority patterns was particularly evident in the interior design of the executive suite at two companies. One had moved the executive area onto a new floor during the 1980s, the other into a new building. The latter was constructed without interior walls—or even offices. On entering the headquarters, a wide atrium staircase brought a visitor onto a broad, third-floor landing area. Here, just beyond an unmarked and unguarded low partition, worked the company's chief executive. His work area was delineated by eye-height L-shaped partitions standing near two sides of a desk, leaving the other two sides entirely open. All conventional barriers to entry were missing. So, too, were the normal physical boundaries for secure discussion. To hold sensitive conversations around such issues as annual compensation, the parties would move to circular meeting rooms set among the low partitions. Even there, only audio privacy could be achieved. The rooms were entirely glass encased, 360 degrees around. Executives meeting in one such setting, for example, looked in one direction onto the work area of the company's general counsel, in another direction onto the work area of the chief financial officer. Room numbers lost meaning; an unfamiliar visitor had to navigate instead by wide boulevards cutting across the executive floor with "street signs" posted at the intersections. The architectural motif was carried to its logical extreme: the boardroom, nestled within the open executive area, was also glass enclosed.

The executive suite of the other company was striking in its contrast with the design of a decade earlier. I had interviewed several of the senior managers of this corporation for a research project in 1980. At that time, the executive area was reached by an exclusive elevator to a high floor. Offices were elegant but entirely conventional in form. Fine nineteenth-century furniture and art lent an ambience of refined status. Numerous executive secretaries added further formality. A decade later, the executive suite had moved down almost to street level, and its denizens no longer enjoyed exclusive elevator service. Here, too, the designers had used a great deal of glass. The offices were enclosed, ensuring conversational privacy, but two and sometimes three of the walls were now of glass from floor to ceiling, eliminating any visual privacy. Secretarial work stations were scattered on one side of the offices, but formal entry was no longer fully guarded. The other side of the most senior offices opened onto a planted courtyard, offering top executives unplanned and unannounced access to one another.

Decentralized Planning and Business Development

A corollary of devolution was to move planning and business development out of headquarters and into the operating units. A corporate office would still facilitate the process, structuring timetables and documents for review but leaving the content of most decision making to operating units outside headquarters. At the same time, the decisions here as elsewhere became more explicitly disciplined around shareholder value.

Some planning and development functions had to remain centrally based. Decisions on whether to "grow" or "squeeze" a division obviously stayed at headquarters. So, too, did decisions on the divestiture or acquisition of business units. The pharmaceutical company, for example, sold a large division during the period of this study. According to those responsible for the divestiture, the division's products no longer fit what had come to be considered the company's core business. What was more important, its earnings were no longer judged adequate. No single precipitating event had moved the company to make the decision at that particular time. But after some years of considering the action, a headquarters consensus had finally emerged among a half-dozen senior managers that the timing was right. Though kept well informed about the decision as it crystallized, managers in the divested division were never consulted about its desirability or even timing.

Smaller acquisitions and divestitures, however, were typically the province of business units, not headquarters. Central management structured a review process but then pushed the final decisions into the divisions that would have to operate, or give up, the business in question. The acquisition aspect could be seen in the electrical-products firm, which received a continuous flow of queries from Wall Street firms in search of buyers for their client companies. Investment bankers sometimes brought offers in person, but more often communicated prospects by mail, telephone, Federal Express, and, increasingly, fax. One major investment bank called daily. During one fourteen-month period, the company logged some 800 transaction offers. Like unsolicited manuscripts arriving at New York publishers, much of these "over the transom" queries were immediately dismissed by the headquarters' director of corporate acquisitions. Of the 800 queries, only 250 were sent for vetting by an appropriate business unit. About one in eight found a business unit that wanted to investigate, the sine qua non for forward movement. In the end, only twenty to twenty-five transactions came to fruition, most well under $10 million but a few over $100 million. Whatever the merits as seen from headquarters, no deals were moved forward until a division came actively to embrace its ownership.

The decentralized acquisition or divestiture decision, however, was predicated on a key condition for completing the deal: a forecast that it would add to shareholder value. A critical test came at the company's "Strategic Capital Review Committee," which evaluated all significant acquisitions, divestitures, and joint ventures. According to several managers serving on the committee, a primary criterion alongside market factors was the transaction's financial promise. The financial promise was calculated using the firm's standard algorithm for determining shareholder value. Proposals embraced by business units that did not measure up were turned down.

A conversion of the planning and development function at the chemical-products company was indicative of how far down the decision pyramid such activity had been pressed. A decade earlier, each business unit authored its own annual plan, but the director of planning actively participated in developing the document. He and his ten-person professional staff also prepared a five-to-ten-page analysis to accompany the plan as it was submitted to the corporate executive committee. The planning staff offered its own recommendations, endorsing some strategies while rejecting others. Often written in a style more persuasive to the executive committee than was the business unit's plan itself, the headquarters' planning analysis was at times accorded more attention than the business unit's original proposal.

By 1990, however, the central planning function had been transformed into a purely facilitating function. The director of planning, whose incumbency had spanned the decade, contrasted his office with that of ten years earlier:

> Now all we do is orchestrate the process. We create guidelines . . . but everything in this handsome pile of data here is generated by them, not by me or anybody in my group. There is not a word that we put in there. There is not a corporate person that participates. It's 100 percent, or at least 99 percent, theirs.
>
> The dialogue is between the unit and the Executive Committee. The Executive Committee is really reading the plans directly. It is actively engaged in dialoguing and critiquing in a line-manager to line-manager fashion, the president of a division to the president of the company.

The direct dialogue was evident in the format of the quarterly meetings between the top one or two managers of each business unit and the company executive committee, a meeting attended by as many as a dozen headquarters managers. The head of corporate planning joined the group, but his function was largely that of recording secretary. Even the responsible executive vice-president rarely joined the conversation. The dialogue was almost entirely between the company CEO and the head of the business unit.

The business units were also expected to guide most of their own business development. Because the divisions operated in distinctive markets, it was presumed that they were best informed about their industry and competition. They could choose to emphasize research, product development, licensing, or acquisition, but it was their choice, not central management's. The business units, as a result, had built their own planning and development capacities.

Other firms had simply abolished the formal planning process altogether. The special-machinery company eliminated its entire planning staff. The pharmaceutical company had moved in the same direction. It had dropped long-term central strategic planning during the mid-1980s, an effort, in the rationale of an executive vice-president, "to push decisions down to the lowest possible level."

When Devolution is Incomplete

Though in most companies consensus on the devolution of decision making prevailed, not all general managers shared in the philosophy. The culture of decentralized responsibility was never fully implanted. Significant resistance could still be seen even in firms that had been devolving authority for as much as a decade.

Sometimes opposition came from above, at other times from below. Whatever the location, the difference often originated in generational schisms in experience and philosophy. In the case of the chemical-products corporation, for example, all twelve senior managers whom I interviewed expressed a commitment to pushing decision making lower into the organization. In a typical framing, the president of a major division offered a singular summing-up of his own managerial style: "I really try to empower people to do their jobs."

Virtually all of the managers of the chemical-products company acted on the commitment, save one: the chief executive. Though believing in the concept of decentralization and given to its rhetoric, the CEO carried other managerial baggage that in practice militated against it. The CEO's inability to live by his official commitment was widely recognized in the organization. As described by the president of one of the major business units, the sources of the conflicting posture were appreciated even if the business impact was not: "He's obviously a bright guy or he wouldn't be where he is, and he's able to amass a lot of information. I think some would say maybe too much for a chief executive. He has an uncanny memory, he had a broad experience in the company, and he works at it. But when you've been at that [CEO] level that long, there's nothing worse than an expert of twenty years ago.'' The chief executive was known to have a more detailed mastery of business-unit planning documents than anybody else at headquarters. The ''uncanny'' memory helped, since planning documents produced by each of the firm's fifteen business units typically numbered several hundred pages. Long work weeks helped too: he was able to absorb much of the material during his two hours of daily chauffeured commuting and late work almost every evening at home.

The regimen created by the CEO's intrusive involvement in detail was evident in the operating experience of the division presidents. One, for example, had negotiated a joint venture with another company to pool their complementary research and development expertise around the development of a promising product. Both sides viewed it as a ''win-win'' arrangement. Yet when the division president sought approval from a review committee chaired by the chief executive, the CEO instructed him to go back to the table to obtain a far more favorable arrangement, even pushing for outright control rather than joint oversight. The division president argued from his earlier negotiations that the other side would not concur, but the CEO insisted. ''There's only one vote at these meetings,'' said the division president. He returned to the negotiating table, and the deal predictably soon fell through. As a result of these and other experiences, said the unit president, ''we are always looking upward. We get a lot of direction from up on top . . . The chief executive feels he wants to push more and more down into the organization, but his personal management style is to get down into it [himself]. He tries not to, but the first thing anybody says [about a plan], 'how would Fred react to this?' ''

Other corrosive effects on creative decision making, management development, and product innovation were also attributed to the CEO's inability to let go. An executive vice-president to whom several of the largest business units reported candidly described his views of the chief executive's business impact: ''When the presidents [of the business units] know the CEO wants to be involved in everything, the presidents really hesitate making decisions. [The CEO] wants to run the company by himself. I think you build a weak succession plan when you have . . . a CEO who wants to be involved in everything . . . What happens at the lower level is that people are afraid to make decisions or *don't* make decisions, because they know that I am going to make it, or the CEO is going to make it. I think that's bad . . . We wonder why we don't have more innovation, why people won't take more risk." Much of the difference stemmed from generational disparities in the definition of what it meant to manage. This same officer observed: "Who do you think you are that you should be making all the decisions for the company based on your extreme lack of knowledge and detail? It's a generational thing. A lot of the older managers, going down all levels, don't feel they're performing unless they can be involved in decisions, minute as they might be . . . The whole organization has got to change. The CEO is sensitive to it, but it's so hard for him to change."

The senior managers necessarily adapted their operating styles to a decision-making climate that they well understood but did not support. One business unit, for instance, had decided to sell an international operation, and it completed the tentative arrangements quickly. Despite the deal's near closure and its clear payoff, the CEO asked his strategy board to review the decision. The executive vice-president responsible for the unit felt he had no choice but to comply with the process. In the end, he successfully defended the decision, and the deal was finally completed. But the compliance did not stem from acceptance. He nursed an alternative vision of how the company should operate:

> My own view is that the CEO or I should work on certain things that no one else is working on. I am going to give [the managers reporting to me] all the help that I can, I'll give them guidance and direction as to where I want to go, but either you win or you lose on your own merits.
>
> What it really comes down to is we have to get top management out of the process in many areas. There is no question that if we are going to get rid of the chemical business, or if we are going to spend $100 million on a chemical acquisition, then I should be in the process . . . But once I say, "OK, I like this, I think that's the direction we ought to go in," then that's it. "Go do it, I don't want to structure your deal."

This executive vice-president hoped and anticipated that his stress on decentralized decision making might one day prevail:

> If I were running the company, we would have more turnover. We have got a lot of guys who are dependent; they are not making the decisions. They complain, "We would like more autonomy" or "We would like this or that," but they are so comfortable with the structure. They are not making the decision, the sense of urgency is not there, they are not moving things

forward fast, and they are touching all the bases to make sure it's in sync with everybody else. That doesn't work.

I would force [the decisions] down, and say: "You have to do it. But at the end of the year I am going to review you, and if you're a good manager, I am going to reward you accordingly. But if you're not, you're going to get another year, and then you are going to get moved aside." I want to put P& L [profit-and-loss responsibility] as far down as I can get it.

He was to have his opportunity. Within a year of the interviews, he had been promoted to the company's presidency. The post was immediately below that of the CEO, and it was widely assumed that he had been implicitly designated the heir apparent. A major proponent of the devolutionary vision was slated to replace the last major holdout for centralized control. The generation gap was closing.

Distributing authority was characterized by elements of both pushing and pulling. Committed to the model, top management found that implementing the principle sometimes clashed with the inertia of traditional behavior among other managers. A chief executive of the transportation company, for example, had campaigned for smaller staffs and larger responsibilities. When he joined the company in the early 1980s, total employment stood near 60,000; by the time he stepped down as CEO in the late 1980s, the rolls had been shrunk to some 35,000 (a reduction that saved an estimated $1 billion in annual payroll). In pushing authority down, he found that some of the firm's long-serving senior managers were not always prepared to accept the responsibility: "I had to canvass people in [the company] and then give everybody a try at what needed to be done. And then, as they showed an inability or unwillingness to make changes, then I had to make changes . . . After five years, I had a lot of blood on my hands. [For instance], I gave one individual all the resources and authority that he indicated he needed to do the job, but he ultimately failed. It was an organizational failure as people would not support him, and I fired him."

On the other hand, a number of aspiring managers were ready to embrace enlarged responsibilities. During the early 1980s, before the restructuring process was initiated, they chafed under the company's centralized bureaucracy. The route to the top was perceived to have been through the mastery of a vast set of rules enforced by headquarters. The procedures reflected in part the regulatory environment in which the company operated. But they also stemmed from a long-dominant traditional managerial style—"kick ass, take names," in the words of one executive who had risen through the ranks. Survivors reported endless examples of inefficient decision making. One account is illustrative.

During the early 1980s, a western regional manager initiated construction of a local plant for manufacturing a product used in the firm's transportation system. The footing for the plant had been built, rock aggregate had been placed in the middle, and the building department was about to pack the aggregate down so it could receive a concrete pouring. But the tamper for packing the aggregate broke. The cost of leasing a tamper for a day was $25, but company rules required headquarters approval for any such rental. As the manager describes it,

> The guys were out there and the machine stopped. They couldn't get it working, and so they sent a request to the building department foreman, and asked him for approval. He had to get it from the roadmaster, and the roadmaster had to get it from the assistant superintendent of maintenance, and he had to get it from me, and I had to get it from the regional assistant vice-president for operations, and he had to get from [the vice-president for operations at national headquarters]. The approval finally came back two weeks later: "Yes, it's OK to lease this tamper for $25."

But the epilogue to the broken-tamper episode transpired before headquarters approval was received. Out of frustration, the local crew chief had leased the tamper anyway without telling anybody. By the time approval arrived, the building had been built.

"Everybody knew the system was so bureaucratic," the manager observed. "It didn't work, we all knew we had too many people, but there had never been a drive to clean house." When the company subsequently initiated a drive to decentralize, he readily embraced the concept. "[We knew] it was the right thing to do. Instead of always having to go to somebody else to get their OK, we started doing things the way we knew they had to be done." An early application of his new-found powers was in the cleanup of transportation accidents. The company had approached accidents in much the same way it had reviewed leasing requests. Nationwide rules mandated a well-worn procedure that the company had been using almost unchanged for nearly a century. As the winds of devolution spread, however, the staff in this region developed its own approach to accident cleanup. It devised a procedure that required less expensive equipment, fewer people to operate, and less time to complete. Concluded the regional manager, "Innovation [finally] began to play a part in the way we did our business."

When Devolution Backfires

Devolution of responsibility also carried the seeds of its own destruction. In placing greater authority in subordinate hands, top management expected better results. But it also anticipated greater errors. Because of the larger performance variability inherent in the decentralization of decision making, averting disasters large and small became more difficult. If too large, the results could put a division or even an entire company at risk.

The downside of devolution became visually evident as I waited for an executive interview at one of the companies. The headquarters setting was typical of that of many large corporations. The offices of the company's four top executives anchored the corners of a rectangular open area; the half-dozen other most senior managers were similarly arrayed just one floor below. Executive-secretary work stations, replete with the latest technologies, guarded each office. A signpost of private power, a company-heliport windsock, fluttered outside. Ordinarily the area's human density would be low, the tenor subdued. The tranquillity was abruptly broken this day, however, by an impromptu assemblage of senior managers. They almost instantaneously converged on a meeting room adjacent to the CEO's office. The chief executive and one of his executive vice-presidents arrived in shirtsleeves. A dozen other managers came without briefing books or other accoutrements of preplanned events. It seemed that all had been summoned on short notice.

The CEO and the chief financial officer were seeking immediate guidance. An international subsidiary of the corporation was led by an ambitious general manager. In the name of entrepreneurial growth, he and his own comptroller had secured local bank loans to expand the operation. They had decided they could ''grow'' the business more aggressively if they had more working capital. The actions had been unauthorized but had gone undetected for more than a year. Local banks believed that the general manager would not have borrowed unless authorized. No natural alarms were tripped, since he was careful to spread the borrowing among a number of banks. When fluctuating exchange rates, hyperinflation, and other unanticipated problems emerged, the subsidiary borrowed still more local funds just to meet the interest payments on the unauthorized loans. To disguise this purpose, the subsidiary falsified sales figures, and that in turn led to a writing of phony invoices. Massive falsification of sales results soon followed in a desperate effort to prop up a tottering house of cards.

The headquarters treasury had finally uncovered the scheme just moments before the managers had been so quickly assembled. "It was amazing how large and extensive it got," rued one company official, "without us knowing it." Five days later, the company publicly announced a loss of nearly $24 million from the operation. Shareholders, of which more than half were institutions, absorbed some of the loss. Earnings per share for the year were reduced by about 10 percent. The corporation's comptroller and its chief financial officer were shaken. The senior manager responsible for this international subsidiary, already viewed skeptically by top management, had a nail driven into his career coffin.

In relinquishing direct supervisory control, central managements recognized the potential of such downside results. The risks were seen as implicit in the definition of devolution. More responsibility had been placed in the hands of subordinates, to fail as well as to succeed. Several of the central managements stood poised to intervene, but only as a last resort. The chief executive of the pharmaceutical company had pulled his headquarters staff back from routine oversight of divisional decision making, while sharpening the stress on results. But he also remained ready to act when devolution backfired or fell short. In the characterization of the company's chief financial officer: "[The CEO] will tell the divisions what he wants, but he won't tell them how to get there. He is only inclined to interfere if they don't seem to be able to make decisions, they're not doing it right, or they stubbed their toes."

Creating a Culture of Self-Reliance

With working arguments akin to Zuboff's concepts of information empowerment (Zuboff, 1988), top managers sought to ensure that other managers knew more about the shareholder-driven strategies and long-run objectives of the company. Wider distribution of information would enable managers to assess whether their actions were contributing to the firm's goals. Without such information, more authority to make decisions was seen as meaningless. With such information, managers would seek even more authority to make decisions. Equally important, the information was targeted to a greater extent at emphasizing shareholder value.

The improved distribution of information passed through time-honored managerial channels, but new forms of transmission opened additional avenues as well. Internal communication at the transportation company was a case in point. To its traditional quarterly magazine it had added a monthly newsletter, a video program series, and an electronic alert system for transmitting significant news and developments throughout the company. In 1989 the company began to distribute annual shareholder reports to all employees, and in 1990 quarterly shareholder reports were added to the distribution. The content of the communications was reoriented as well, establishing and reinforcing the primacy of shareholder value. "We want the employees to learn," said the vice-president for communications and public affairs, "that the company is being managed for the benefit of the shareholders, and that decisions we make with regard to facilities and operations have that at their root." A driving concern was the building of a new culture: "How do you make 35,000 employees understand that the whole point of this [company's business] is returning earnings to shareholders? How do we get our employees to understand that the company is not run for the convenience of our shippers or our employees, that the first calling is for the shareholders?" In 1990, the monthly employee newsletter began to report the company's stock prices and a range of related business indicators. A mid-year issue, for instance, contained the daily closing prices of the company's stock for the month of May. Another chart displayed a weekly tracking of the company's service performance. Elsewhere, in responding to a nonexempt employee's letter objecting to the limited number of employees eligible for incentive compensation, the vice-president for human resources took the opportunity to remind readers of their common ground with the shareholders: "Employees of this company can, and should, benefit—along with the owners of the company—from outstanding financial success." Among the ways to engineer such sharing, he suggested, were expansion of stock ownership plans and performance-based bonuses. No concrete proposals were advanced in his brief response, but the implicit alignment message was clear.

The intensified emphasis on communicating shareholder value to employees was also evident in an internal publication of the retail-services company. One monthly magazine, distributed throughout the company's supervisory ranks, had a circulation in 1991 of more than 50,000. Published since the 1970s, it had made virtually no reference to shareholders until 1985. Then, for the first time, appeared a report on the company's annual-meeting. Thereafter the annual-meeting report became a regular feature, periodic reminder of the supervisors' ultimate source of authority. The report's prominence grew considerably during the next five years, more than doubling in space by 1990.

The chairman's speech at the company's annual meeting was also quoted, to stress the linkage between employee performance and share value. Stated the 1989 message: "We are proud of our record of [stock appreciation and dividends], tributes to the hard work of our employees . . . who focus on the operating fundamentals of our business. As shareholders, many of them have the same interests as you, and, consequently, you benefit from their hard work and dedication." The appreciated value of the company to shareholders was also summarized by one line repeated in each year's article. The chairman annually compared the current value of one share of stock to its value in the mid-1960s. By the end of the 1980s, he was able to inform shareholders—and all those with supervisory responsibilities—that the ratio had reached almost 250:1.

As in building and sustaining any common culture, executives used both ceremonial occasions and regular meetings to reinforce the company's core values among their managers. The linkage between individual performance and collective achievement was repeatedly stressed. For instance, one of the main exhibits that the special-machinery company's chief executive and chief operations officer consistently used in formal management meetings was a report of the firm's return to its shareholders. The chart was shown, for example, at the general management meeting held every four months. Here the CEO typically offered an extended presentation of recent developments in the firm's earnings per share. Upon delivering the general message, he then turned to the individual units and specific events that were helping or hurting that performance. Similarly, the company ran a management education center adjacent to headquarters, making appearances by senior management a regular feature of the experience of managers brought in from around the country. Senior managers reminded participants that each was responsible for overall performance, and that overall performance had but one criterion. A senior vice-president who frequently made training program appearances characterized the main objective: "[We stress] the idea that you personally are contributing—or are not contributing—to the earnings performance, and that what you do in your particular operation can definitely make a difference on the shares' performance."

Building and sustaining a culture is always an incomplete process. Pockets of resistance, cynicism, and indifference remained. Observed one manager: "We talk in glowing terms about shareholder value, and this corporation has probably done a very good job of educating people as to the catechism of value. I'm not sure that the religion has been instilled."

The lower the ranks, the more difficult the inculcation. Bringing the rank-and-file employee into the culture required more ingenuity because there was less to offer. For general management, understanding and acting on the concepts and logic of shareholder value were soon reinforced with enlarged business budgets and higher compensation. For lower levels, the tangible consequences became less evident, making the educational task more daunting.

Despite such constraints, several of the companies were determined to spread the gospel. An initiative by the electrical-products maker was instructive. It had succeeded in creating the alignment culture at the top and then sought to move it to the bottom. As a priority for the 1990s, the chief executive pressed the importance of "value creation for all audiences." The headquarters manager primarily responsible for making it happen described the task: "The biggest challenge we've had . . . is to communicate shareholder value. There's nothing more pressing, more important, more concentrated in all of our communications than share-holder value. That's something that makes an awful lot of sense when you are talking to the security analysts . . . But we have found that not even 10 percent of our employees are shareholders, and they don't understand what [shareholder value] has to do with anything." Still, those most responsible for the program remained convinced that shareholder value would be more readily understood and accepted as a company goal than traditional barometers. Managers theorized that, for employees, it would carry greater legitimacy and tangibility. According to the firm's director of strategic planning:

> Shareholder value . . . is something that people can get motivationally and emotionally tied to, more so than profits. Why would anybody say: "Hey, I like [income after taxes] as a percentage of sales, I want to maximize that"? I think they would rather say, "I want my share price to go up, and I want to beat [a competitor] in share price. And I want to read that in the [*Wall Street*] *Journal.*"
>
> I don't think people necessarily have to understand [it] . . . In communicating with the engineer or the shop worker, how can they understand share-holder value? Well they don't have to understand shareholder value, they just have to read the [share] price in the paper, and that price relates to the things that happen in the business.

From informal feedback, top management had nonetheless concluded that the alignment culture had made few real inroads at the grassroots, despite some downward education efforts. A new, more aggressive initiative was intended to overcome that. The corporate communications office brought nearly three dozen communications specialists from the company's various business units to an informal meeting with the chief executive. In a script prepared by the headquarters communications chief, the CEO focused the agenda: "How do you get the employees to buy in as owners?" He wanted one main message delivered: " 'You are important and what you contribute is important.' How you get that across to [more than 100,000] people is our greatest challenge."

In the spirit of decentralization, the meeting of the specialists with the chief executive was treated as a kind of internal press conference. Headquarters provided the division specialists with photographs, a camera-ready article, and audio tapes on shareholder value. It was then up to them to fashion a communication program to best deliver the message within their own business units. As described by the responsible headquarters manager: "We really want them to come in to hear from [the CEO's] perspective what's important, and then let them ask all the questions so they can figure out how to best communicate to their own employees. We can't do that here . . . That's why we want to involve the local communicators a lot more. If they can understand what [the CEO wants to say], they can figure out how to communicate to their employees." To monitor progress, headquarters added several questions to a standard corporation-wide employee questionnaire. It asked if the employees had "heard of Shareholder Value" and whether they had learned about it from supervisors, higher management, company publications, or electronic media. The agenda was simply to ensure that the rank-and-file absorbed the basic concept. In the summary assessment of the vice-president for corporate relations: "We don't need to educate everybody on [our shareholder-value rubric and decision rules], but we sure do want them to realize that every decision should be made on the basis of 'does it add value?' "

Measuring Decisions and Results

A corollary of the deemphasis on control was a reemphasis on results. If the process of reaching preset objectives was of lessened concern, the outcome was of greater concern. Moreover, the specific manner in which the results were stressed and ultimately measured derived directly from the emphasis on ownership value.

Measurement tools for company and internal valuation exercises were available from a number of consulting firms (for example, from Alcar, McKinsey, Stern Stewart, and Valuation Research Corporation). Other consulting firms specialized in translating the valuation measures into schemes for management compensation (for example, Hewitt Associates; Hay Management Consultants; Towers, Perrin, Forster and Crosby). General instruments for helping to make shareholder value operational in decision making were available as well (see, for instance, Rappaport, 1986; Coperland, Koller, and Murrin, 1990; Reimann, 1990; Sikora, 1990).

Despite the external services and internal efforts, the concept remained fuzzy at best in the minds of many managers. When I asked for his operating conception of shareholder value, the chief financial officer of one of the corporations turned the question back on me. "You probably know more about it," he said, "since you've thought about it more than I have."

Still, agreement on the basics had become widespread. Shareholder value was generally understood to be some combination of share dividends and appreciation, accumulated over several years. All of the firms had taken steps to specify the concept so that it could be used in guiding decisions and assessing outcomes.

At the electrical-products firm, a single operational definition was employed to judge an array of actions. It was used, for example, as a central criterion throughout the biannual strategic review of its sixteen business units. A week prior to its strategic-review hearing with the company's top management, each business unit submitted a forty-page planning document, fashioned around one "primary objective": to "make your business unit *worth more to* [*the company*] than it's worth today." To this end, the business units prepared an assessment of the major alternatives they foresaw. For each segment, a business unit calculated a "business-as-usual" value, and this then served as a benchmark for evaluating the anticipated additional value of proposed alternatives. The literal bottom line for the presentation to top management was the forecast growth in what was termed the "warranted market value" (WMV) for each of the segments and the overall business unit. WMV furnished a numerical measure derived from a formula based on the return on equity, the cost of equity, and an anticipated growth rate. It was designed to approximate what an outside investor would assign to the segment or unit, thereby providing an operational surrogate for share price and dividend.

Central management repeatedly focused attention on the singular importance of this one measure of performance. "Shareholder value is our *internal* corporate driving force," commented the company's president at the annual retreat with his top management in 1988. "We expect our business units to perform like successful corporations . . . This is what investors expect from established corporations, and it's what we must expect from our established business units." As a result, he affirmatively warned, "value-generating businesses deserve additional resources: more people, more capital, more strategic money."

To ensure that the value-based planning process was understood by all practitioners, the company's planning department mounted short courses on the subject for the top management of all of its business units. The course title was unambiguous: "How to Build Shareholder Value." The message was also unequivocal: "We need to communicate that [the company] is managed to continuously grow shareholder value." During an offering of the course in early 1987 to executives of one of the company's major business units (which would have ranked well up the Fortune 500 list if it had been an independent company), the unit's senior management was told that shareholder value remained the central criterion in decision making in (1) comparing alternative strategies, (2) evaluating investments, (3) deploying resources, (4) considering acquisitions, (5) shutting plants down, (6) exiting from aging business lines, and (7) cutting employment. In comparing investment strategies, for instance, the managers were reminded that "the alternative that promises the highest WMV is the preferred investment." To make the process operational, the course offered a detailed exercise in calculating WMV for three strategic alternatives, and another exercise in determining whether an acquisition candidate looked promising according to the same criteria.

In each major area of decision making, the company had constructed algorithms favoring alternatives that emphasized value. Business-unit managers had little incentive to retain a product, plant, or operation that was not contributing to their unit's performance at acceptable levels. Nor would they see advantage in acquiring a line that would not do the same. Disposing of a "loser" would increase a unit's operating profit margins, which in turn favored the managers' year-end bonus calculation. "There is so much corporate pressure to improve margins," observed the director of corporate acquisitions, "that an intelligent general manager will do his best to get rid of businesses that are not strategic to him, that are not contributing high margins." On the acquisition side, without a strong "value story," a business unit would find it difficult to sell an acquisition proposal to a company review committee. Most general managers would not even bring such a recommendation forward if it appeared to run the risk of diluting the unit's income after taxes, a key criterion for assessing annual performance for the unit and its management. A number of otherwise potentially appealing acquisitions brought by headquarters to the business units were thus rejected because of the measurement criteria already instilled in the units by headquarters.

Other companies undertook analogous efforts to measure the contributions of business units to overall shareholder value, and several developed equally elaborate algorithms for estimating a unit's contribution to its dividends and stock growth. None contemplated issuing separate classes of stock for their business units, as General Motors had done with two of its acquired subsidiaries (Electronic Data Systems, and Hughes Aircraft and Delco Electronics). But several had undertaken planning exercises around the creation of "phantom stocks" that would more systematically permit such calculations.

Short of that device, companies evolved less precise ways of making management action parallel company objectives. One of the more common mechanisms was seen in a complex rating of the special-machinery corporation's sales branch operations. Its twenty-nine operations were ranked monthly and annually on their net income and other measures assumed to have long-term impact on shareholder value. The ratings were circulated to all branches (a sample is shown in Table 3.1), leaving no secrets about which operations were, or were not, contributing to shareholder prosperity. The vice-president for marketing and sales, author of the monthly comparative assessment, used it as an explicit device for stimulating earnings:

Table 3.1. 1990 ranking of 6 out of 29 sales branches of a special-machinery corporation.

Location	Overall ranking	Net income before taxes		Pretax percent return		Net income 1990 v. 1989		Sales increase 1990 v. 1989	
		Thousands of dollars	Rank	Percent	Rank	Thousands of dollars	Rank	Percent	Rank
Seattle	1	1,451	4	7.31	3	449	5	43.8	4
Denver	2	919	13	6.95	5	(15)	15	32.8	7
Scranton	3	1,657	2	6.63	9	434	6	10.6	19
Houston	27	(415)	28	−3.81	29	(282)	25	0.7	26
Chicago	28	(460)	29	−1.71	28	(1,368)	29	7.4	20
Atlanta	29	92	25	0.89	26	(371)	27	−0.7	28

Source: Records of the special-machinery company (1990).

If our earnings are going down, we say, "Hey guys, we can't let this happen." The board and the Street are looking to see what we are doing. Our whole objective that we set for everybody is improvement of our earnings over the prior period on a continuing basis and what do we have to do to make that happen . . . So we don't look kindly on an operation that is making less earnings this year than last. I want to know for damn sure why that's happening.

The pressure is always on us to improve our earnings over the prior year or the prior period. We keep the pressure on ourselves . . . We believe the way that you get your stock price up is to improve your earnings per share, and you get your earnings per share going because you get better earnings out of each operation in the business.

Contraction of Central Management

The increase of ownership influence placed top management in a kind of double bind. It had devolved more authority into the operating units of the organization, relinquishing much day-to-day control. Yet at the same time it was under intensified pressure to assure that all units were contributing to the firm's financial performance. In contrast to earnings in an era when managerial power went largely unchallenged, lackluster results now invited bargain hunters, proxy fights, and early retirements.

While placement of more authority in the divisions pointed toward a reduction of central staff, the pressure to produce could thus also have pointed to the opposite. To increase the firm's value to its shareholders, more oversight was required to redirect investments, reshape the culture, dispose of unprofitable divisions, and more generally discipline the company's operations. An enlarged headquarters headcount could therefore be seen as essential to implement the new ownership-related discipline.

However valid may be the argument for hiring more corporate managers to promote shareholder value, the opposite occurred. The organizations I studied had generally moved toward fewer reporting levels. Less detailed information was required from the operating units, and less frequent review of their decisions was exacted. Central staff functions were curtailed as well. Strategic planning, human resource, finance, purchasing, and other staffs were streamlined as many of their responsibilities were moved into the operating business units.

The chemical-products company, for example, had cut its headquarters staff of more than 2,000 to under 1,000 during the 1980s. The net reduction to the company, however, was probably less than a fifth the number, since a majority of staff members were simply reassigned to similar work within specific business units. One headquarters function with some thirty-five staff members was completely eliminated, yet most of these just moved their offices to the divisions. Still, their movement out of headquarters was consistent with the devolution of authority into the operating business units. Several of the companies explicitly used a headquarters employment cap as a means for forcing devolution. The chief executive of the pharmaceutical company imposed a freeze on the central headcount soon after he took office in the mid-1980s. Any additions to the headquarters rolls required his personal approval. The measure was not primarily aimed at cutting costs, though that was a welcome by-product. It was done simply to diminish the capacity of central managers to retain staff and thereby maintain direct control.

One case illustrates how far the central-office downsizing can go. The special-machinery company grew more than ten-fold during the 1990s, leapfrogging over many competitors. In 1980 it was not counted among America's 500 largest manufacturers. Two years later it had reached the lower rungs of the Fortune 500; by 1985 it ranked above 400; and by 1990 it had risen near 200. During this same period its corporate staff was cut by some 90 percent (from approximately 320 to thirty), and its headquarters facility correspondingly shrank.

Housed in a modern but modest two-story clapboard building in an isolated rural setting, the central management team in 1990 numbered six general managers, three attorneys, five tax specialists, five accountants, and three internal auditors. When I asked the chief operating officer at the end of an interview if it would be possible to interview his directors of strategic planning and of human resources, he said, "You just did." So extensive had been the flattening of the organizational chart that this officer had become fond of saying that "we are a mile wide and a quarter-inch deep."

At the start of the 1980s, central staff had included forty-five individuals responsible for manufacturing and thirty people responsible for contracting. By the end of the 1980s, a single person remained for manufacturing, and only one person oversaw contracting. The reductions went hand in hand with a radical cutback in the amount of formal reporting, and a sharp increase in the amount of field authority. Prior to the headquarters downsizing, for example, all contracts exceeding $100,000 required central approval. After the downsizing, only contracts exceeding $1 million required higher-level attention, and then only for an open review of whether it was the best contract, not for formal approval. Similarly, before the contraction of central management, the three major manufacturing plants devoted considerable time to preparing plans for review by the forty-five-person manufacturing division at headquarters. After the contraction, all such reporting was abolished. The chief operating officer contrasted the decision-making climate before and after. The first he inherited upon joining the manufacturing staff; the second, he helped create:

> If there was a problem with a manufacturing plant . . . [since] these forty-five people needed something to do, they would fly down to [the plant locations] and get a five-year forecast [from the plant managers] and bring it back. Then they would have staff meetings for three or four days a week and talk about all these plans. We really didn't do anything that made the product better, got us more competitive, or got us closer to our customer.
>
> I just couldn't understand what we were accomplishing by these meetings. [They] had nothing to do with the product, or selling the product, or making the product, or reducing product costs of improving product quality . . . [The plan] would be analyzed to death because you had a big staff and you had people "pro it" and people "con it." They never got anything done.

Similarly, the requirement of central approval for contracts exceeding $100,000 meant that action had been slow. External contracts at this company called for the manufacture and installation of its special equipment according to customer design. The company was facing challenges from smaller, leaner competitors which had better products, were more responsive to customer needs, and were faster to act. As a result, observed the chief operating officer, "All this [approval process] did was to give you a high degree of certainty that you weren't going to get the job. By the time you submitted your bid, the job was halfway done."

The review and approval procedures and their staffs had been completely abolished. The new headquarters building, as a result, was a fraction of its predecessor's size. The company's director of investor relations, a senior vice-president with several other major responsibilities in his portfolio, delighted in bringing Wall Street analysts to visit. The modest physical structure served as a useful metaphor for the firm's operating culture:

> One of the points that we make is that we have a limited overhead, that our corporate expenses do not include airplanes, apartments, staffs, and

bureaucracies. We tend to operate very lean and push that right down through the operations as well . . . We don't have poison pills, golden parachutes, or employment agreements, and most of the corporate people have ownership in the company of a substantial nature.

The story of [the company] is to a large degree this building. The story is of not a lot of bureaucracy or corporate hierarchy. A typical investment analyst arrives at this building, looks at it, and says, "Where's [the company]? Where's this three-and-a-half-billion-dollar company?"

The headquarters downsizing can be systematically illustrated with data from the large electrical-products company. Continuing an expansionary phase dating to the 1970s, headquarters had grown during the early 1980s. Then, as it introduced an aggressive shareholder-value culture, strategic plans, budget decisions, executive incentives, and a host of other actions came to be viewed through the lens of shareholder value, and so did central-management headcount. A 1987 training document for top management of one of the company's major business units summarized the point: "We structure our organization [to] minimize management levels."

Employment numbers at most large manufacturing firms declined during this period, so it would be no surprise to see some reduction in management numbers. While manufacturing employment as a whole fell little during the 1980s, employment by the 500 largest firms dropped substantially. The Fortune 500 employed 15.9 million in 1980, but only 12.4 million a decade later (Autry and Colodny, 1990). This represented a 23 percent decline, against a 4 percent decline for manufacturing as a whole (see Figure 3.1). Consistent with the trend, the electrical-products firm had shrunk its employment by 17 percent during the decade.

The total number of corporate managers, defined by the company to include the heads of all major divisions and functions, fell even further, from over 300 in 1984 to under 200 by 1990 (Figure 3.2). General managers with staff functions dropped from 31 percent of the total in 1984 to 18 percent by 1990. In 1984, this corporation employed about one general manager for every 400 employees, but by 1990 the ratio had declined to one general manager for every 600 employees (Figure 3.3).

The paring of senior management is also evident in the skeletal organizational charts in Figure 3.4, which confirm the streamlining of the reporting hierarchies. In 1984, the general managers of the company's twenty-three business units (divisions that carried profit-and-loss responsibilities) collectively faced thirty-seven managers between themselves and the chief

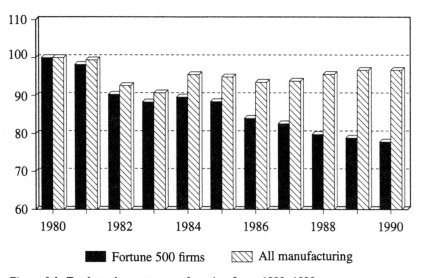

Figure 3.1. Total employment, manufacturing firms, 1980–1990.
(Index: 1980 = 100.).

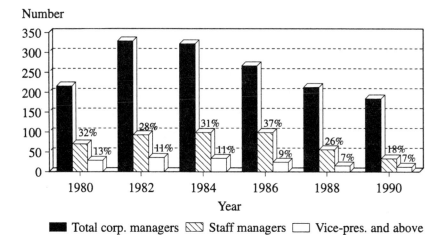

Figure 3.2. General corporate management, electrical-products firm, 1980–1990.
Includes division directors and presidents; corporate vice-presidents and
above. (Percentages are for managers relative to total corporate
managers.)

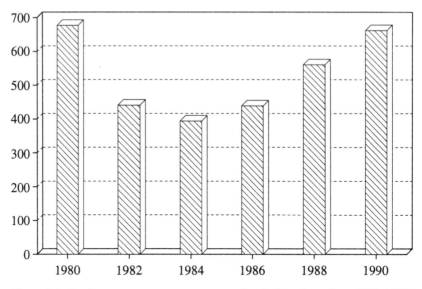

Figure 3.3. Employees per corporate manager, electrical-products firm, 1980–1990. (1990 figure is estimated.)

executive. By 1990, following the elimination of almost an entire layer of management, the heads of the company's sixteen business units faced only eighteen managers between themselves and the CEO's office.

As the traditional Weberian pyramid gave way to a leaner and flatter organizational chart, in no case was the acknowledged motive to empower the workforce, to give managers greater control over decisions, or to improve the quality of work life. To some managers these were of course laudable by-products of the decentralization. But the organizational alignment was result driven, not process driven. The actions were not taken because management believed in decentralization for its own sake. In fact, most managers displayed little intrinsic interest in the subject. The steps were instead simply derivative of management's commitment to increase shareholder return. Senior managers had evolved an organizational design that worked. The results were the basis for its legitimacy.

The logic of contracting central management to streamline decision making constituted a kind of template for organizational design within business units as well. As restrictions on headcounts were lifted but more performance responsibility imposed, some division managers readily cloned what they saw at headquarters. Others did so only after prodding by top management, but in either case the outcome was the same: fewer layers of general management and fewer managers in each layer. As business units became more oriented toward results and less constrained in how to achieve them, downsizing often appealed to unit heads. The pharmaceutical company offered a case in point. Its central-office headcount had been frozen for eight years. As devolution took sway, the chief executive would tell the divisions that profitability required improvement, and invite them to report back to him on how to do so. Since employee compensation was a major factor in any unit's costs, the plans were often returned with significant personnel cuts.

Conclusion

During the late 1980s and early 1990s, company structure came to be driven in part by a changing ownership environment. The restructuring that followed ushered in a new organizational principle giving special shaping to a range of organizational elements. Their precise forms varied from firm to firm, reflecting unique histories and market positions. Yet the forms shared generic elements, including the devolution of authority, distribution of shareholder-value information, application of new criteria in decision making, and contraction of headquarters management.

Aspects of these elements had appeared before, and for other reasons. What was distinctive was the systemic alignment of the organizational changes around enhancing shareholder value. Rather than hoping for better results from alterations in single organizational components, company management sought wholesale redesign of the organization. Intrinsic to the strategy was a better-informed workforce. Companies thus also sought to apprise its employees of the role of shareholder value in setting company objectives and evaluating results.

Alignment efforts should be seen, however, as being as much a matter of process as of outcome. Internal resistance was evident in the higher ranks, and the concept was often poorly understood in the lower ranks. At times the efforts would backfire, as foreshortened oversight allowed for larger mistakes, mistakes that served to embolden opponents of devolution. And the right course of action was never crystal clear in any case. Companies viewed the efforts more as successive approximation than as definitive implementation of a received model.

The observed alignment efforts suggest that efforts to resolve agency-

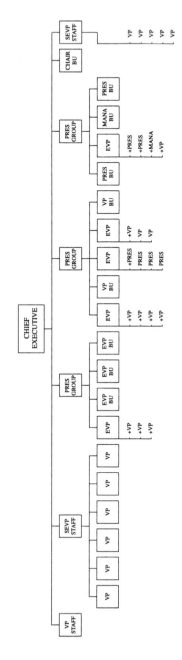

1984

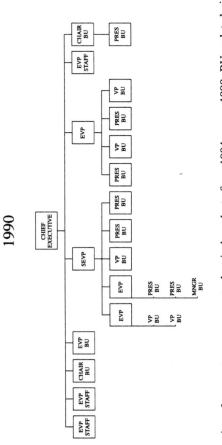

Figure 3.4. Organization of corporate management, electrical-products firm, 1984 versus 1990. BU and + designate business units. SEVP = senior executive vice-president. Chair = chairman.

principal problems between top managers and owners should be seen as one instance of a broader set of problems concerning organizational alignment. The agency issue is often viewed as a conflict between the individual interests of company officers and shareholders (Jensen and Meckling, 1976; Fama, 1980; Eisenhardt, 1989; Perrow, 1986, pp. 224–236). This focus is not surprising, since agency problems become most visible in the personalized oppositions that erupt between owners or would-be owners and company executives. Yet underlying many such struggles for control are fundamentally differing conceptions of how the firm should be organized and the criteria that should be used to guide decision making and evaluate performance. Closing the gap between company principals and their agents is a matter of aligning not just individual behavior but also organizational structure.

FOUR

Intensified
Management of Managers

The organizational logic of ownership-disciplined alignment ramified into the organization's management of its managers. Managers throughout the company received more authority to succeed, and more rope with which to fail. Their selection and grooming thereby acquired greater salience. If the right manager was picked to fill a position, the rewards to the shareholders could be larger than in the past; if a mistake was made, the costs could be larger as well. As a result, a premium was placed on the management of managers, a trend reinforced by the more generally observed focusing of human resource planning on broader organizational questions (Greer et al., 1989).

The intensified management of managers inverted the traditional allocation of managerial time and exercise of control. Centralization had placed a premium on senior management's direct involvement in a broad array of company decisions. Control was exercised through direct review of actions and policies. Decentralization, by contrast, meant that more managerial time was spent on selecting the right people to make the decisions, less on the decisions themselves. Control came to be exercised through more careful selection of the decision makers, and by linking their decisions more closely to shareholder value. The selection process sought to ensure quality decisions; the compensation system sought to align the decision objectives to what shareholders wanted.

The traditional conception of the manager was altered in the process. In the heyday of the large, hierarchic bureaucracy, large-scale corporate organization had created what William H. Whyte (1956) had aptly dubbed the "organization man." Managerial behavior, as David Riesman (1950) chronicled, had become "other-directed," acutely sensitive to organizational norms of behavior. In the traditional impersonal and rule-laden company hierarchy, managers good at mastering the organization's culture and codes found themselves moving into increasingly responsible positions, a process well documented by Robert Jackall (1983, 1988). But they also discovered little reduction in the oversight of their decisions once there. By contrast, in the rule-minimum life of an aligned firm, the other-directed organization man, and sometimes woman, was more likely to falter. Conformity to organizational cues would no longer suffice as a guide to decision making. Nor could it serve nearly so well as a proxy for success or promise. Independent judgment and results were now requisite.

As ownership-disciplined alignment reconfigured the management of managers, it addressed some organizational problems but created new ones at the same time. Devolution permitted divisions to customize their compensation systems and succession rules. Yet in putting more authority for human-resource policies in the hands of divisions, transfers among divisions, so critical in the past to the creation of a future cadre of general managers, became more difficult. The contraction of general management jobs at headquarters further reduced opportunities for leadership development.

This chapter identifies leading elements of the intensified management of managers, both advantageous and problematic. It begins with examination of company techniques to enhance management information systems—in this case information on managers themselves. It then turns to the increased investment of top management time in managing managers; altered selection criteria for appointing managers; enhanced incentives in managerial compensation; efforts to make managers themselves into owners; and, finally, the balkanization of managerial development.

Though aspects of these elements were partially driven by market and other forces, they were also systemically tied to the organizational alignment efforts. Changes were explicitly predicated on enhancing shareholder value and measuring performance outcomes with the same yardstick.

Knowledge of Management and Managerial Positions

A major organizational consequence of intensified management of managers was the creation of stronger formal and informal information systems to track and analyze the stock of management talent. The systems were designed to provide senior managers with more effective tools as they found themselves devoting increasing fractions of their day to management succession.

Actions by the financial-services company, which employed more than 80,000 people, illustrate the development of such tracking systems. The company's chief executive had increasingly emphasized "people-building" skills, and in the mid-1980s he created a new post: there would henceforth be a full-time management-development specialist. Carrying the title "vice-president for executive resources," this specialist was the CEO's right-hand person for molding a cadre of people-building managers and then, in the specialist's words, "fusing it into the system."

The program focused on two tiers of managers. The specialist established a system to track approximately 150 young "high-potential" managers who were expected to enter general management eventually. They were carefully monitored and evaluated. Particular care was taken, for instance, in assigning them to new responsibilities. The guiding principle was that their development required continuous "stretching." Yet overstretching, the placement in a position too far above the person's current abilities, was also viewed as a danger, for both the person and the organization.

More central to the specialist's role was the tracking of approximately 300 individuals (known as the "Corporate 300") who had already reached or promised to achieve general management levels. The top of the pool was occupied by one hundred senior managers who served either on the company's highest policy-setting committee or as heads of major business units. The remainder of the pool consisted of senior people in each of the business units who were viewed as having the potential to reach the top of the pool. The generic line defining the top was the level at which the managers were seen as "creators," not simply "creatures," of the company's culture.

The specialist and two associates sought to become personally acquainted with each of the Corporate 300, a task requiring substantial travel to this multinational's far-flung offices. In mid-1990, for instance, the specialist spent several days with a senior manager who headed one of the smaller business units. The unit had been losing money, and the specialist sought to enlarge the company's understanding of how the unit's president fared under duress. He met with the unit's personnel staff, its senior managers, and finally with the president himself. Already alarmed at the impact his poor numbers might have been having on headquarters' perceptions, the president was eager to talk and to listen as well, concerned about where he stood in the eyes of both his boss and the chief executive.

In keeping with the people-management philosophy, the specialist also made contact with each senior manager's immediate subordinates. The purpose was to create a fuller portrait of the person's capacities as viewed from both above and below. A formal information system built on current electronic technologies contained extensive data on both sets of managers, but it was complemented by a soft information system, or what is perhaps more aptly termed a knowledge system, constructed from the specialist's own observations and assessments. He became, in his own words, an "internal headhunter," searching for people builders. But he was also prepared to retool the "people abusers."

To build a detailed and comprehensive information system, the specialist and his staff interviewed fifty division heads and the managers just below them. To each they posed a set of key questions:

1. Who are the people builders here, and who "built" you?
2. Who are the people "abusers and bullies" that drive people out?
3. If you were [the CEO] and wanted to change the culture, what would you do?

Transcripts of the specialist's interviews around these questions, unedited except for removal of each commentator's name, were periodically reviewed with the chief executive. Certain managers' names came up repeatedly, some as builders, others as abusers. Profiles were compiled on both groups, laden with detailed accounts of how they had behaved and reacted in various circumstances.

Equally important, this system also built knowledge about the other side of the placement equation. Half of the specialist's job was to assay the senior management positions themselves. Depth information was acquired on unique requirements of the positions as they became open, data that formal job descriptions could never hope to convey. Those who had held the positions were of course acutely aware of their demands, but the specialist's task was to extract such information on the top 300 positions and place it at the ready disposal of the chief executive and several others responsible for executive appointment.

The value of this new capacity was evident during a major reorganization of the top ranks of the firm in 1990. The reporting structure was radically redesigned to integrate customer contact that had previously been divided among several separate divisions. The extensive redesign, which included a number of senior reassignments around a reconfigured organizational chart, had been carefully prepared by the CEO. In accordance with a stress on decentralization, the chart was made flatter. Two layers of management in two of the company's major divisions were slated for elimination. So portentous was the restructuring that, to avoid rumor and adverse effects on morale, an announcement was communicated worldwide to all offices at the same moment through a fax dispatch. In the announcement, the chief executive identified the specific reassignments of each of the senior officers and those reporting to them. He added that although "the important changes appear to be at the top of the organization, the true purpose is to broaden and focus our effort." But he also warned in closing that "we have much to do." In assessing his managers' capacities for their new responsibilities and in preparing the new reporting structure, the CEO had drawn extensively upon the knowledge system concerning his people and concerning his positions that the specialist had placed at his disposal.

The knowledge system drew information up the reporting hierarchy but, consistent with the devolution principle, pushed it down as well. It could not have been otherwise. Gathering information without giving information would have violated the culture of decentralization. It would also have violated an implicit rule in any organizational setting that requires reciprocity for any information sharing, whether up and down a hierarchy or across divisions (von Hippel, 1987; Schrader, 1992). Without some trading, the information well would have soon run dry. The executive specialist appreciated this iron law of antioligarchy. And given his frequent contact with the company's inner circle of top management and detailed knowledge of senior managers in the far reaches of the firm, the specialist possessed invaluable information to share. Cognizant of the implicit obligations, he would volunteer, during visits to dispersed company operations, to offer informal presentations on "what [the CEO] is thinking." The comments were carefully scrutinized for hints of how headquarters perceived the operation. After five years of work on these issues, the specialist had created an informal knowledge network that acquired a life of its own. In unacknowledged exchange for the information he had shared or could share, managers among the Corporate 300 would tip him off when colleagues were ready to move or about to resign.

Other companies tracked their upper echelons with analogous methods. Though varying in scope and specifics, all such methods were intended to generate detailed information with which top management could better match their people and positions. The knowledge system at the electrical-products firm, for instance, was overseen by a senior staff person responsible for "executive resources." The latter were the company's top 1,200 to 1,400 individuals, defined by two lists: (1) those currently occupying 400 key positions and the identified potential replacements (up to three) for each, about 1,200 people; and (2) those holding some 1,400 positions eligible for incentive compensation. A third data base was available as well: a "management readiness" roster comprising people throughout the company who had been identified as being prepared for general management responsibilities. While most employment decisions were now entirely made by the business units, appointments to the incentive positions were still centrally directed.

Whenever an incentive position opened, the director of executive resources would secure an updated description and then build a list of some twelve to fifteen candidates. The top two previously identified potential replacements were automatically included from the first list. The remaining candidates were drawn off the second and "management readiness" lists. From extensive discussions with those most familiar with the position and those most knowledgeable about the candidates, the director would gradually consolidate a rank-ordered "consensus" short-list of three. The final short-list and supporting documentation then went to the chief executive for ultimate review, rumination, and decision.

Managerial Investment in Managing Managers

Direct observation of executives at work reveals a dozen or more recurrent roles, ranging from resource allocation to conflict resolution (Mintzberg, 1973; Kotter, 1982; Donaldson and Lorsch, 1983). For reasons foreshadowed in the devolution of decision making already described, the daily time budget of senior managers was shifted away from some traditional tasks and toward the internal management of subordinates.

Virtually all of the line managers recognized this change in their organizational lives, and the topic evoked exceptionally animated discussion. The linkage between the policies of decentralized decision making and the emphasis on the management of managers was explicit in the minds of many senior managers: devolution was seen as necessitating such action.

The heads of the functional divisions and business units of the pharmaceutical company, for example, conducted an extended assessment of their own people every year as part of the general division or unit review. To sharpen the focus, a key question was always: Who could best replace the senior managers reporting directly to the division or unit head? The division and unit heads in turn would conduct a candid review around much the same question with the company's chief executive and chief operating officer. Three sets of names were on the table: their own replacements, replacements for all of their directly reporting managers, and high-potential managers at any level. The latter were to be watched, nurtured, and singled out for broader assignments. The chief executive had declared management development and succession a major priority because so much authority had been vested in the lower ranks. In the capsule summary of the chief financial officer, "There are two important jobs [our CEO] has. One is people and management succession. The other is when not to spend money. So you can see the orientation here. 'You guys are given the responsibility, and the only thing I'm going to do is to approve your stuff if I think it's a good idea.' "

Similar developments were evident in the electrical-products firm. A senior manager, the executive vice-president for human resources, offered an account typical of most. He had served as general manager of several business units during the period when the company adopted shareholder value as a guiding principle. Prior to the restructuring, "there was a list of 'ready now' kind of people to be put into general manager jobs. As unsophisticated as it sounds, . . . it was . . . a situation of picking the next guy who came up at the top of the chart. If I was the number one guy on the chart, I got the job. It was almost done without real consideration of how my capabilities might fit the situation." The process of selecting general management was reorganized during the 1980s to incorporate a new company emphasis. "We began to be much more astute in defining job requirements," observed the executive vice-president; the company moved away from job descriptions and toward what came to be known as "position profiles." The profiles identified key characteristics of the business unit, including the main issues that it would face during the next several years. They itemized the specific skills required of a general manager—skills that differed sharply according to whether the unit was, say, slated for growth rather than "milking" or closing. A profile specified the kind of relations the person in the position should be expected to create within the unit, with other units in the company, and with the supplier and customer worlds.

Such profiles meant that a more fine-honed match could be made between the individual and the organization. For those who were matched to general management positions, intensified training was added in strategic planning and value-based management. Before the restructuring, the attrition rate for failed general management assignments was estimated to range from 30 to 40 percent. After the improved selection and training procedures were in place, the attrition rate dropped significantly.

An executive vice-president of the electrical-products firm responsible for three large business units, and a veteran of several of them, had incorporated the new emphasis on management selection into his business routine. A long-time manager at the company, he had come through its wrenching mid-1980s restructuring with special appreciation for the importance of carefully selecting his managers:

> We spend a lot of time [reviewing managers]. When you get into the restructuring arena, the people are even more important: thinking through, planning, strategizing, shifting, moving, and positioning people. This is more important than it is in a stable, orderly [setting in which] "he's going to retire and everybody is going to move up a notch in domino progression" . . .
>
> [Now], in a period of contraction, say you have five candidates. They're all good, they're all capable, they're all qualified. We need to *really* make sure we pick the best one who can actually do the job . . . Who are the guys who can make it happen? Who are the guys that can get the job done? . . . Who are the real aggressive people who are willing to bite the bullet and make the hard decisions?

Answering such questions in this company required intensified focus on immediate subordinates and even on those that they in turn managed. Detailed information two levels down was required for succession planning. And it was also required for credibility with the chief executive.

In preparation for the annual review with the electrical-products CEO, the executive vice-president would spend at least two hours with every manager one and two levels below him. The review process necessitated scheduled meetings with some fifty individuals. This executive vice-president would then devote three hours of his annual business review with the chief executive to discussion of the managers. The appraisals were specific, emphasizing both financial performance and people management. This could be seen in the written assessment of one division manager who reported directly to a business-unit head. As we reviewed the annual written report on this unit head, the executive vice-president, his boss's boss, observed: "*Great* guy. Really does a super job. He's a wonderful manager, and everything else . . . But the line on this guy is that you wouldn't want to work for him. He's a tough son-of-a-bitch. He's a dictator, a hard-nosed SOB. You wouldn't want to spend a weekend with him . . . He's a top but tough manager.'' By traditional criteria, the division manager was an able performer. He won a special award for his unit, which included a cash prize of $250,000, and his division ranked at the top in operating profits in the business unit. Still, the management of managers had become a necessary criterion for advancement along with financial performance. As a result, both the written record and the first-hand assessment of his superiors were in agreement: he was now considered "not promotable."

In line with the organizational logic of shareholder value, the management of managers was formally added in one guise or another to the lists of executive objectives at all of the companies studied. It appeared as a major consideration for managerial appraisals and performance review. At one of the companies, for example, the top forty managers received annual written ratings on only six criteria, people management among them:

1. Knowledge and judgment
2. Administrative capacities
3. Leadership
4. People skills
5. Line-management abilities
6. Staff skills

Similarly, in 1991 the retail-services firm proposed to include people management among its leading performance criteria as it revised its short-term incentive plans to create a "system more closely tied to an individual's performance" (1991 company document). After extensive informal consultation with the senior managers to be affected, "people" skills were formally introduced as one of five main criteria. The appraisal system was further specified to include the motivation, development, and turnover of one's employees.

At the chemical-products company, the management of managers had recently been added as one of its formally stated performance objectives. "I think we do a hell of a lot better job today," said the chief financial officer, "in worrying about succession and management development, and in making it part of the management process . . . than we did ten years ago . . . [Now] we literally make management succession a part of the objectives of each of the managers." As part of the process, he met annually with the company's executive committee, consisting of its top four officers. The discussion focused in detail on the four or five senior people in each of the five functional areas reporting to him (finance, treasury, comptroller, tax, and information services). "I go through each of my groups. I talk about who's good, what I see where these guys ought to be going, and what they need to do to round-out." As a master of detail himself, the CEO would expect in-depth knowledge about each of the individuals. The chief financial officer and other senior managers who represented their units before this committee understood that "they better damned well know their business" if they were to survive.

The breadth of managerial assessment at this company was well illustrated by the annual review of one of its major business units. Approximately 200 of its senior people were on incentive pay, and every year the president of the unit would discuss the incentives and performance for each of the 200 people with the chief executive. This review alone consumed twenty hours or more of the CEO's time, a process repeated with each of the other units as well.

Managerial Misappointment

Even with the strengthened filtering, poor performers nonetheless occasionally rose through the hierarchy. Some had proven adept at "managing up" until reaching a level where individual performance became more measurable. Others had been strong performers but later received an inappropriate assignment or were elevated too high. Whatever the cause, the failures furnished visible reminders of the need for careful review of both person and position.

One case from the financial-services firm was used within the company to reaffirm the importance of extracting full information before a match was made. A "high-potential" young manager (age thirty-nine) was assigned to head the company's operations in another country. His credentials appeared solid: he held an MBA degree, had a decade of experience with the company, was familiar with the company's operations in two other countries, and seemed motivated to go overseas again. He had already been labeled a "star performer," and was seen as ready for a significant challenge. The country office to which he was assigned carried a staff of 200, a considerable jump from his largest previous staff of fifteen. The operation had been well run and was regarded as highly successful, an auspicious moment for taking charge. The match, however, proved an enormous mistake.

In accepting an overseas assignment in principle, the young manager had assumed it would be in Europe or in some other developed region. He had never anticipated receiving the actual assignment, which was to the capital of a developing nation. In selecting this ambitious manager "to run the country," the company had assumed that he was volunteering for any major overseas location. It had not foreseen that both he and his wife would despise the actual setting. But the die was cast. On arriving in the foreign city, the couple disdainfully refused to entertain local customers. For major clients, this constituted an opening faux pas, and others were to follow. The manager was unwilling to learn the local language, reigned in staff members who had built close client relations, and took little cognizance of the culture's special emphasis on personalized business relations. Staff turnover soared, especially among the high performers. A vice-president of the company directly familiar with the case ascribed much of what became an obvious mismatch to poor organizational intelligence. The special problems should have been foreseen: "If we had really dug in and knew this guy, we would have seen in [the earlier assignment] he was pretty aloof. He was great with clients, great with the seniors, [makes a] great presentation, and knows his business. Talking about business, he gets all charged up, very enthusiastic. But he was very very aloof, never built a team, and liked to do a deal himself." Before the reassignment, the overseas office had been a profitable operation in a growth market with large potential. Within two years the revenue stream turned negative and the operation began posting major losses. The young manager's fast rise was eclipsed, at least for the moment. He was reassigned to another job and was working under a cloud, though the company took special pains this time to place him in a position that it knew he would master. In the meantime, it now needed a replacement with special skills to manage what had become a "turnaround situation," a far harder post to fill than the one in question just two years earlier.

When managers failed to shoulder the responsibility afforded by decentralization, greater blame fell on their shoulders as well. The logic was straightforward: under decentralization, failures were more a matter of individual shortcomings, less a product of shortfalls in oversight or organization. It followed that intervention took longer, but was more deeply personal when it came. A troubled business unit within a large division at the pharmaceutical company offered a confirming account.

Located in the Midwest, far from both divisional and company headquarters, the long-successful unit suddenly reported severe financial problems. The abruptness of the downturn in the $200 million operation came as a surprise, and, worse, the causes remained unclear to headquarters. The company's senior human-resources official was dispatched to evaluate. Following extensive discussions with management personnel, he returned deeply disturbed about the unit's leadership. The unit remained an authoritarian backwater, its anachronistic ways taking a toll on employee performance. The unit president, who had been recently promoted, was known to be an abrasive "browbeater." But he had obtained good results in his previous post, and the division head to whom he reported had thought he would be able to "smooth out the edges." The president had been instructed and then coached to transcend a management style no longer in favor.

The unit's results had plummeted nonetheless. An exacerbating factor was the introduction of new information systems to manage inventory and customer relations. Though desirable moves in principle, in practice the systems proved extremely troublesome during installation, and the technical problems were further worsened by the president's autocratic style. Because of the decentralized context, however, headquarters learned of the problem belatedly. "Everything's OK," the unit president had repeatedly reassured his boss. "I've got it under control."

In an ironic twist on the company's policy of decentralization, devolution had been interpreted by the unit president as license to manage in his own centralized fashion. As described by the senior vice-president for human resources:

We keep preaching decentralization: "You guys are out there to run your own businesses" . . .

[The unit president's attitude was], "Nobody knows this business like me" and "you corporate types are so far removed from reality." The basic personality, business instinct, and style he had were made worse because we as a company keep preaching independence and decentralization, and he really took it to heart . . .

He was in [a midwestern city] and he was a long way away from his boss and his boss's boss, so the environment made what was basically a tenuous situation at best more and more difficult. The basic problems were there, but our structure and style made it worse.

It was a chastening experience. Customers were driven away, product launches delayed, and management energies drained. Free giveaways were later offered to win back alienated buyers. The company's back-of-the-envelope estimate of the one-time loss was somewhere between $5 million and $15 million, possibly more. In the final analysis, the unit president's management style and that of several colleagues, not the unit's organizational design or its technical problems with the information systems, were diagnosed as the primary cause. The incident reinforced the company's resolve to manage management succession better. In the words of the same human-resources official, "We have to remind ourselves from time to time how important our deliberations are when we put senior people in brand new roles. The classic good worker doesn't necessarily make a good foreman. We all learned quite a lesson. You just can't say, 'We'll coach him, and we'll counsel him, and he'll be OK' . . . We've talked more about personalities, styles, and the fits now because of this." The company's chief operating officer and the general manager of the division responsible for the unit concluded that the unit president was no longer redeemable. They developed a severance package to force the president out of the unit—and out of the corporation—and subsequently also forced out the head of the unit's manufacturing operations and several senior managers as well. These managers had been given authority to succeed, and they paid the ultimate price for failing to do so.

Incentives in Management Compensation

As ownership-disciplined responsibilities devolved into the organization, managerial compensation schemes were redesigned as well. The new alignment pressures led firms to expand and refine their performance-based compensation schemes. More managerial income was made contingent upon company or division performance in all of the companies studied, and it was more closely linked to measures of shareholder value.

The observation that higher proportions of managerial compensation were placed at risk was consistent with assessments of many observers (Berger, 1991; Baker, 1990). One consulting firm's comparison of the compensation of senior managers of a set of major companies it tracked between 1982 and 1989, for instance, revealed that long-term compensation based on a company's performance rose from 16 to 31 percent of the executives' total pay (Hyman, 1991). Another consulting firm's study of compensation for the top seven to eight officers of a set of approximately forty-five large manufacturing and service firms revealed comparable trends. From 1982 to 1990, fixed compensation (base salary, benefits, and

Percent

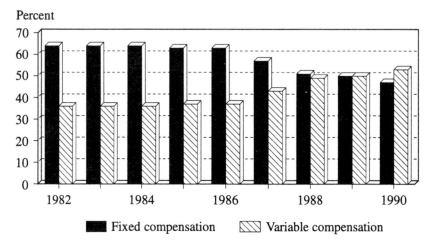

Figure 4.1. Percent fixed and variable executive compensation, large companies, 1982–1990. Fixed = base, benefits, and perquisites. Variable = annual and long-term incentives. (Source: Private surveys of Hewitt Associates.)

perquisites) declined from 64 to 47 percent of total executive compensation, while variable compensation (annual and long-term incentives) rose from 36 to 53 percent (see Figure 4.1). Especially pronounced was the relative growth of long-term compensation, more than doubling over the decade from 16 to 33 percent (Table 4.1 and Figure 4.2).

All of the companies I studied reported that managerial compensation had become increasingly tied to performance. So widespread had become the trends that they came to be accepted as natural and necessary aspects of current management practices. The increased risk in managerial compensation contained four main components. First, more managers were placed on contingent compensation schemes. Second, the contingent element was more directly linked to indicators of shareholder wealth. Third, companies sought to connect company performance more explicitly with managerial gain in the minds of managers. Fourth, forms of managerial ownership were developed for top managers of business units.

Spreading Contingent Compensation

Top company managers had long had a substantial fraction of their compensation at risk. Contingent compensation was now extended to include

Table 4.1. Percent fixed and variable executive compensation, large manufacturing and service companies, 1982–1990.[a]

	Fixed compensation			Variable compensation	
Year	Base salary	Benefits	Perquisites	Annual	Long-term
1982	44	15	5	20	16
1983	44	16	4	19	17
1984	44	16	4	18	18
1985	43	16	4	18	19
1986	43	16	4	17	20
1987	40	13	4	17	26
1988	37	11	3	18	31
1989[b]	36	11	3	19	31
1990	34	10	3	20	33

Source: Hewitt Associates (1991), private surveys.

a. Hewitt Associates annually surveyed a nearly constant sample of approximately 45 large manufacturing and service companies (acquired firms were replaced by firms of similar sector and size). Compensation is for top seven or eight officers.

b. Company revenue in 1989 averaged approximately $9 billion.

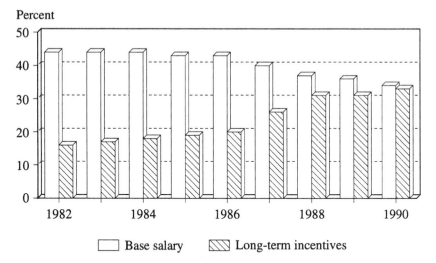

Figure 4.2. Percent base salary and long-term incentives, executive compensation, large companies, 1982–1990. (Source: Private surveys of Hewitt Associates.)

hundreds and, in several cases, thousands of managers. Compensation was made more contingent upon business-unit and corporate achievement, not just personal performance. The gradient for performance was steeper, opening opportunities for sharply increasing one's income, but also for sharply decreasing it.

The scope of the change can be illustrated with evolving policies of the large transportation company. The annual bonus plan, based on both individual and corporate performance, was limited in 1988 to 65 top executives and 525 marketing managers. Two years later the list was expanded to include more than 2,875 additional managers, or about 80 percent of the salaried workforce. The gradient for rewarding company performance was steepened as well. Among senior managers, a top performer in a year of top company performance would now receive a year-end bonus payment equal to the size of the manager's base salary; a poor performer in a year of poor company performance would receive no annual bonus. The firm's payoff matrix for this executive group appears below. A value of 0.55 for mid-company and individual performance, for example, signified that the annual bonus would be set at 0.55 times base salary.

		Company performance				
		High	2	3	4	Low
Individual	High:	1.00	.85	.70	.55	.00
performance	Medium:	.85	.70	.55	.40	.00
	Low:	.70	.55	.40	.25	.00

On the premise that the next tier of managers contributed less to overall company performance and accordingly should have a lower gradient, all matrix figures were reduced by 30 percent. The top performer in a year of top company performance would thus receive an annual bonus of 0.70 times base salary (down from 1.00 times base). For the lowest managerial grade in the bonus pool, the matrix numbers were contracted by 60 percent, so that the top-grade performer would see a bonus equal to 0.40 times base salary. Whatever the gradient, it was explicitly intended to align management and shareholder interests among all those carrying significant responsibilities in the company. In the words of the chief executive who had initiated the change, "By putting everybody on a bonus system, [we] created such an interest in this company . . . Every person in the whole company worries about it and thinks about what they can do . . . The targets are there and everybody knows what it takes."

Like the emphasis on management succession, the expansion of contingent compensation was a direct, logical corollary of decentralization. If management decisions were not to be externally controlled, the managers required their own inertial guidance systems to ensure good decisions, where "good" was now defined as enhancing shareholder value. Performance-based income was elegant in its simplicity. In the conception of one senior vice-president of the special-machinery company, "We allow them to make the decisions they need to make on a day-to-day basis, but that is then also how we compensate them. Their compensation, in addition to their base salary, is based on the P&L [profit and loss] of their operating unit. So they have the responsibility and authority to manage it. If they do it well, they get paid well, and if they don't, they don't get paid."

Each company fashioned its own unique approach, though the basic principles were much the same. The formula of the chemical-products company, for example, was similar to that of the transportation firm; but the specific features were custom designed. The company had promoted incentive compensation during much of the 1980s, and by 1990 some 20 percent of its salaried workforce received part of its compensation through stock options and annual incentive bonuses. Year-end compensation for a given manager was a mixture of individual, business unit, and company performance, the latter measured as earnings per share. Each individual was assigned a basic incentive figure that was a percentage of base pay, but the actual individual bonus could range from zero to twice that number. The business unit's performance added or subtracted up to 20 percent around this base figure, and the company's performance contributed another 25 percent either way. As was common among the companies, the higher the managerial level, the greater the basic incentive figure. Among the business-unit presidents, the contingent fraction of total compensation varied from 26 to 38 percent; among the top dozen officers of the firm, the contingent part constituted 30 percent to more than 60 percent of the total.

As in other areas of corporate change, the rhetoric of contingent compensation was widely shared but implementation sometimes lagged. The retail-services firm occupied the slow end of the change spectrum. Variable compensation for the firm's top 100 managers consisted of an annual bonus and a single long-term incentive, the stock option. The performance of all of these managers except the top twenty with title of senior vice-president and above, was annually evaluated through an open two-stage review process. First, the eighty managers were assessed on a rating sheet by each of the top twenty. Then, the top twenty would assemble for a full day in January to review the written rating for each manager, share the information upon which it had been based, and adjust the final assessment. Although the process was formally open, an informal norm had been long established that the annual incentive bonus was to serve as no incentive at all. It had become a thirteenth paycheck, granted almost automatically. Virtually nobody received an amount smaller than that of the year before, and the size of the increment had become a function more of seniority than of performance. The winds of change were blowing even here, however, as a new system aimed at incentivizing this short-term measure was finally developed in 1990. In contrast to the way changes had come about in the other firms, change in this case had been initiated not by senior managers but rather by several outside members of the board of directors. Serving on the boards of other companies that had moved well into the forefront of incentive compensation, they had pressed top management to move this company to the frontier as well. With the appointment of a new chief executive, their advocacy had finally fallen on more receptive ears.

Linking Contingent Compensation
to Shareholder Value

Performance measures used in calculating managerial compensation became more closely linked to indicators of shareholder value. This was of course critical to the entire system of alignment. If managers were being rewarded for A whereas the shareholders were hoping for B, results would be forthcoming, only they wouldn't be the right ones (Kerr, 1975). Effectively translating shareholder value into measures of managerial performance, and those measures in turn into management income, involved several steps.

Since the new measures and the formulas for their numeric conversion were still under development, the steps were approached in experimental fashion. The optimal path without introducing unwanted distortions remained unclear. The designers of compensation systems faced several decisions, the outcomes of which could not be fully known in advance. The decisions were framed around four dimensions:

Absolute versus relative measures of company performance. Absolute measures track the company over time (for example, the rate of growth in share price and dividends). Relative measures adjust these figures for the performance of a comparison set of companies. Comparison could be with companies in the same industry, firms of the same general size, or some company index such as Standard and Poor's 500. Research generally confirmed that large companies typically incorporated both absolute and relative measures. A study of 1,049 major firms from 1974 to 1986, for instance, revealed that changes in the compensation of chief executives generally depended in part on changes in the company's return to shareholders, but that the compensation changes were also adjusted for a company's performance relative to the industry and, especially, the market as a whole (Gibbons and Murphy, 1990).

Complex versus simple measures of performance. Streamlined measures are presumed to be better understood and acted upon by large numbers of managers, but more complex measures could more accurately measure shareholder value.

Company-wide versus business-unit measures of performance. The appropriate weighting of company, business-unit, and even subunit performance in calculating a manager's compensation could be varied considerably according to the manager's responsibilities, degree of company decentralization, and other organizational factors.

Choice and specification of measures of performance. An array of measures for capturing various features of company performance is available. Those that are chosen must be translated into quantified internal measures that managers can understand in their day-to-day decision making (see Ehrenberg, 1990; Rock and Berger, 1991; Foulkes, 1991).

Among the most common ways of linking long-term incentives to shareholder value was the stock option, which found universal application among the seven corporations. The ultimate value of stock options to the managers depended on the rise of the company's share price over several years, a straightforward device making compensation contingent upon a major component of·shareholder value.

Among top managers, additional long-term incentive schemes were designed to further focus managerial attention on operational actions that would generate shareholder value over a period of time. At the transportation company, any such schemes were to include several objectives, according to a 1989 internal company planning document:

> the compensation program should be simple in design and well communicated;
> the performance measures should reflect shareholder-value creation;
> the program should motivate executives to focus on long-term strategy;

the system should align management and shareholder interests by providing financial incentives to build shareholder value over the long term.

In line with these considerations, one main incentive vehicle for several years at the transportation company was a four-year performance share unit plan. Under this plan, a set of shares was held by the company for distribution to its top managers if the firm performed well. The shares were vested at up to 15 percent per year if performance objectives were met by the company. Performance objectives in this case consisted of annual targets for operating cash flow and return on capital, viewed as the two primary determinants of the company's shareholder value. To adjust for economic fluctuations beyond the control of top management, the remaining 40 percent of the shares were vested at the end of the four years if the company performed well compared to a comparison set of firms. The annual vesting for this incentive scheme was structured by matrix figures similar to that for bonus allocations. The figures below identify the fraction of the annual potential set of shares that were to be granted to the executives under varying performance conditions:

		Return on capital (% of target)				
		100	90	80	70	<70
	100:	1.00	.85	.70	.55	.00
Operating cash flow (% of target)	90:	.85	.70	.55	.40	.00
	80:	.70	.55	.40	.25	.00
	70:	.55	.40	.25	.00	.00
	<70:	.00	.00	.00	.00	.00

The transportation company, however, became dissatisfied with this compensation scheme during the late 1980s. Confronting the design questions above, the company devoted considerable energy to the development of alternative systems of measurement and reward. In 1990, an internal task force recommended that the firm focus on a new measure, defined as cash flow return on investment, which the company saw as more closely related to shareholder value. The company was persuaded in part by a consulting firm's study showing that such a measure correlated more highly with companies' market value than did alternative measures.

Indicative of the uncertainty in finding the optimal path for implementing shareholder-oriented compensation schemes, the board of directors balked. It delayed full implementation of the revised system, fearful that the new system could distract management from what it considered an even higher priority—namely, paying off a large debt load resulting from a late 1980s restructuring of the company. Top management remained committed, nonetheless, to implementing its contingent compensation system. It kept the old measures in place, while experimenting with and gradually implementing the new system. Said the chief architect of the process, "We wanted to focus the attention of this management team on . . . long-term and total shareholder return. [Companies in our industry] have traditionally measured their performance in very traditional account- ing ways—net income, earnings per share. This company, with the intro- duction of this compensation program, [has begun] shifting toward a measurement that reflected long-term total shareholder return." Early returns were gratifying. At the end of 1990, a large fraction of the salaried workforce received for the first time a year-end bonus based on individual and company performance. Informal feedback, according to the vice- president for human resources, revealed that the aligning impact was as had been expected:

> All you would hear about from people is, "Damn, can you believe what I got in my paycheck?" For people who had never seen this kind of thing, it was really an incentive . . .
>
> I think what it did was to energize the people of the company toward the financial goals of the organization. The older feeling was, "I'll just stay here, do my job, and get my paycheck. All I have to do is just stay out of trouble and I'll be OK."
>
> Now people are thinking it's really worthwhile to do the extra things to save the money . . . Those kinds of thoughts never would have occurred to people in the old days. So it's a motivator, a driver to change behavior.

Still, companies moved slowly in this direction at best. Variable com- pensation had come to occupy a larger fraction of total income, and a larger fraction of managers were brought into its net. Change was less advanced on the third key component, the performance factors on which the compensation was made contingent. A survey of approximately 350 large manufacturing and service firms in 1985 and 1990 revealed that the leading performance measure for long-term management performance remained earnings per share (Table 4.2). The second most widely used measure was net income. Both represented a partial measure of shareholder value, but neither could be viewed as comprehensive. What is generally

Table 4.2. Percent of large companies using primary measures for assessing long-term senior management performance, 1985 and 1990.

Measure	1985	1990[a]
Earnings per share	30	29
Net income	24	23
Return on equity	24	20
Total shareholder return	4	13
Return on capital	4	13
Return on assets	0	13
Other measures	14	5

Source: Hewitt Associates (1991), private surveys. The surveys comprised some 350 large manufacturing and service companies.

a. The median company revenue in 1990 stood at $6.0 billion. The 1990 column sums to more than 100 percent because some companies reported two or more measures to be primary.

seen as the more complete measure, total shareholder return (dividends plus appreciated stock price), was the primary measure in 1985 at only one in twenty companies. By 1990, slightly more than one in ten companies had made it a primary compensation tool.

The widespread acceptance of contingent compensation principles, and their still underdeveloped linkage with shareholder interests, were also confirmed in a 1990 survey of seventy-nine directors of major firms who served as chairs of their board's compensation committee. Virtually all asserted the importance of linking executive and employee compensation to the generation of shareholder value. But they were less sanguine about their recent success in doing so (Table 4.3). Other evidence suggests that

Table 4.3. Survey of chairs of board compensation committees reporting linkages between company compensation and shareholder interests, 1990.

Statement	Percent who strongly agree	Percent who agree
It is especially important that shareholder interests be linked to executive compensation programs	83	17
It is important that our compensation programs link employee and shareholder interests	71	28
Our company does a good job of linking executive and shareholder interests	38	54

Source: Hay Group (1991).

they had not done so in the less recent past. A study of executive salaries and bonuses for seventy-eight companies in 1977 and 1980 revealed that movement in a firm's share price had virtually no bearing on changes in executive compensation (Kerr and Bettis, 1987).

The Problems of Asymmetry and Measurement in Linkage

Although the principle of linking managerial compensation with share-holder value was reasonably widespread, the practice of linkage still faced two major hurdles in implementation. One was an asymmetry stemming from a clash between individual preference and organizational logic. Managers naturally sought reward for favorable performance and no loss for the unfavorable, whereas the logic of ownership-discipline dictated symmetry. The second hurdle concerned measurement: it was easy to state the principle of rewarding a contribution to shareholder value, but it was difficult to measure individual performance. Isolating unique contributions in complex organizations could prove intractable.

The asymmetry hurdle. The organizational linkage of executive and shareholder interests implied that adverse results for investors should be followed by adverse results for managers (O'Byrne, 1991). Yet any ideal-ized version of the symmetry model was simply not observed in practice. Rather, companies carried a pronounced tilt in favor of rewards over punishment.

Executives were assured of substantial income even in the event of much red ink. Generous base salaries guaranteed that catastrophic company losses would never ''zero-out'' executive income, short of outright dismissal. The magnitude of the assured base can be illustrated with ITT's 1991 compensation of its top five officers: the chief executive, chief financial officer, general counsel, and two executive vice-presidents received fixed salaries, respectively, of $1.4 million, $725,000, $625,000, $514,167, and $380,000 (ITT Corporation, 1992). They could and did earn considerably more from a variety of short- and long-term incentive packages. But there would have been no starvation here had even the sky fallen in.

Incentive schemes themselves generally favored the upside over the downside. Stock options, one of the most common long-term incentives, illustrate the skew. Given the opportunity to purchase a number of company shares after a set period of time, typically one to five years, the purchase would by prearrangement be made at the current prices. The positive incentive was clear: if the shares had performed well over the period, the executive received the difference between the current and original price. If the shares had not done well, however, the executive had only to do nothing. Poor stock performance would be unpunished, except for the fact that the executive would witness a missed opportunity. Adverse stock movement would not take away from the executive's base compensation, and, as a result, extremely adverse movement was no worse for executive compensation than no movement. Other incentive devices, including what are generally termed performance units, performance share grants, restricted stock grants, and stock appreciation rights, worked much the same way, rewarding strong company performance and zeroing poor performance (Rock and Berger, 1989; Foulkes, 1991; Crystal, 1991a, 1991b). However, such schemes still implicitly placed some downside risk on the executive in much the same way that a salesperson on commission tangibly feels the consequences of sales shortfalls. When variable compensation was a relatively large proportion of the total, poor company performance could leave an executive with a fraction of the expected income. That expectation might have been far beyond the dreams of most Americans, but failure to attain it could nonetheless have been perceived by the executive as a major personal loss.

One of the seven companies I studied experienced a disastrous year, and its impact on executive compensation was instructive. While most of the firm's business units had delivered reasonably good earnings for the year, one unit had produced a huge loss. So great was the deficit that the financial health of the entire company was severely eroded, with earnings, dividends, and share price nose-diving. For the general manager of the troubled unit, company compensation dropped to zero when he was abruptly dismissed (though even then, he was given a generous long-term consulting contract worth more than $100,000 annually). Other managers in the unit were dismissed as well. No top company officers lost their jobs, but they did suffer a sizable drop in personal income. Compared to compensation in the year before, the total annual compensation of the top five executives declined by more than two-fifths. The unit's debacle again brought a tangible reminder of the downside risks assumed when authority devolved. As vigorous as the executive selection of unit managers may have been, mistakes in the absence of rigid oversight magnified quickly into a substantial sting of the top executives' own paychecks.

Because of the complex structure of executive compensation, in which long-term incentives were only weakly related to a given year's company results, the relationship between total executive compensation and annual firm performance was imprecise at best. Such loose coupling was evident in the 1990 compensation for the chief executives of the three U.S. automobile manufacturers. Annual reports and proxy statements for two of the three firms reported an adverse year for both company and top officer. General Motors Corporation had lost nearly $2 billion in 1990 and cut its dividends by nearly half. Its chief executive personally felt the impact: despite his promotion during the year to the company's highest office, his total compensation was cut by more than a third (from $2.21 million in 1989 to $1.44 million in 1990). With analogous financial results at Ford Motor Company and Chrysler Corporation, the Ford CEO saw his total compensation drop by 60 percent, but, defying the logic, the Chrysler CEO enjoyed a 15 percent increase. Still, the general thrust was consistent. When General Motors suffered another adverse year in 1991, losing $4.45 billion, the largest annual loss in history for any U.S. company, its executives further felt the price. GM's top seven managers saw their combined income drop by 42 percent (Levin, 1992a).

The measurement hurdle. Significant measurement problems also abounded. The size of this hurdle was generally an inverse function of a manager's location in the hierarchy. Hierarchy, here, is not defined as the traditional organizational pyramid; rather, it is a function of the extent to which a managerial position carried responsibility for the performance of an operating unit, and the extent to which that unit contributed to the company's total value. The farther a managerial position was from one of these pivotal locations, the more difficult it was to develop an algorithm, a procedural rule, for accurately tying compensation to the creation of shareholder value.

The actions of the chief executive and several top officers seemed to affect stock price and dividend payouts to such an extent that the linkages appeared obvious to those involved. Below the executive suite, however, the contingency in compensation lost much of this self-evident quality. The contributions of subordinates and staff specialists in theory should have been measurable, but the problems and costs of doing so rapidly escalated. Moreover, the risks of misspecification also expanded, heightening the error of rewarding A while hoping for B. The electrical-products manufacturer was cognizant of the pitfalls here. Many senior managers were committed to expansion of the contingent compensation system, even to hourly workers if possible. But they moved cautiously and experimentally, slowed by concern about the distorting effects of improper measurement. Contingent compensation could serve to discipline organizational energy around defined objectives, but it could also badly misfire when poorly specified.

With regard to managers heading a company's major business units, individual actions carried relatively visible impact on a company's shareholder value, making a variable-pay algorithm for such executives more straightforward. Even here, however, the precision of the linkage was partly a function of the unit's contribution to company wealth. One indirect indicator of the salience of the contribution was the expressed concerns of both buy- and sell-side analysts when they arrived for a company visit. In addition to top management, they often sought to meet with heads of major business units. But they typically preferred contact with the heads of the units most responsible for overall company performance. If those units performed well, investor interests were well served, and vice versa. In one company, so dominant was one of the operating units that its president had nearly as much direct contact with company investors as did the company's top executives.

The more distant the manager and unit from the central process of defining a company's contributions to its investors, the more difficult it became to define an accurate compensation scheme for that manager or unit. Organizational implications of this value-measurement hurdle, however, ran contrary to a well-known organizational law of inverse uncertainty. Rosabeth Kanter (1977) observed that uncertainty in decision making increased in the highest reaches of an organization, where the information required to reduce risk is less available and where the decisions, though fateful, may not bear fruit (or bring famine) for years to come. Linking pay to performance should thus be more difficult, by this argument, the higher one moves in the decision-making hierarchy. That is one reason that the sharing of social characteristics should become, as Kanter also argued, more common among managers at the top. Yet the value-measurement hurdle led to just the opposite on both fronts, with more measurement precision and less social similarity expected at the top. A study of a mid-sized manufacturing firm in 1985 confirmed what would be anticipated by the argument of the value-measurement hurdle: annual managerial bonuses were found to be predicated on individual performance to a greater extent among high-level managers and those who worked at headquarters than among managers located elsewhere in the company (Kahn and Sherer, 1990).

The relative net balance of these contrary organizational forces varied from firm to firm. Among companies where the logic of management-disciplined alignment still prevailed, the law of inverse uncertainty was likely to have the upper hand. Conversely, among firms where the logic of ownership-disciplined alignment had made inroads, that law was likely to have less bearing. The organizational mix was always a relative one, with the two forces varying from firm to firm and year to year as a function of investor power or preemptive management moves in anticipation of it.

When the balance tipped more in favor of ownership-disciplined alignment, several consequences were observable. First, contingent compensation was likely to be more widespread, the contingency gradient steeper, and the contingency more linked to shareholder value at the top of the organization—all tendencies that were seen among the seven companies.

Second, top managerial appraisal was likely to be based less on social similarity and more on measurable performance (this, too, was observed, as noted below).

Third, compensation among top managers of the business units tended to vary according to the the units' measurable contributions to company value. In the past, a unit's size may have been a good predictor of compensation, since it connoted risk and responsibility, two of the traditional drivers of compensation. As the balance shifted between the two competing organizational principles, however, the divisional heads were likely to see their total compensation related less to sheer size and more to measures of their contribution to the enterprise's dividends and share price. That in turn was likely to alter managerial behavior, encouraging risk in the pursuit of reward. Consistent with this expectation, Galbraith and Merrill (1991) found in a study of seventy-nine business units in technology-intensive firms that when managerial compensation was more incentive based, the units were more likely to favor R&D over marketing expenditures, to invest in capital equipment, and to diversify their product lines less.

The three-way linkage of performance, compensation, and shareholder value, then, was seen by many managers as a targeted direction for company change, but one that would require solving numerous operational problems along the way. The introduction of symmetrical upside and downside risks ran against a corporate tradition of relative income security, even for risk-prone executives. And general measurement problems, whatever the asymmetry issues, accelerated as one descended the company hierarchy.

Well-honed individual measurement systems at any level also threatened other performance objectives. Company support for cross-functional teams, interdivisional cooperation, and collective identity were undermined when management incentives played too much on harnessing narrow self-interest and too little on mobilizing collective energies. Efforts to align through privatized incentives ran the risk of misaligning a host of group incentives.

In the Minds of Managers

Contingent compensation schemes, however designed, were only as effective as they were comprehensible. To ensure that the senior managers understood how one's total income for the coming year depended on performance, companies sought to communicate their plans in detail. The human-resources office of the transportation company, for example, annually provided each manager with a detailed breakdown of the various forms of compensation that could be expected during the coming year. The consequences of the past year's performance were also presented graphically. The charts for two managers in 1990 appear in Figure 4.3 (though managers received only their own chart). Since the components of compensation followed complex rules and had various tax implications,

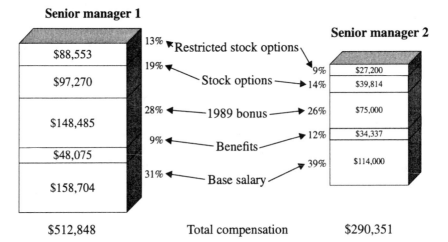

Figure 4.3. Compensation of two senior managers, transportation company, 1990.

the company furnished each manager with a customized document (an "Executive Compensation Portfolio") of some seventy-five pages explaining how the components operated and precisely what the manager could anticipate at year's end. "As an executive with [the company]," the 1990 version of the booklet began, "your actions and decisions determine in large part the future course and success of our operations . . . [Your] consistent dedicated efforts to meet [the company's] mission will significantly impact the financial rewards available through your compensation program." Stock options and related long-term incentives were offered, the manager was reminded, "as an incentive to focus on shareholder interests."

Some incentive mechanisms spoke for themselves. If tangible, they required little company explanation. One such device was a restricted stock grant. At the transportation company, some 130 top managers received such grants as part of their compensation. Although they paid nothing for the shares, they could not sell them for a defined period, and shares were forfeited if the executives left the company before the end of the period for any reason. During the restricted period, however, the rewarded managers received dividends from the shares. These quarterly payments, often substantial, provided an immediacy that stock options usually lacked. The vice-president for human resources at the transportation company offered himself as his own best example of the consequences: "The most notable change has been since we started giving the restricted stock grants to these top 130 . . . Every quarter I get a divided check—I get a divided check from my ownership position. It's amazing how that's a continual reminder of what my responsibilities are as an owner, because when I get a divided check, I'm an owner of this company that is driven by the overall financials . . . We own stock now in a company that we have very direct control over."

Well informed of the precise ways in which their compensation was linked to the company's performance, many top managers could forecast their year-end income long before year's end. Several confided making frequent mental calculations, even daily, with the changing stock price. At the transportation company, many of the officers held 10,000 to 20,000 shares of the company's stock, and a one-dollar gain in the stock value on a given day could mean a $10,000 to $20,000 personal gain. A one-dollar drop had equally tangible consequences.

At the special-machinery company, where stock was an even greater component of the compensation formulas, the chief operating officer received some 70 percent of his compensation in company shares. The skew toward stock over cash dated back seven years, and as a result he had accumulated nearly a third of a million shares in the company. "I am one of the most interested shareholders in this company," he said. "I tend to think in earnings per share." When asked how often he checked his company's price, he said "every morning, every night, and . . . probably about ten times a day." Management obsession with stock performance was reflected in the entry to the executive office building, where the visual field contained only two objects: a receptionist desk guarding the portals and a display posting a number. Updated three times a day, the posting contained the current price of the firm's shares. While the electrical-products company offered no such visual posting, it did provide a continually updated audio posting. Executives could call from anywhere to obtain the moment's quote, and many did. The chief executive himself regarded the stock price as a kind of daily personal report card.

The chief operating officer of the special-machinery company confirmed that the large ownership stake strongly colored his views of numerous company decisions. For instance, the state in which the company was incorporated adopted an antitakeover law in the late 1980s, and the company promptly "opted out" of the law's coverage, meaning that it could not invoke the statute's protections if an unwanted takeover bid materialized. "I feel strongly," the officer said, "that anything that would prevent the takeover of a company from a management that wasn't effectively managing it or getting full value for its shareholders is a big negative for its shareholders. It's a big negative for me. I think about it that way." The negative also translated into opposition to golden parachutes and special management contracts that financially protect managers in the event of a hostile acquisition. Though sometimes viewed as an ambiguous form of antitakeover defense, they were seen in this company as an unambiguous device for protecting management against shareholders. Many investment bankers had suggested to the company that prudence dictated the adoption of golden parachutes and similar devices. Though certainly reluctant to lose his executive position, as would be likely in the event of a takeover, this manager's ownership stake outweighed his managerial interests: "We have no [golden] parachutes or [management] contracts anyplace in the organization. As a shareholder of the company, I really don't think that those are the right things to do, because it gives the shareholders the impression, myself included, of an 'entrenched management' kind of philosophy. If we're not doing the job, and somebody can pay the shareholders more money for this company, by God they should do it.''

Transforming Managers into Owners

New forms of "internal ownership" were created for top managers of business units, giving each manager benefits and risks as if he or she were the unit's founder-entrepreneur. Several of the companies, for example, created compensation schemes that permitted the heads of business units that had had a highly successful year to earn seven-figure incomes. Conversely, poor years could yield five-figure incomes, but in an exceptionally good year unit managers' compensation could exceed that of their boss or other top executives.

The electrical-products company sought to take matters a step further. It experimented with strong performance-based compensation schemes for several years, and in 1990 it moved to transform its business units into almost stand-alone units. In its search for organizational models, it had studied the organization of the nation's largest buyout firm, Kohlberg Kravis Roberts. It sought to understand how KKR had been able to exercise effective financial oversight yet at the same time give vigorous ownership incentives to the top managers of such holdings as RJR Nabisco, Safeway Stores, and Duracell. Combined with decentralized decision making, the strong KKR ownership incentives appeared to offer an exceptional chemistry. The report from Duracell was illustrative of what might be achieved. With the backing of KKR, Duracell had moved from a division of Kraft to a stand-alone company in the KKR stable. KKR retained some 87 percent of the company's ownership, but management held the balance, creating a culture of ownership that the electrical-products firm found appealing. Some 350 managers possessed significant equity in the company, and compensation was built around further increasing that stake. A characterization by Duracell's chief executive summarized the model under study (Kidder, 1990, pp. 27, 32): "After Duracell went private, our people started negotiating targets *up,* not down. It was a complete reversal of what typically goes on in large companies . . . When managers become owners, they begin to think a lot harder about taking money out of mature businesses and investing in growth areas . . . It's certainly not happening because all of a sudden we put in new controls at headquarters. In fact, today we have fewer controls than we had as part of Kraft. What's different is that the proposals for change are coming from the bottom up rather than the top down.''

With sixteen relatively independent business units of its own, many similar in size to some KKR holdings, the electrical-products manufacturer looked for ways to create an internal KKR equivalent. The strategic-planning director described the company's initiative to do so through a high-level working group on compensation:

> We had shareholder-value based planning . . . and we had a vision of outstanding returns to shareholders through 1995. We needed something to get us there, and that something we have called ''ownership.''
>
> We put together this task force to work on compensation and measurement because we wanted to see if the whole compensation system is lined up for shareholders interests. Are we measuring the right thing?
>
> But it wasn't too long before we said: You can't just change the compensation, you have to empower the people. We can change the compensation system and it will help matters, but only if we connect it to an empowerment culture where people will see that their actions influence the business, and that they can actually act as owners.

The task force urged that each business unit have the power to create its own forms of organizational empowerment and compensation. The company subsequently adopted a policy of encouraging all units to increase their contingent pay but at the same time allowing each almost complete freedom to design its own system. Under the policy, for instance, each unit could opt to extend contingent pay to all of its employees down to the shop floor; it could also decide to make all of the pay contingent on five- or even ten-year growth in its contribution to the company's share value. The task force recommendations and subsequent company policies were aimed, in the words of the chief planner, simply at ''getting people to think like owners, and to empower them to act like owners.''

The ownership scheme appealed to senior line managers, both for what it promised them personally and for the management tool it placed at their disposal. An executive overseeing two major business units described the virtues:

> Every compensation program that we've had until now, with a few exceptions, is one where the upside is capped and the downside risk is nonexistent. We set our targets, and if we hit 100 percent of those targets, that's what we get. We get no incentive financially to drive them up.

What we're looking at now are approaches whereby the sky's the limit! If I were a business-unit general manager running a business, and we take one of these approaches whereby I am going to be compensated long term on value creation, I can become a millionaire. The more I generate, the more I make. At the same time, these approaches have downside risks.

Those downside risks nonetheless generated alarm as the ownership concept was introduced down the line. Subordinate managers feared that some of the company's debt would be shifted to their shoulders, and that their operating units could be partially sold to outside investors. When this executive first met with his own management team to introduce the concept, the initial reactions were of shock. Following a round of "shock therapy," however, he pushed ahead, still convinced of the course's correctness and convincing others along the way. "We're well enough along right now that by the start of next year we'll have a new plan in place that will increase the sense of ownership without taking on any of the more drastic actions [such as shouldering debt], and we'll have a realistic downside. But the biggest difference is that a guy several levels down can break the bank."

From Social Similarity to Managerial Performance

The enhanced stress on managing managers for results can be expected to erode one of the most commonly observed social features of managers in senior positions: their social similarity. Traditionally, homogeneity has extended to virtually every feature of the managerial persona—attire, language, club memberships, gender, race. In *Men and Women of the Corporation* (1977), Rosabeth Moss Kanter persuasively argued that social similarity has long served as a surrogate for trust. In hiring and promoting people similar to themselves with whom they comfortably work, managers have sought to reduce the problems of risky appointments inherent in any personnel actions but especially fateful at the senior levels. The result was widespread social homogeneity. To note just two traditional signs also observed in the present study, of all the senior managers interviewed in the seven major corporations, only three were women and none were racial minorities.

If social similarity served as a convenient predictor of managerial performance in the past, shareholder pressures can be expected to undermine such a utility. Social similarity was, after all, a surrogate, and it suffered from the inexactitude that characterizes any indirect measure. Enhanced shareholder vigilance and the attendant stress on managing managers thus carried a corollary: social similarity should be of diminished value in managerial appraisal and assessment, and greater diversity should be expected in managerial ranks. A related corollary was that realigned companies would be more likely to view managerial diversity as an opportunity for more effective learning than as a problem to be solved. The rhetoric of managing diversity should give way to learning from diversity.

The intensified search for performance over similarity was, in fact, evident in the way the chief executive of the transportation company had appraised his senior personnel during a radical restructuring of the managerial ranks during his five-year tenure. He confessed to having learned to look beyond similarity and comfort in his wrenching search for better company performance. He had been with the company only a short period before his elevation to CEO, and since he was unfamiliar with many of the firm's managers, among the most difficult initial tasks was to judge the reliability of the advice he was receiving: "There was a difficult period when I was trying to diagnose the information. Information was flowing to me, but everybody put a spin on it, every problem was somebody else's fault, people had a whole series of excuses for what was done and what was not done, and I was getting a lot of self-serving information. It took me a fair amount of time to figure out what was going on." So unreliable was much of the information that he became skeptical of even his own direct impressions of the managers he inherited:

One of the things I learned was that . . . initial impressions did not conform well with job performance over a certain period of time. It's not like the Ivy League, where people have lots of similar attributes and they're selected on those attributes. There are some people that don't speak English very well who turn out to be terrific managers—sensitive, innovative, and smart.

There are other people who make good presentations, who seem to be excellent textbook managers, [but] who turn out under pressure to not do as well as one might think. It took a while for me to figure out who the good people were and who the bad people were. I moved people around until I got somebody in a position who would take the kind of steps that I think were indicated.

The executive described one case where initial judgments of similarity or comfort proved on the mark, but also two cases, one positive and one negative, where they proved highly misleading:

[Case 1] I had somebody working for me who I was very uncomfortable with at the visceral level, but I had no objective evidence that there was a problem. All I knew was that I was uncomfortable. [Later], I fired him. If I had done it by instinct, I would have done it much sooner, but I held myself to the standard that results do matter.

[Case 2] One person that disappointed me a great deal was smart, knew the business, was very personable, was personally loyal to me, but could never—or was unwilling—to take dramatic enough action in a fair way. He would only make small changes, changes at the margin, as opposed to stepping out . . . In the end I solved that problem by changing the person. I found somebody else who could do the things that needed to be done.

[Case 3] Another individual in marketing I was not initially impressed with, but the results kept rolling in year-in and year-out, and I ended up promoting him. When I did, I had a little session with him and I apologized for being so slow to recognize his potential. I tried to let the objective results dominate the personnel moves.

In more aggressively moving beyond impressions, financial results and people management were recurrent emphases. But there was also a heightened preference for independent judgment, especially if it focused on reducing costs and enhancing returns. Acceptance of the conventional frameworks for business decisions that took certain fixed costs for granted was immediately suspect to some. While sensitivity to prevailing business norms remained a prerequisite for success, the inner-directed norms of the professional entrepreneur acquired greater emphasis. The president of the special-machinery company described his reactions when prospective senior managers visited the company:

If somebody comes in and says my fixed costs are so much, my variable is so much, and I'm locked in with these fixed costs, you know he's the wrong guy . . . [But] if a "different" person comes in the door, you sort of know [that he or she is the right kind of manager].

They look and say, "Gee, the overhead in that plant is high." [They say] there is no such thing as a fixed cost, we have to get our break-evens down, we have to run our machines flat out, and we have to lower our prices by 20 percent [since] right now we are getting killed by only 10 percent by the competition. If they are [also] innovative and creative, they are going to work out.

In a vision whose generic elements were expressed by many of the managers with whom discussions were held, this executive offered his idealized picture of the managers he has sought to recruit over a decade of building an organization and culture focused on shareholder value:

> A person coming in here that we hang on to and that really does well could be a person who just wouldn't fit in a larger organization. He or she is an independent thinker, questions things that are going on continually, doesn't accept the status quo, knows what our competitors are up to, knows where our shortcomings are, is constantly working with research and development, is constantly working with manufacturing and sales or whoever it may be to make things better, is out there in the marketplace talking to customers and distributors, and really has a strong, keen awareness of what's going on.

Balkanization of Managerial Careers

A concomitant of intensified decentralization in companies with multiple business units and divisions was heightened variability in human-resource policies among them. Uniform company-wide practices gave way to customized arrangements reflecting the unit's conditions and managerial preferences. Although this was one of devolution's necessary outcomes, the variability among the units gave rise to greater balkanization within the company. Much standardization remained, but compared to the previous, more bureaucratic configuration, alignment led to more customized and less standardized practices.

An example in the human-resource arena can be seen in the formation of an employee assistance plan at the chemical-products firm. With origins in alcohol assistance programs, employee assistance plans (EAPs) were expanded or created at many large companies during the 1970s and 1980s to provide assistance in a range of areas including substance abuse, stress, divorce, health, family conflict, and other problems potentially affecting work performance (Roman and Blum, 1987). Some programs take a special focus, as does Johnson & Johnson's "Live for Life" program, which concentrates on employee exercise and health throughout the company's many business units. Despite initial opposition to its costs and skepticism about its purpose among heads of some of the company's business units, the chief executive mandated its implementation throughout the firm.

The chemical-products company established an employee assistance plan for headquarters employees, but left it up to the business units to decide whether and how to create their own. The central EAP provided a model for the units and conveyed top management's commitment to the concept, but implementation was left entirely to the business units. Some subsequently created such programs; others did not. Central management no longer even tracked which ones did. Prior to the devolution of the 1980s, the company would have established a task force to study the issue, and then mandated a policy for all units to follow. The postdecentralization result left unanswered the extent to which employee problems were addressed in units choosing not to create an EAP. But the human-resources office at headquarters had decided it was no longer a corporate issue, at least not of a magnitude to justify overriding its policy of devolution.

More troublesome were the analogous consequences for career movement between units, the sine qua non for general management development. Without experience in at least several of a company's business units, a manager was often considered to lack the breadth of experience, informal networks, and credibility to move effectively into the central ranks. As salary scales, compensation packages, and managerial grades evolved autonomously within the business units, moving from one to another became more daunting. It was in part for this reason that the chemical-products company had retained a partially centralized salary structure, despite a company philosophy and divisional pressures to the contrary. The firm's chief human-resources officer described the downside problems: ''If you've got these five business units with various salary schedules, then how are you going to pay the corporate people? Are they going to get the high schedule? Or an average? . . . The most devastating thing, it would take about five minutes in this organization, once you split the salary schedules, for every employee to know which is the high-paid unit and which is the low-paid. The difficulty in moving people between units would mount significantly.'' Still, since the firm recognized that its business units operated in diverse product markets and faced variant competitive pressures in the market for managerial talent, it gave these units flexibility within the centrally set structure. Early managerial careers now developed more within the operating units, less in the company as a whole, though there were exceptions. In the summary assessment of the human-resources chief:

> One of the consequences of this reorganization was to lessen the movement of people between the divisions and business units at lower levels. [We] officially recognized that we were in a lot of different businesses, and we said, ''Let's make these units autonomous and free-standing, give them their objectives, sit back and don't encumber them with a lot of bureaucratic corporate red tape, and let them do their thing.'' Then, as one of the natural results, . . . they would tend to look [for managers] within their own

organization rather than have to go through some corporate mechanism that forced them to look across the company.

As a result, movement at the lower levels across divisions and business decreased, while promotions within increased. Mindful of the continuing need to develop general managerial talent, however, the company retained a corporate mechanism for cultivating those identified at an early stage as having high potential. The mechanism was characterized by its manager as "a very aggressive corporate-run, corporate-owned, corporate-mandated management-development and management-succession planning activity." It was from this group, a small fraction of any managerial age cohort, that the firm's future leadership would be cultivated and then drawn. According to the vice-president for human resources, "Once an individual gets identified with a certain level of potential within a business unit, then . . . the corporation [gets] heavy-handed in making certain that this individual starts to move between business units . . . The common denominator is . . . who can be an operating-division president, who can run a $200 or $300 or $700 million business."

Career lines had been similarly reconfigured at the electrical-products company. Replacements for the top 1,400 incentive-compensation positions remained the prerogative of headquarters management. But most other replacements had become business-unit decisions. The contrast with the policies of a decade earlier was stark. Then, a roster of 30,000 managers and professionals was centrally operated. Now, that data base had simply been closed. Then, some 30 percent of exempt appointments were of people moving from one business unit to another. Now, that fraction had dropped by half.

Conclusion

Aligning managerial and shareholder interests was still an organizational frontier. Few devices were yet of long-standing proven utility. The management of managers was thus approached experimentally, as were many organizational design questions. It was a trial-and-error process, as firms tested and tinkered with alternative schemes.

The implementers were moving inductively through accumulating experience toward what an academic research literature was already confirming in the area of executive compensation. One study, for example, focused on the compensation of the top seventy-five managers at each of some 250 large corporations in the early 1980s (Abowd, 1990). It found that when executive compensation was built around traditional accounting measures of company performance, such as company return on equity, it did not well predict subsequent company performance. By contrast, when compensation was driven by shareholder-value measures, such as change in total shareholder return (defined here as dividends and capital gains per share over a period, divided by the beginning share price), it did predict subsequent company behavior. (Related results can be found in Leonard, 1990, and Ehrenberg, 1990.)

The companies studied here had all moved in this general direction. Performance criteria were now more extensively applied to the compensation package and more deeply extended down the managerial ranks. The contingent criteria were more explicitly tied to shareholder interests. These changes in compensation were taken in conjunction with corresponding changes in management oversight and staffing. Less top-management time went into approving business decisions; more went into implementing management succession and reviewing subordinate performance. To facilitate the process, the firms created better information systems pertaining to the managers and the positions to which they would be appointed.

Alignment efforts, however, should not be confused with alignment outcomes. Many of the initiatives were taken with few precedents to build upon and little certainty of outcome, and new problems were often generated in solving the old. This could be seen in the large losses that could now follow a poor executive choice. It was also evident in the weakened internal market for general managerial talent. And, in any case, alignment in the management of managers stopped far short of its logical possibilities. Variable compensation was more extensively used, yet most compensation of most managers remained essentially fixed, impervious to individual or company performance. Information for management succession was improved, but the usual limits of "bounded rationality" still resulted in some poor appointments. Organizational alignment was thus a process of testing and retesting, with organizational outcomes by no means assured.

The process of ownership-disciplined alignment tended to introduce change in many organizational components. Discussions of agent-principal problems in the corporate context frequently focus on incentivizing managers as agents to perform just as their principals, the shareholders, would want. Most efforts to overcome the alignment dilemma were narrowly conceived, and sometimes apparently reduced to designing compensation schemes that effectively constrained individual behavior. But we have seen that companies actively confronting the agent-principal dilemma found it necessary to evolve a host of related changes, from devolved decision making to centralized knowledge systems. The changes far transcended the roles and incentives of the chief executive and his immediate associates, or any other set of individuals. The introduction of a highly contingent shareholder-focused compensation system for top management, shorn of the numerous related changes chronicled here in Chapters 3 and 4, was a move in the right direction but did not go far enough. The agent-principal conflict was an organizational problem requiring an organizational solution.

FIVE

Aligning Shareholders

Organizational alignment was driven by shareholder pressures—real, anticipated, or feared. Alignment efforts were not limited, however, to internal company changes. The agenda included externally directed change as well. Organizational design was brought into better alignment with shareholder objectives, but shareholders were also brought into better alignment with management objectives. Companies met shareholder challenges with challenges of their own.

Some corporate response should have been anticipated from the elementary principles of organizational politics. The application of influence is rarely unilateral, with all give and no take. Attempts by one institution to control another are almost always met with countermeasures. Finding themselves on the receiving end of pressure politics, large corporations were as likely as any other organization to resist.

Managements were hardly shy about holding their own in any such conflict. Most executives had come to office in an era when the tenets of free enterprise were taken to mean virtually complete autonomy. Deference, it seemed, was due no one. Moreover, many managements had already learned that countermeasures would work when limitations on their autonomy were sought by outside institutions. Companies had successfully mobilized against many of the regulatory constraints imposed on business during the 1960s and 1970s (Vogel, 1989; Himmelstein, 1990). Now, with new constraints coming instead from their shareholders, defiance would come naturally.

Openly doing so, however, was another matter. Shareholders, after all, held a uniquely privileged position. Other claimants, whether elected officials, environmentalists, or bankers, could make demands and raise the costs of operating. Yet, to the thinking of most executives, they had no special call on management. As a matter of political reality, their power would be respected, but the moral basis for many of their demands would not be. Owners, by contrast, occupied hallowed ground. If private enterprise meant anything, a company's ultimate source of legitimacy could only be its ultimate source of capital. The rhetoric of one participant would be echoed by many (Seely, 1991, 36): "Shareholders come first, other capital contributors thereafter, and other constituencies in the order that they contribute to the long-term profitability of the business. Public companies are not in business to reward creditors, inspire devotion of their employees, win the favor of the communities in which they operate, or have the best plants or products. These are all means to an end—making shareholders richer." Seeking to resist or reshape shareholder demands would thus seem to contradict the very concept of corporate ownership. It would certainly contravene much business wisdom. Rejecting or managing demands from other constituencies should be expected. Opposing shareholder pressures would be ironic and, to some, heretical.

Resistance to shareholder demands would be especially problematic for companies that had restructured in the name of increasing shareholder value. Their alignment efforts had been undertaken in part because the company's organization was viewed as increasingly incapable of yielding the return that shareholders deserved or wanted. Challenging stockholders would therefore run against the grain even more at these firms than at companies where owners had long been ignored anyway.

We should therefore expect management resistance to shareholder demands to be couched in carefully formulated rationales. Aligning shareholders to company advantage might be redefined as building investor relations. Lobbying investors for proxy votes could be labeled as prudent action on behalf of the greater shareholder good. Adopting an antitakeover defense might be recast as protecting "shareholder rights." In some instances such rationales would no doubt correspond to reality; in other cases they would surely mask it. Whatever the correspondence, the fact remained that investor demands could be resisted and managed.

If aligning shareholders was a conceptually unnatural act, the practical actions would not be. Companies had already built sophisticated offices for orchestrating their relations with a host of external constituencies, ranging from the White House and the media to antiapartheid activists. Most of the nation's largest companies had established full-time public affairs offices by the 1980s (Post et al., 1983). Professional staffs, under the direction of a senior manager often reporting to the chief executive, had mastered the use of media contacts, political action committees, company foundations, lobbyists, and an array of other devices for controlling and shaping the company's public environment (Handler and Mulkern, 1982).

Yet shareholders placed demands on the company's doorstep that were distinct from those of, say, congressional candidates or recycling advocates. Working with shareholders would not be the same as working with reporters for the *Wall Street Journal* or representatives of the city mayor. Still, many of the generic skills could be carried over. Extending the management of public affairs to the management of shareholder affairs was thus a natural generalization of political action that companies had already learned to do elsewhere. External constituencies had long ago discovered payoff in "lobbying the corporation" (Vogel, 1978). Corporations now found that lobbying the shareholder could yield rich dividends as well. Offered one investor relations consultant: "Marketing stock can be more important than marketing a product" (quoted in Mahoney, 1990). The manager of investor relations at the retail-services company confided that his function had come to be known inside the company as "financial marketing."

Whether viewed as financial marketing or investor management, a company's actions were intended to inform and influence its shareholders. If shrewd steps slid into deceitful tactics, shareholder alignment could shade into shareholder manipulation. Fraudulent actions are certainly not unknown in the securities industry, as readers well know from such accounts as James Stewart's *Den of Thieves* (1991). Still, federal regulations required fair disclosure of company information, and large investors harbored few illusions about company agendas (O'Barr and Conley, 1992). The two parties could be seen as working with—and sometimes against—one another for their own advantage, employing tactics well known to each.

The Rise of Investor Relations

In its successful resistance of a takeover by NL industries, Lockheed's management met with most of the company's large institutional investors (Blumenthal and Wartzman, 1991). In its unsuccessful resistance to the AT&T takeover, NCR's management had done much the same (L. J.

Davis, 1991). In its sustained resistance to Carl Icahn's proxy fight for control, USX's management worked a similar circuit (Hicks, 1990). Crisis management evoked actions in each case that were direct extensions of what many companies had learned to do in more methodical fashion. If the 1970s saw the professionalization and organizational implanting of the public affairs function, the 1980s witnessed the same for the investor relations (IR) function (Mahoney, 1991a, 1991b).

Until the 1980s, to the extent that shareholders occupied management time at all, investor relations was often the province of the chief financial officer (CFO). As shareholder questions would periodically arise, the CFO would take time from an otherwise full schedule to respond. Investor relations then entailed little more than public relations and occasional crisis management. Contact with shareholders was largely episodic, reactive, and unorganized.

At decade's end, by contrast, the investor relations office had often become a full-time professionalized operation. Exceptions remained. Investor relations at the special-machinery and transportation companies were still directed by part-time executives who carried a portfolio of other responsibilities. But at the other five corporations, a manager was assigned full time to the function, sometimes assisted by one or more professional staff members. Moreover, the office typically reported to the top of the organizational chart, either through the chief financial officer or some other senior officer (Table 5.1).

Whatever the title or reporting structure, all of those responsible for investor relations were in regular conversation with both the chief executive and the chief financial officer. The investor relations manager occupied

Table 5.1. Title and reporting structure of the manager of investor relations, seven corporations, 1989–1991.

Company	Title of manager of investor relations	Executive to whom IR manager reports
Pharmaceuticals	Vice-president	Executive vice-president
Special machinery	Senior vice-president	Chief executive officer
Transportation	Vice-president	Chief executive officer
Chemical products	Vice-president	Chief executive officer
Retail services	Vice-president	Chief financial officer
Electrical products	Director	Chief financial officer
Financial services	Senior vice-president	Chief financial officer

an office proximate to, if not within, the executive suite in all seven companies. Often, he had worked with and knew well all of the company's top managers.

At the financial-services company the position had traditionally been staffed as a largely reactive post. Until the late 1980s, an individual from the investment side of the bank would be temporarily assigned to the role as a step in career development. Since the position did little more than respond to investor queries, it was assumed that the right background for the job was familiarity with the investment community. As the position was redefined to play a far more proactive role, the chief executive and one of his top people tapped a general manager with some twenty years of experience in several major branches of the company. Because of his senior status, he had long worked with those who ran the company's major divisions, and now he regularly communicated with them on investor issues. The senior status also facilitated full access to the company's most critical information flows. All written reports received by the CEO were routed to him as well, and he was a regular participant in the company's top budget and planning meetings.

The central place that investor relations had come to occupy in the organizational chart of many companies is evident from two surveys conducted by the National Investor Relations Institute, the professional association of company managers responsible for investor relations. In 1985 and 1989 it asked its company members to characterize the organization of their operations. The responding firms were generally large, with approximately two-thirds of the companies in each survey listed on the New York Stock Exchange. In both surveys, investor relations managers had been in the field for an average of more than five years, and some two-thirds reported to the company's chief financial officer, chief executive officer, president, or chairman. The 1989 survey reported that 26 percent of the managers served on a corporate standing committee (such as a management or steering committee), and 52 percent had personal contact with the board of directors (National Investor Relations Institute, 1985, 1989).

Shareholder Communications

Managing investor relations meant, first, active communication with the company's shareholders. Rather than passively allowing analysts and investors to draw their own conclusions from publicly available but generally bare-bones sources, companies preemptively sought them out. More information would be more aggressively distributed, and more certainly controlled in content.

The growth of company investment in investor communications can be illustrated with data compiled by the retail-services firm. The company's program was distinctive in that it devoted a larger proportion of its time to contact with individual investors, and it maintained exceptionally good records of its communications. Otherwise, its activities were relatively typical. As can be seen in Table 5.2, the frequency of communication with investors sharply increased during the end of the 1980s. The number of contacts with investors of all kinds more than tripled between 1986 and 1990.

One of the retail-service company's communication innovations was the introduction in 1989 of periodic conference calls for analysts and top management. A conference call in mid-1990, for example, included the company's chief executive, chief operating officer, and chief financial officer. After extensive review of the company's performance, they fielded questions from analysts and investment managers. Would the company "be willing to borrow money in order to repurchase stock"? Could they "continue to take costs out" of operations? Had the recession made "their outlook more cautious now"? Detailed responses followed, and in case

Table 5.2. Investor activities of retail services company, 1986–1990.

Activity	1986	1987	1988	1989	1990[a]
Contact with analysts and portfolio managers:					
Telephone discussions	481	585	487	635	585
Individual contacts	30	50	120	300	180
Individual visits	22	35	50	70	72
Group presentations	16	22	20	18	17
Conference calls	0	0	0	3	6
Telephone contact with brokers	n.a.	20	75	218	227
Contact with individual investors:					
Telephone discussions	170	231	150	270	632
Written communication	114	178	201	328	754

Source: Company records (1991).

a. The 1990 data for contact with analysts and portfolio managers are through November; the 1990 data for other items are through September.

management's general posture was still not clear on closing, the director of investor relations concluded with the statement, "We are very optimistic about our long-term business opportunities and hope that message came through in our discussion" (company records, 1990).

The communications programs of the financial-services firm followed a similar strategy. The investor relations director and his professional staff maintained regular personal contact with virtually all of the firm's major analysts and investors. The contact ranged from frequent informal telephone conversations to major meetings in which analysts and investors sat with the firm's chief executive. A specially prepared newsletter ensured a steady but controlled flow of company information. One newsletter issue, for instance, highlighted comments at an analysts' meeting by two of the company's officers, focusing on the firm's European strategies; another issue summarized the chief executive's observations at a meeting of institutional investors and analysts, where he stressed the firm's emphasis on globalization.

Although the shareholder base often numbered in the tens of thousands and sometimes exceeded 100,000, investor relations managers usually focused company resources on the several hundred largest shareholders. In 1985, prior to the wave of institutional activism, more than two-fifths of investor relations managers' contact time was already devoted to buy-side analysts and portfolio managers, according to companies surveyed that year by the National Investor Relations Institute. By contrast, less than one-fifth went to individual shareholders (Figure 5.1).

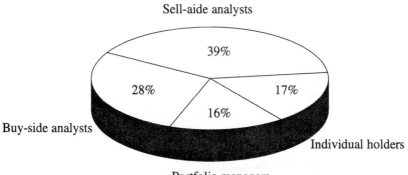

Figure 5.1. Percent allocation of company investor relations time. (Source: National Investor Relations Institute, 1985, p. 2.)

Institutional investors reported increased effort by companies to contact them. Annual surveys of institutional investors from 1985 to 1989 revealed continued expansion in the amount and quality of information supplied by companies, the willingness of firms to meet with investors, and the frequency with which companies initiated contact with the institutions (Table 5.3). In every year of the survey, the institutional investors reporting that their contact with companies, often at the initiative of the firms, had increased during the previous year far outnumbered those reporting decreased contact.

Recruiting, Retaining, and Changing Investors

The investor relations agenda extended far beyond keeping investors well informed. It was also designed to keep investors. It was intended to attract new investors. And it was sometimes organized to change the mix of investors. Such efforts entailed not only delivering more information to the investment community, but also more disciplining of the information around management's central message to shareholders. When that message was not readily understood or appreciated, the agenda also became one of "educating" shareholders.

Recruitment, retention, and change dominated investor relations office at the retail-services firm. The passive model of responding to investor inquiries had given way during the mid-1980s to an active model of stimulating inquiries. In the informal culture at headquarters, the investor relations manager had come to be viewed as responsible for "investor recruitment" rather than relations. "I think of our job," said the manager, "as recruiting investors, not having relationships with them." The defining vision far exceeded information exchange: "We don't just look at the supply side. We want to create demand. And creating demand is getting out there and talking to people about your story over a long period of time . . . There's no reason that [our] stock can't fit into a lot of portfolios . . . My [investor relations] group has a motto that 'our job is to sell stock.' When we're doing something that isn't selling stock, we've got to think real hard about doing it."

In developing strategies for reaching new investors and retaining old ones, the investor relations office had turned to the company's marketing department. In one major initiative, for instance, the IR office sought to increase the number of individual shareholders who directly reinvested

Table 5.3. Percent of institutional investors reporting increase or decrease in contact by companies.[a]

	1986		1987		1988		1989	
Type of company contact	Increased	Decreased	Increased	Decreased	Increased	Decreased	Increased	Decreased
Information provided by companies to investors:								
Quality of information	35	7	29	0	30	5	38	10
Amount of information	54	2	37	4	43	5	51	3
Direct contact of companies with investors:								
Company's willingness to meet	33	2	41	2	47	7	56	3
No. of companies initiating contact	55	10	47	6	46	5	65	5
(No. of surveyed investors)	(572)		(601)		(630)		(602)	

Source: Greenwich Associates (1990).

a. The increased percentages reflect the proportion of responding investors stating that the flow of information had increased significantly or somewhat; the decreased figures reflect the proportion stating that the flow had decreased significantly or somewhat. The percentages reporting no change are omitted from the table.

their dividends in additional company stock. The marketing department assisted in the preparation of a letter to all individual shareholders urging such reinvestment, using one of the company's well-known advertising symbols to promote the message.

The retail-services company viewed the recruitment of individual shareholders as an end in itself. Small holders were considered more likely to invest for the long term and less likely to vote against management. The company's campaign during the late 1980s for the individual investor had shown success: between 1986 and 1990, the number of shareholders rose by more than 150 percent (from under 50,000 to well over 100,000). Individuals held 44 percent of the company's shares in 1986 but 48 percent in 1990, a change almost the precise reverse of the overall trend in individual shareholding (Table 2.2). Yet recruitment of individual stockholders was also viewed as a means to another end, the stimulation of institutional interest. Though without confirming statistical evidence, managers believed that the enhanced individual demand for its stock had in turn enhanced the interest of institutional investors. Concluded the investor relations manager: "One of the reasons we think we've been so successful on the institutional side is they know we're creating demand on the individual side."

Other companies chose to focus more on the direct recruitment and retention of institutional investors. The fact that institutions were large in scale and small in number simplified targeting, though even here selective focus was required, since the large-investor community still comprised some 2,000 institutions. Various selection strategies were devised, but among the most common was to focus on large holders deemed relatively underinvested in the company. "Underinvestment" often meant that an investor held less of a stake in the firm than in a comparison set of companies, frequently the firm's competitors. The presumption, not always well founded, was that investors viewed competitors as largely equivalent alternatives. The decision to invest in one competitor over another was seen as hinging on small differences. A company might therefore promote its securities by explaining away the differences and better drawing the attention of such underinvestors.

At the financial-services firm, for example, changes in the holdings of the major investors were tracked on a daily basis, and investors whose stakes in the company dropped or were substantially below those in other companies in the same industry were directly lobbied for more. A "relationship manager" and a backup manager were assigned to each of the fifty largest institutional investors. Only several years earlier, the fifty largest had not even been fully identified. According to the firm's senior vice-president for investor relations, "Five or six years ago we didn't know for sure who the top fifty were. Five or six years ago the approach was a reactive approach. The phone rings, you answer it . . . Because we have aggressively gone out to determine who our shareholders are, we now have a much better idea both of who our shareholders and who our potential shareholders are." The financial-services firm divided the more than 2,000 institutions it tracked in a data base into six basic classifications reflecting their investment strategies. One category, for instance, included the investors that indexed their funds, a group for which recruitment efforts would be pointless. Other categories included active investors tiered by size and by investment style. Subgroups of the latter were placed on the prospect list: "We always have a targeted list of investors," observed the IR manager. "When you match their appetite against the [actual] holding of us, we identify those who we should be a logical holding for, but aren't. Those are the ones that we contact proactively."

The pharmaceutical company did much the same. It systematically tracked institutional holdings in ten other major pharmaceutical companies. One of its measures of an institution's commitment was the percentage of the fund's holdings invested in the company compared with its holdings in the company's primary competitors. Investor holdings varied considerably among the competitors (selectively illustrated in Table 5.4). One investment company had placed only 0.1 percent of its holdings in the pharmaceutical firm, while averaging 0.8 percent investment among

Table 5.4. Holdings of four selected institutional investors in the pharmaceutical company under study and in ten other pharmaceutical firms, 1990.

Institutional investor	Percent of holdings in pharmaceutical company	Holdings in ten other pharmaceutical companies	
		Average percent	Range of percent
Insurance company	2.1	0.6	0 to 2.0
Commercial bank trust	0.9	0.5	0 to 1.6
Public pension fund	0.4	0.7	0 to 1.3
Investment company	0.1	0.8	0 to 1.7

Source: Company records (1990).

the ten competitors, and ranging as high as 1.7 percent investment in one. An outside firm that had compiled the comparative figures (along with the identities and telephone numbers of the fund managers) reminded the pharmaceutical company to use the information to "contact the right person at institutions who own your competitors but not your company" or to "target institutions that are moving into your industry" (company records, 1990).

The firm made similar trackings of sell-side analysts whose assessments and forecasts also affected shareholder retention and recruitment. Overly pessimistic analysts, such as underinvesting investors, might be singled out for special attention. In one case, the investor relations director had also learned to couple the trackings with an implicit quid pro quo. His staff systematically compared the analysts' forecasts for the company's quarterly and annual earnings with the firm's actual performance. Within hours of the company's announcement of the quarterly and annual results, the first telephone calls were placed to the analysts who had been overly optimistic in their predictions. It was they, the investor manager reasoned, who most needed—and therefore would most remember—the company's immediate assistance in explaining their errant forecasts.

Working to moderate sell-side analysts' expectations was a widely practiced art. One research study also suggested a tinge of practical self-interest. Analysis of the predictors of turnover among chief executives of 408 large firms in 1983 found that a frequent precursor was the firms' falling short of analysts' published expectations for company earnings per share. Expectation shortfalls proved to be a better predictor of CEO exit than such traditional performance shortfalls as adverse stock price movements and declining rates of return on equity (Puffer and Weintrop, 1991).

Communication efforts were also aimed at retaining investors, especially when investors were confronted with dismaying results. Announcement of results from an adverse period would typically be followed by a blitz of telephone calls to and from both sell-side analysts and buy-side investors. Another financial-services firm, for example, used a conference call for that purpose after each quarter and after all major mergers and acquisitions. The chairman would seek to explain the underlying issues to analysts from both sides of the investment community. The latent function, confided the senior vice-president for investor relations and corporate communication, was to "get the analysts off the numbers and onto the core operating strategies and the long term" (discussion among investor relations managers, 1990).

Investors' Impatient Message

Refocusing investors on the longer term would be no easy feat. Their eagerness for short-term results was widely perceived to be an operating fact. Outside the firm, the intensity of short-term investor demands was a matter of continuing policy and research dispute (Rappaport, 1992; Competitiveness Policy Council, 1992; National Academy of Engineering, 1992; Jacobs, 1991). Inside the firm, however, for most senior managers the matter was already resolved. "Short-termism" was an environmental "fact," widely recognized and widely lamented. Limited time horizons among major investors had become an operating factor that senior managers recognized but never fully accepted.

The pervasiveness of management concern can be seen in a 1989 survey of investor relations managers by the National Investor Relations Institute. When the managers were asked to identify their major concerns regarding their company's "relationship with the financial community," one response dominated: more than half singled out the short-term perspective of sell-side analysts and institutions (Table 5.5).

So widespread was the critique of investors' focus on short-term results that it had become a virtual cliché. But the aura of short-term demands constituted a real constraint that many managers felt they could not ignore. The impact was probably nowhere more evident than at the chemical-products company. The picture that emerged there was one of intense concern with short-term shareholder pressures, more so than at the other six companies. Nonetheless, it was a concern shared in some form by all.

The chemical-products company managers reported that investor issues had generated little direct concern a decade earlier. Shareholder interests had been appreciated but could be safely ignored. One former unit head

Table 5.5. Major concerns of investor relations managers for 721 companies, 1989.

Percent of companies	Major concern
55	Short-term perspectives of sell-side and institutional holders
22	Lack of interest on buy-side
9	Lack of market makers
2	Too much interest on buy-side
13	Other
15	None

Source: National Investor Relations Institute (1989), p. 10.

recalled his earlier attitude: "When I was a president of a business [unit] here, I would say, 'Screw Wall Street—I'm going to do it my way and build for the future.'" He was now the company's vice-president for external affairs, including investor relations, with some 30 to 40 percent of his time given to contact with institutional investors. His understanding of shareholder pressures had changed accordingly:

> To some extent in [this company] there was a feeling of "The hell with shareholders. We're running a business here, we're making good business decisions, and we're not running a business for the sake of impressing the 'Street.'"
>
> The performance of the company on relatively short-term time frames, like the quarterly reports, while anathema to us in many respects . . . I nonetheless recognized was part of the atmosphere in which I had to work. If you're going to play that game, and you want to get the stock up, and you really think you are undervalued, you're going to need the help of the people who prescribe those ground rules.

With a greater sensitivity to investor issues than that expressed by any other executive, the external affairs manager had come to respect the power of the investment community. On this premise, he had defined his investor relations role within the company to include internal education: "I have been an instrument in this company in getting senior managers to recognize that we have to home in on those quarters."

Senior managers throughout the chemical-products company had become more aware of the shareholder demand for consistent short-term results. One long-time executive who presided over half of the company's major business units reflected on the changing ground rules:

> I can't think of a time in my industrial career, some twenty-four or twenty-five years, when [we have been so] particularly intensive in looking at short-term earnings. I think the advent of the takeover, both the hostile and the white-knight, and all this merger mania have put enormous pressure from Wall Street on public companies to perform in the short term and show projections that look good for the long term.
>
> You are forced into looking at your short term far more than you were in the past because there is an immediate and direct implication if you don't get the short-term results and you don't meet expectations on the outside. Your stock goes down, and that puts you in another category of being rumored as potentially being a takeover candidate. So it's just a total preoccupation . . .
>
> We've had to make a lot more people far more aware of the short term

than we used to. It used to be you could manage it at the top, and if you had a little glitch you could explain it and get by. Today, you're living under a microscope, and everybody has got everything on a computer of everything you're supposed to do, and if they don't like it, you get put into a downward slide . . . Short-term performance is what drives it.

In addition to pressing periodic expense reductions to help short-term earnings and other financial measures, this manager sought organizational change as well: "The biggest difference is," he observed in reference to the rise of investor pressures, "a few years ago I could manage the whole process from in here. But [now] I have had to get my operating presidents more involved in why we are doing things so they don't think we're nuts." He had brought them "into the loop" so that they could better appreciate the reasons for what otherwise might not always seem organizationally rational.

The quarterly pressures infused staff functions as well as line functions. The company's top financial person observed: "Wall Street has altered our thought process and our management process. We worry about quarterly earnings. Whatever the aspects are that go into them, we worry about them. It used to be that you could convince yourself that you're in this thing for the long term. The perception is that that's not really true anymore." To facilitate the structuring of quarterly and yearly results, the chief financial officer projected end-of-quarter and end-of-year sales and earnings on a weekly basis. He confessed that he could not do much to affect the results—that was the job of the operating-unit heads and the group executives. ("I don't make the shit, I don't sell the shit, I just keep the score.") But the information he now provided could be used by line managers to trim expenses, book sales before quarter's end, and delay product starts until after quarter's end.

Another of the company's group executives had come to rely on such projections in guiding the work of the various business units reporting to him. Direct personal contact with investors and analysts had only reinforced his belief that the quarter and the year were a necessary working frame:

There's no question that the outside analysts have a significant influence on the company. We feel that we are required to increase earnings every quarter. There's no question about it. We begin to fuss about it in the last month of the quarter, and we really start to look at the earnings to make sure that we can move up versus last year, to the extent that we use some reserves and things like that to ensure continuing growth.

I don't feel that it's had the effect of reducing our research . . . But it's so pervasive in the company that we feel that we have to increase our earnings in order to hold up the stock price, in order to prevent us from being acquired or criticized. At the [weekly] officers' meetings, we always talk about the earnings. It's just an ingrained idea that we have to increase earnings . . .

I meet with the analysts . . ., and they don't focus strategically. They like it if you have a new product coming and they talk about it, but it's always "What do next quarter's earnings look like?" We have got some major shareholders who come in after these quarterly meetings, and they're interested in what research is produced . . . They'd like to know what the positioning of [our new] products is, and what competitive products might be coming, and how we will look. But that's always at the end of the discussion.

The pervasiveness of the concern was also evident one level down in the organization. Reporting to the executive vice-president, the head of one of the chemical-product company's largest business units was asked if the influence of institutional shareholders and analysts tangibly reached his office: "Yes, there is no question. Definitely. Do we do things because of it? Yes." Yet he insisted that the bow to Wall Street was without sustained downside: "Do we do things that are deleterious long term? I think I can honestly say no." He echoed an impression shared by most of this company's senior managers that they had been able to shield the company's core decisions. The short-term pressures were well recognized. But so long as earnings displayed relatively consistent quarterly growth, other decisions could be effectively shielded from investor pressures. The business-unit head was thus both responsive and protective, as he explained: "Because you front-end load this tremendous distribution system that we have, you have the ability to move materials into your system . . . So we can move dollars around in a period of time, say a thirty-day period of time, to accomplish certain objectives. If a quarter is slow, we may go out to our dealers and agents, and load them up somewhat . . . But in my experience we have not made a wrong decision or a strategic decision to reflect those [shareholder or analyst] concerns."

Educating Unmotivated Learners

Management concern for short-term shareholder impatience was widespread, and it was here more than anywhere else that companies sought to direct their educational efforts. The purpose was to convince current or potential shareholders that periodic dips in earnings were little more than that. The company's long-term strategies and prospects, and the market's ups and downs, should be taken into account, it would be argued, in judging a company's value and prospects.

In meetings with analysts and investors, for instance, one of the chemical-product company's officers would initially review the firm's quarterly or annual financial performance. The discussion of immediate performance issues addressed the most pressing questions, and it helped establish credibility for what followed. He would then turn the discussion to the company's plans for the next three to four years. The purpose was to refocus thinking around a broader time horizon for judging the company's past and future performance. He perceived that he would not always bring the audience along with him. Nonetheless, after responding to the investors' rash of short-term queries, he repeatedly moved discussion toward long-term strategic issues confronting the firm and industry.

Yet since class attendance was not required, the effectiveness of such educational efforts depended on motivated learners. Many company managers came to believe, however, that certain fund managers were impervious to almost any message. (Some fund managers reciprocally complained about the unresponsiveness of company managers, according to a contemporaneous study by O'Barr and Conley published in 1992.) It seemed that certain investment overseers were too busy, others too uninterested, and still others too ill-informed to appreciate a message. Complaints on all counts were illustrated in an informal exchange among approximately twenty directors of investor relations. They belonged to an exclusive investor relations association drawn from the nation's largest corporations. The exchange followed an outside expert's invited review of recent developments in shareholder activism.

The investor relations manager for one company opened the exchange by recounting how he had written to all of his major investors, asking them to comment on or ask about any issues of concern. "How many do you think I heard from?" he asked, as his fingers formed a zero. Another IR director reported that he had called the proponent of one shareholder resolution on governance submitted to his company, hoping to encourage its withdrawal. The individual who answered reportedly said that his wife belonged "to some group that we don't know much about" and that she had simply submitted the proposal on the group's behalf (the group, it developed, was the United Shareholders Association). An IR director for a third corporation reported contacting one of the largest public pension funds, well known for its activism, but reacted with dismay when its managers appeared to have little interest in or knowledge about his company even though the pension fund was one of the company's largest investors. Still another IR director asserted that "people like [the top manager of one of the largest funds] just want to be kissed by our CEO and be recognized. The rest is irrelevant." Contrary observations were notable for their absence.

The privately expressed cynicism toward the learning interests of some investors reflected in part the problems of delivering an unwanted message. Investors did not always constitute a receptive audience. The reaction of a president of an investment fund specializing in buyouts, with funds drawn in part from large institutional owners, was symptomatic. On hearing a summary of these comments by the investor relations managers, a ground with which he was already well familiar, he waved off further description. "They're all brain dead," he declared. Some of the gap between companies and investors would prove unyielding to any educational effort.

Mobilizing Shareholder Support

When company communication and education failed, and shareholder dissatisfaction with a company's performance remained, some investors quietly decreased their holdings. As noted in Chapter 2, however, others had taken their grievances to the proxy process. A few spearheaded shareholder proposals; larger numbers would quietly join in support. This switch of investor expression of dissatisfaction from exit to voice would change the investor relations function from recruitment and retention to persuasion and mobilization.

Leading the proxy charge were several large public pension funds and members of the United Shareholders Association, though others took the initiative as well (see Table A.7 in Appendix 2). Their proposals would require firms to take actions ranging from rescinding poison pills to removing incumbent directors. The impact of a proposal on a company was almost a linear function of the number of shares voted for or against the resolution. The outcome thus depended on the relative capacity of the two sides to mobilize shareholder support. During the proxy season, the period leading up to a company's annual meeting, some investor relations managers saw their role virtually transformed into that of a campaign manager.

When a shareholder resolution was placed on a company's proxy ballot, the investment community became a political as well as a financial constituency. The formal rule was simple: those proposing the resolution needed the vote of a majority of shares to win passage; management required a majority to ensure defeat. Informal interpretations could sometimes turn a formal shareholder defeat into a de facto win, as managers still felt it prudent to take actions that a failed proposal had advocated. Conversely, some resolutions were nonbinding, and managers did not always follow the actions recommended by winning advisories. Whatever the formal provisions, when large proportions of shareholders voted against management, the message was usually heard and sometimes heeded.

The investor power in such messages could be seen in the aftermath of six shareholder proposals attracting large antimanagement votes at the USX Corporation annual meeting in 1990 (Table 5.6). Four were defeated, several by only narrow margins, and two passed, though both were advisory. USX took several subsequent actions even though it was formally obliged to take none. It modified its poison pill, introduced limited classified voting, and in 1991 created separate classes of stock for its steel and oil businesses, a step in partial response to the spinoff resolution of Carl Icahn, the company's largest investor (Investor Responsibility Research Center, 1990b, p. 13; Hicks, 1991).

Table 5.6. Shareholder proposals and voting at the annual meeting of USX Corporation, 1990.

Shareholder proposal	Sponsor	Percent who voted in favor
Require minimum stock ownership by directors	C. Rossi	31.9
Ban golden parachutes	N. Rossi (USA)	39.2
Spin-off steel business	Carl Icahn	42.9
Repeal classified board	Gilberts	46.8
Confidential voting	E. Rossi (USA)	51.3
Redeem or vote on poison pill	R. Porth (USA)	53.5

Source: Investor Responsibility Research Center (1990a), p. 86.

Defeat of shareholder proposals was thus not just a matter of securing a bare majority of votes for management. A decisive majority could also serve to deter future resolutions and discourage takeover initiatives requiring shareholder approval. This became particularly important during the late 1980s and early 1990s, as takeover strategies shifted from tender offers and junk-bond financing to struggles for board control through the proxy process.

When a company sought to mobilize its investors against a shareholder proposal, the voting of many shares could be well forecast, necessitating little direct solicitation. A company-managed pension fund and employee stock-option plan would be safely in management's column; certain public pension funds would predictably side with a pension-fund-sponsored resolution; and some funds could be expected to sit on their hands. Management's sense of these divisions, enriched by information from consulting firms (usually specialist "proxy solicitors"), well mapped what social science research confirmed. In one study of voting on antitakeover amendments proposed to shareholders by managements in 1984, for instance, institutional investors were divided into three groups: (1) investors most potentially sensitive to management voting pressures, such as insurance firms, banks, and nonbank trusts; (2) investors that could most readily resist management entreaties, such as public pension funds, mutual funds, endowments and foundations; and (3) an intermediate group, including corporate pension funds, brokerage houses, and investment counsel firms. Analysis of 288 antitakeover amendments proposed by 191 companies revealed that when the percentage of a company's stock held by pressure-sensitive investors was higher, the negative vote was lower. Conversely, when the percentage held by pressure-resistant investors was higher, the negative vote was higher. When the intermediate-group holding was higher, the vote fell in between (Brickley, Lease, and Smith, 1988).

The voting of many shares, however, was in doubt until they were cast. Moreover, except at a handful of companies that had adopted confidential voting policies, the votes could be in doubt even after they were cast. Proxy solicitation rules permitted companies to recontact investors after they had sent in their proxy statement. If an institution could be persuaded to change its vote, to do so it had only to submit another proxy statement. Statements were dated, and only the latest entered the final tally. Voting early and voting often was not only legitimate but also, for companies without confidential voting, a provision that could be used to advantage.

Preserving a Shareholder Rights Plan

Since direct lobbying of stockholders could materially affect the voting outcome on a shareholder resolution, companies confronted with a resolution on management policy or governance would usually launch a campaign to get out the vote. The tactics would seem familiar to those experienced in partisan campaigns for public office, though there was little self-conscious use of campaign strategies from the formal political process. Still, the investor relations office often came to resemble a campaign headquarters.

This corporate mobilization of investor support to defeat a shareholder resolution is illustrated by two examples, both drawn from among the seven main companies. Both resolutions concerned shareholder rights plans, or poison pills. Both companies created teams of senior managers to defeat the resolutions through aggressive solicitation of sympathetic shareholders. Neither company was certain of the outcome. Since the shareholder proposals were a matter of public record, to protect confidentiality neither the companies' product areas nor the dates and figures of the shareholder proposals are reported here.

A shareholder rights plan is generally designed to encourage would-be takeover parties to negotiate with the board of directors. If a board rejects a takeover offer but the acquirer still seeks control through the acquisition of stock, the poison pill provision grants existing shareholders the right to buy stock in the company (or acquirer) at a discounted level when the hostile acquirer reaches a specific level of holdings. It proved to be one of the most widely implemented takeover defenses during the late 1980s. Among the 500 largest manufacturing firms, by 1985 poison pills had been adopted by 34 percent of the companies; by 1990, the proportion had risen to 62 percent (Figure 2.8).

In the first case, the company was presented with a proposal from the California Public Employees' Retirement System to withdraw its shareholder rights plan or submit it to a shareholder vote. The company had not previously received a shareholder proposal from a public pension fund, but it quickly formulated a strategy to defeat the proposal. Seven senior managers were grouped into a "proxy solicitation team" to spearhead the fight. Each member received a six-page summary of the company's posture on why rescinding the poison pill would be in neither the company's nor the owners' interests. The shareholder rights plan was put in place, they were told, "to protect the interests of our shareholders and to enhance the value of their investment in the event the Company is faced with coercive or unfair takeover tactics . . . [It] strengthens and protects the Company and its shareholders in the most flexible and fair way." In further pursuit of the high ground, the team was also informed that Calpers had evidently never asked its own participants if they approved Calpers' tactics. Now Calpers was urging the company to ask its shareholders if they favored the company's tactics: "To whom is the State Retirement System accountable?" (company document, late 1980s).

The investor relations director assigned team managers and three board directors to call the firm's major institutional investors. Six temporary employees were hired to telephone all individual shareholders whose holdings exceeded some 1,000 shares. The primary goal was to secure a better than 80 percent vote against the proposal. A secondary purpose of the calling to the institutions was to renew communication with some major investors that had not been contacted for some time. "We like the idea of calling up institutions once a year and just talking to them," observed the IR manager. "We used the proxy solicitation process as an excuse."

Calls to the institutions were carefully scripted to elicit the identity of the person who would cast the votes for the holder, how many shares were at stake, and how the investor planned to vote. When an institution disclosed its intention of voting against management, the investor relations director and the chief financial officer then considered whether to launch a "second strike." A major company pension fund, for example, had signaled an interest in supporting the Calpers proposal. The target company's IR manager called the fund's analyst, and the chief financial officer called the CFO at the other company, the individual to whom the pension fund manager reported. Both were urged to reverse the pension fund's stand. The callers implicitly invoked what two researchers have termed the private pension-fund golden rule: "Do unto other companies' pension funds as you would have their pension funds do unto your company" (O'Barr and Conley, 1992).

The campaign of visits, calls, and follow-ups was premised on the belief, expressed in company planning documents, that "there is a direct relationship between the shares voted in support of management and our efforts." The strength of the relationship was not clear, but it was at least clear that their actions made some difference. The company pension fund that was resolicited subsequently turned in favor of management, as did some other initially negative investors. Since votes could be cast at any time and repeatedly until the annual meeting, the IR manager maintained a daily tally and frequently updated a projection of the outcome. The final count, however, felt short of management's initial target of at least an 80 percent negative vote. The final vote: 67 percent for management, 33 percent for Calpers. Yet it was decisive enough to discourage new shareholder resolutions in the immediately ensuing years.

During the next four years, neither Calpers nor any other public pension fund returned to seek reform of this company's governance. Still, the takeover environment of the late 1980s had engendered organizational anxieties that could not be shaken. Though no stalker had ever been identified, "never say never," warned the investor relations manager: "Other companies waited until it was too late [to build investor relations] . . . Although we would like to think that there are some strengths that we have . . . anything can happen. I think the eighties proved that . . . All we can do is to keep erecting picket fences that someone has to keep jumping over."

The second case entailed a similar company effort to turn back a proposal to rescind a poison pill. This firm had adopted its "share purchase rights plan" two years earlier. It was justified by the chief executive officer as a plan with "provisions to protect shareholders in the event of an unsolicited attempt to acquire the Company." In the view of the CEO, it was "a sound and reasonable means of addressing complex issues of corporate policy created by the current takeover environment" (company document, mid-1980s). A public pension fund proposed to put the plan to a shareholders' referendum, and again management vigorously opposed the challenge to its authority.

After marshaling its arguments, management set out to marshal its votes. As in the early stages of a political campaign, predictions on how groups of voters were likely to vote guided the allocation of company resources. Individual stockholders could generally be expected to side with management. Many institutional shareholders, however, could not be expected to do so. Since institutions owned more than three-fifths of the company's stock, large-scale defections among them could lead to a management defeat. With the help of an outside firm specializing in proxy solicitation, the firm initially estimated that only half of its institutions at best were currently in management's column. The company feared that many institutions' penchant for short-term calculus could bring out a large negative vote. The campaign director cautioned senior management: "A large number of our shares are held in accounts managed by big investment managers, many of whom employ short-term investment strategies. We are, therefore, in danger of losing the [shareholder proposal] vote unless we are able to enlist the help of beneficial owners who, like ourselves, are concerned with long-term development'' (company document, late 1980s).

Warning that ''our position will be an uphill fight,'' the campaign manager designed several tactics to encourage voting by favorable parties and discourage voting by unfavorable parties. The tactics varied with the size and perceived preference of the shareholders, and certain groups required distinctive approaches:

Small institutions. Small institutions were expected to side more often with management than were large investors. The proxy solicitor would contact them first, and problematic institutions would then be approached by the company's senior managers.

Company pension funds. Many company pension funds were expected to be sympathetic to management. Senior managers were to contact their counterparts at such companies. They would urge their counterparts to press fund managers for a favorable vote.

Foreign institutional investors. Various foreign institutions held substantial positions (two British investors, for example, each held more than 200,000 shares), but they tended not to vote. Still, anticipating a sympathetic response, senior managers solicited their support through telephone appeals.

Large, antimanagement investors. Several large institutions were already known to favor the shareholder resolution. They were to remain untouched, with the hope that ''because of administrative difficulties they may not be able to vote their shares.'' The proxy solicitation firm would normally help a company's owners resolve such difficulties, but here it rendered no assistance.

Drawing on these and other distinctions, a comprehensive roster of each major investor was created to guide company campaign actions (a sample of which is reproduced in Table 5.7).

Company pension funds were regarded as the most sympathetic group of investors, since many were directly overseen by company managers who were likely to be unsympathetic to shareholder challenges, at least by instinct. Still, federal law required that pension funds be administered for maximum financial benefit to the participants. Some company pension fund managers would interpret the legal environment to encourage voting

Table 5.7. Large company's plan for contact of major investors regarding shareholder governance proposal, by type of investor.

Type of investor	Percent of company's shares	Action plan
Company pension fund	1.12	"Will be difficult"; company should pursue early; executive VP to contact company.
Company pension fund	0.55	CEO to contact company.
Company pension fund	0.35	CEO to call CEO of company.
Public pension fund	1.30	No action; an "adamant" proposal supporter.
Public pension fund	0.97	Proxy solicitor "says [pension fund] is not adamant and should make effort to change vote."
Commercial bank trust	0.60	Proxy solicitor to make first contact.
Commercial bank trust	0.47	"Generally against us, but we should try."
Investment company	1.16	Chief operating officer to call top fund manager.
Investment company	0.82	"Firm supports [pension fund] proposal but may not do much to get shares voted."
Investment company	0.74	"They are 'studying the matter.'" Proxy solicitor reports that "they would normally vote in favor of [pension fund] proposal." CFO has already contacted fund manager.
Investment fund	0.43	"Had thought we would get their vote. Now appears they will vote against us. Make strong effort."

Source: Company records (late 1980s).

against management if it would arguably enhance shareholder power. No vote could thus be taken for granted among even this naturally sympathetic constituency. As a result, the company's chief executive wrote the CEOs of a large number of firms whose pension funds were soon to be voting on the shareholder proposal. Making note when appropriate of the fact that the recipient CEO's company had also adopted a shareholder rights plan, the chief executive made a manager-to-manager appeal:

"I believe that you share my concern with the current [takeover] climate and would view favorably our response in adopting the rights plan. I am therefore soliciting your assistance in our efforts to secure wide shareholder support for management's opposition to the shareholder proposal. As I am sure you are aware, managers of large funds and particularly pension and other employee benefit funds often tend to vote automatically for proposals such as the one submitted to our meeting. It is our understanding that pension managers engaged by your company hold shares in [our company] and I would appreciate your contacting those managers to advise them of your position on the shareholder proposal, and to encourage them to vote with our Board of Directors and *against* the proposal'' (company records, late 1980s).

As with so many relations among top managers across firms, favors implicitly engendered reciprocal obligations. It could thus be important for the appeal's recipient to display some form of sympathetic response, even if he or she did not or could not turn around the pension fund's vote. Given the widespread cross-company investing by company pension funds, the targeted company would know that it might later have to seek a return of the favor. The corporation in question used past voting of its own pension fund to advantage here. When one of the senior vice-presidents was placing his calls to other companies, on some occasions he was able to remind the call's recipient that his company had voted favorably on one of the recipient's proxies in earlier years. He might also allude to concerns shared by managements almost anywhere, as evident in this paraphrasing of his basic message: "We would like your vote on these corporate governance issues. We think that there is a problem out there as a result of the ability of the Icahns and the Pickenses and the Steinbergs to be able to stampede boards. We think that much of that is not only bad for the long term, but in the short term people could buy companies cheaper as a result."

The soliciting managers in this instance could also play on concurrent reciprocal possibilities, as their own company was itself receiving a spate of similar letters from senior managers of other companies also facing shareholder resolutions. One incoming letter from a major equipment manufacturer, for example, described its effort to defeat a similar rescission of its poison pill, closing with the hope that "we can count on your support." Another letter from one of the country's largest food producers also sought backing against a shareholder proposal to eliminate a shareholder rights plan. Worrying that "this shareholder proposal activity may well thwart management actions designed to promote the long-term interest of all [company] shareholders," it also pressed the company's managers to "urge your fund managers to vote 'AGAINST' this proposal" (company records, late 1980s).

Some five months before the annual meeting, the proxy solicitor classified most of the major investors in four categories, ranging from "virtually certain to vote against management" to "almost certain to vote with management." Some 22 percent were deemed almost certainly negative, and another 22 percent were seen as questionable at best. With a near majority in doubt, management redoubled its efforts, urging parties leaning against management to consider abstaining instead. When the vote was finally tallied, more than two-thirds had voted for management's recommendation against the rescission. A number of companies had been targeted with similar resolutions during the same proxy season, and the sense of collective reciprocity among managements that the wave may have created could have been a factor in the final voting. An attorney who had facilitated the writing of the shareholder rights plan at a number of the companies declared vindication: "Pill 30—Institutions 0" (press release caption, late 1980s).

Conclusion

The alignment of company organization with shareholder interests, in response to or anticipation of shareholder pressures, had brought a range of changes to the higher circles of management. Whether acceptingly or grudgingly, management could no longer afford to ignore the amassing of investor power. The tenor of company recognition of this new environmental reality could be seen in a 1991 summary assessment of the editor of a newsletter for corporate investor relations managers (Mahoney, 1991c, p. 1): "Institutional investors are driving everything—buying and selling of shares; movement of stock price; decline of brokerage analyst clout; investment modeling; reduction of shares held directly by individuals; shareholder influence on corporate strategy, structure and decision-making; international investing; whether companies can stand off hostile takeovers." While not fully genuflecting, management culture acquired new respect for the shareholder public, at times even for their short-term spirits. The respect did not extend to any presumed investor prowess in how to manage. The chief executive of Contel Corporation, a large telecommunications services company (annual sales of about $3 billion), offered a public assessment that would be privately expressed by many: "There is a move by pension funds to assert that they can assist management. But I have never seen a list of great triumphs of those who manage money who go out to manage a company. There is nothing to tell me that these state pension groups in New York, California and New Jersey know anything about how to run a company'' (Wohlstetter, 1990).

Still, as agency theorists might expect, or at least find gratifying, the agent-principal conundrum was moving toward some resolution as principals acquired the political wherewithal to better control their agents. Agent resistance to the new forms of control would come as no real surprise, since their interests were still distinct. Management opposition was widespread, and antitakeover defenses were widely adopted during the late 1980s. Subsequent efforts by institutional investors to dismantle the defenses were vigorously resisted.

More problematic for agency theory was the agents' proactive management of the relationship. Companies learned to communicate more effectively with their investors, but they also learned that they might be able to change the investors as well. Reeducation of shareholders was the first act of alignment in that direction. If investors were insisting on short-term performance, efforts were made to move them ''off the numbers and onto the core operating strategies and long term.'' When they could not be so moved, as was usually the case, new investors were sought. When investors were there only for the short-term gain, there was no love lost in any case. ''I don't think we have to be loyal to shareholders who are not loyal to us,'' observed the vice-president for external affairs of the chemical-products company. ''If we do a crappy job, they ought to kick us out and change the management. But if T. Boone Pickens comes along and puts us in play, and opportunistic shareholders want to make megabucks while they chop up the company and shut down plants and fire people . . . I see no shareholder-value responsibility in things like that.'' If shareholders old or new still insisted on pressing management for change, companies would circle the wagons, erecting a host of governance devices to thwart what was viewed as unwarranted intrusion into managerial prerogatives.

The picture, then, is not one of passive company acquiescence in the face of enhanced shareholder power. Firms fought back, and in the course of resisting discovered that they could alter their ownership structure. The relationship between agents and principals thus bore a certain symmetry. Organizations became better aligned to meet shareholder interests. But shareholders were also better aligned to meet management interests.

The concentration of management attention on control may have been accompanied by lack of attention elsewhere. As for traditional company constituencies, ranging from suppliers and employees to the local community, better shareholder alignment could connote worse alignment for them. More responsiveness to investor demands for higher returns may have brought, for instance, less responsiveness to worker demands for higher security. But even such specific questions as changes in employment totals following a leveraged buyout were the subject of empirical dispute (Long and Ravenscraft, 1991), and the lasting impact of heightened shareholder awareness on other constituencies remained to be seen. In the absence of renewed political mobilization on a par with major owners, however, the interests of these other stakeholder groups may have been at risk. Greater shareholder return could induce lesser stakeholder return.

SIX

Restructured Agendas for
Political Action

The managerial revolution had freed company executives to pursue company political strategies with little direct reference to shareholders large or small. To be sure, political actions, whether giving money to charities for the homeless or to candidates for Congress, were justified in company terms. Articulating a linkage between disparate political actions and company prosperity was the art of public affairs (Weaver, 1988). Whether or not the rationale was persuasive, the political agendas were pursued with little guidance or interference from investors.

During the 1970s and early 1980s, the agendas had focused on public policy, and the level of action exceeded that of the immediate past. Business mobilized to combat what it viewed as inhospitable public opinion and costly government regulation. Survey trends confirmed that public attitudes had turned disrespectful (Lipset and Schneider, 1983). Managers might have found solace in the fact that the public had turned against almost all major institutions, not just business. Yet many set out to remake their firm's political environment, drawing on an array of old and new tools. To the traditional repertoire of lobbying and public relations were added political action committee (PAC) donations to candidates for office; mobilization of employees and other "stakeholders" on behalf of company legislative objectives; involvement of company managers as volunteers in community affairs; contribution of company money, products, and services to nonprofit organizations; and investments in advocacy advertising and "cause-related" marketing.

The subsequent reemergence of ownership power reshaped how those tools were deployed. Investor demand for accountability had direct impact, as companies sought better discipline of political action around the enhancement of shareholder return. Greater discipline of political action was translated simply into less action. More return to shareholder dividends implied less budget for political outreach. But it was also translated into redirecting the company's political energies. Following a decade of resistance to state intervention, companies now sought state protection.

Contracted Corporate Action

For companies whose emphasis on profits had been expanded and whose time horizons had been shortened, political outreach was an easy target for cost cutting. Company political actions produced long-term gains, but they typically yielded few short-term benefits (McGuire, Sundgren, and Schneeweis, 1988). Companies under intensified ownership influence or threatened by raiders could be expected to reassess the costs of operating a full-service public affairs function.

To explore the extent to which such actions were taken, let us look at two major components of corporate political action: first, the giving of company money to nonprofit organizations through charitable donations; second, the giving of managerial money to candidates for federal office through political action committees.

Charitable Giving

Studies of individual firms facing or experiencing ownership change revealed that charitable giving often wavered when a firm's ownership was under challenge. This was evident in the experience of a large manufacturing company (with annual sales in the range of $2–5 billion) that I had followed during a period in the late 1980s when it was targeted in a hostile takeover bid. The company was not one of the seven focal firms treated in this book, but I conducted interviews with key managers in similar fashion several times before and after the takeover initiative. The hostile bid was vigorously resisted through a variety of measures, including the introduction of an employee stock ownership plan. The company also encouraged a fraction of the workforce to accept early retirement. For those who remained, salaries and wages were significantly reduced to fund the stock ownership plan.

Because of the takeover uncertainties facing the company and its employees, annual company solicitation of employee contributions to the

United Way was delayed, and the company's contribution budget was frozen. Some of the impact, however, was felt in passing only. Incumbent management ultimately prevailed against the hostile suitor, and an air of guarded normalcy gradually returned. A newly acquired commitment to leaner production and higher earnings came to dominate. With stability restored, the company reinstituted its annual solicitation of United Way contributions from employees. Similarly, the director of corporate giving was successful in recovering much of his annual budget.

Other evidence nonetheless suggests that intensified shareholder power exerted enduring downward pressure on business investment in giving programs. One inferential shard comes from systematic comparison of companies that were controlled by top management with firms that were dominated by owners. Detailed study of corporate contributions to non-profit organizations in the Minneapolis–St. Paul region found that firms classed as owner-dominated generally made significantly smaller charitable contributions than did those deemed to be manager-controlled. The giving difference remained even when a range of other company character-istics was taken into account (Atkinson and Galaskiewicz, 1988). Though cross-sectional, the evidence implies that more ownership influence may translate into less generous giving.

Corroborating data come from managers themselves. Chief executives and their likely immediate successors were surveyed in one study of 255 major firms in 1988. Most reported that they faced increasingly turbulent environments, and that the turbulence had cast a shadow on company commitment to giving. Moreover, the expected successors were more likely than the current generation of CEOs to expect their company's giving level to decline because of the harsh economic climate (Yankelovich, 1988). Outlooks do not always translate into action, but the results suggested that the next generation of executive leadership had taken a more skeptical view of this avenue of political action.

One of the best general barometers for the level of company commitment to charitable donations is the percentage of pretax net income (PTNI) contributed to nonprofit activity, and it is useful to examine its movement during this period. The percentage of pretax net income carried the special advantage of taking into account the ebb and flow of company earnings, which can strongly influence the amount of giving even when a company's commitment remains constant (Useem, 1987).

During the 1960s and 1970s, companies contributed about one percent of their pretax net income to charitable activities (Figure 6.1). This "one-

Percent of pretax net income

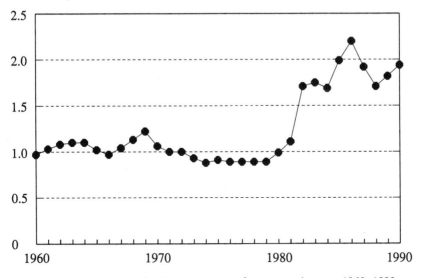

Figure 6.1. Corporate contributions as percent of pretax net income, 1960–1990.
Data for 1988–1990 are estimated. (Source: Council for Aid to
Education, 1991.)

percent rule'' had steadily prevailed until the early 1980s, when company
convention abruptly moved toward a two-percent benchmark. Corporate
commitment further pushed to a historic high of 2.20 percent of PTNI in
1986. Thereafter the giving rate declined to 1.92 and 1.77 percent in the
succeeding two years, the largest such decrease since the early 1950s. The
trend again reversed itself during the next two years, though not enough
to regain the high-water mark of 1986. Corporate giving appeared shaky,
but the bottom had not dropped out.

Political Action Committee Giving

Akin to aggregate trends in corporate contributions to nonprofit organizations, overall company giving to national political candidates did not
display unambiguous decline during the late 1980s. Yet like charitable
giving, after nearly a decade of rapid growth, PAC support leveled out.
The number of corporate committees even dropped slightly between the
1987–1988 and 1989–1990 electoral cycles. And the incremental growth

in PAC spending between cycles was the slowest of the decade (Table 6.1 and Figure 6.2).

Also akin to corporate giving, company investment in political action wavered when company control was at issue. This was shown in a detailed interview study of public affairs managers at thirty-eight major companies in 1988–1989 (Clawson, Neustadtl, and Scott, 1992). Several of the firms had undergone restructuring as a result of a change in ownership, and the resulting turnover in top management adversely affected their PAC operations.

One company, for instance, was taken private by a major buyout firm in 1987, then quickly sold to another group of managers and outside investors, and was facing the possibility of still another ownership change at the time of the interview. PAC funding depended on voluntary management contributions, and the preoccupation with ownership restructuring had severely undercut efforts to increase participation rates and to increase gifts from past contributors. Still, though PAC income suffered because of the uncertainty, the company remained committed to restoring its level of political action. "We know that public policy is extremely important to us," observed the PAC manager, so "we just have to do a better job in the new company in carrying the level of solicitation to lower levels of management and increasing the participation by all levels of management."

In another case, ownership of a publicly traded company was sought by one of the well-known takeover figures. The bid was defeated, but

Table 6.1. Number of corporate political action committees and their total contributions to congressional candidates, 1977–1990.

Electoral cycle	Number of PACs	Contributions (in millions of dollars)	Percent change in contributions from previous cycle
1977–78	784	9.5	—
1979–80	1,251	31.4	230.5
1981–82	1,557	43.3	37.8
1983–84	1,809	59.2	36.7
1985–86	1,906	79.3	33.9
1987–88	2,088	89.9	13.3
1989–90	1,965	100.8	12.1

Source: U.S. Federal Election Commission (1991 and earlier years); Matasar (1986), p. 34.

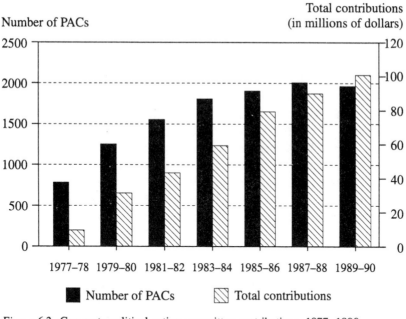

Figure 6.2. Corporate political action committee contributions, 1977–1990. (Sources: U.S. Federal Election Commission, 1991; Matasar, 1986.)

many of the top managers resigned under pressure, and the company was later divided into two separate firms. The turmoil of the transition made solicitation particularly difficult, according to one of the PAC officials: "There had been a lot of upheaval and people dropping out . . . When a raider comes after you, people start thinking, 'Oh my god, should I really be giving to the United Way and the PAC,' and they started dropping out . . . I think it is really rude to solicit people for the PAC when they have got so many other things on their minds like keeping their job."

Statistical analysis of PACs among privately and publicly held companies suggests that the greatest impact may be felt when a corporation is taken private. In a reanalysis of PAC data for publicly traded companies in the 1982 election, Burris (1989) found little difference between owner-controlled and management-controlled firms in the likelihood of operating a political action committee. However, among the nation's largest privately held firms, the likelihood of operating a PAC was substantially lower. In 1982, of the 100 largest private companies, 14 percent had formed a PAC, whereas of the 500 largest publicly traded industrial firms,

56 percent operated a PAC, a disparity that was partly but not entirely attributable to size differences. Evidence presented later in this chapter confirms that when large publicly traded companies were taken private, PAC contributions declined in the aftermath.

Ownership challenges and turnover more permanently reduced the level of political action through the reduction of employee ranks. Voluntary gifts by managers are a PAC's lifeblood, and fewer managers meant fewer gifts. Funds for charitable purposes also depended on employee numbers, though less precisely: a portion of the giving budget at many large companies was programmed to match employee gifts with corporate funds. The thinning of employee ranks among large firms therefore also thinned such company-supported contributions. Furthermore, the reductions meant that fewer managers and employees were available for volunteer programs, which companies commonly encouraged to improve community relations.

PAC funding may have been harder hit by employment downsizing than was charitable giving. PAC funds come primarily from senior management ranks at headquarters, while employee matching-gift programs draw support more widely. We have already seen that alignment tended to bring disproportionate reductions in headquarters staffing. Consistent with this, a study of establishment-level ownership change between 1977 and 1982 showed that central-office employees were shed more often than production employees. Employment growth was 16 percent lower in central offices that changed ownership than in those that did not, whereas employment growth was only 5 percent lower in production establishments that changed ownership compared to those that did not (Lichtenberg and Siegel, 1989).

Political Action for Shareholder Value

Corporate political action that remained after the tightening was itself reprogrammed. Both charitable and PAC giving were more closely linked to shareholder objectives, at least in principle. In practice, such linkages could not always be readily identified or easily demonstrated. Still, among those overseeing the programs, giving for its own sake became less valued, accountability and payback more so.

The tightening of the reigns was evident at the transportation company, which had long operated a charitable foundation. The giving program was built and operated for nearly a decade by a single senior manager (a "one-man band," in the words of a successor). Because the director enjoyed the confidence of the chief executive, the operating constraints were small and the giving budgets large. Grants of more than $50,000 required approval by top management, but even here the review was considered cursory. The foundation's annual budget reached 1.5 percent of pretax net income, and the company contributed more than $10 million annually to a broad array of causes, especially those near headquarters.

As a new chief executive brought the transportation company through a wrenching restructuring, however, charitable giving—along with virtually all other company programs—came under scrutiny. The CEO obtained board approval to reduce contributions to 1.0 percent of pretax net income, tightened oversight of the giving process, brought others into allocation decisions, decreased a preference for causes near the home office, directed funds to more often reflect employee preferences, and initiated a year-long review of the foundation's guiding principles.

Senior managers of the transportation firm recognized that charitable giving could not be strictly defined around company objectives. To too openly do so would defeat its public relations value. In any case, tangible payoffs could not be readily drawn from many otherwise deserving causes. "It's just hard to make a connection between a battered women's workshop on some Indian reservation and our business purposes," observed the foundation's new director. "It's a crying need, and it's a need felt in the community, but it really does not advance our business purposes, except in a way that people appreciate your good citizenship efforts. It's a very tenuous connection." Still, a central concern in the foundation's review was the extent to which it could more systematically promote company purpose. Observed the responsible manager, the vice-president for public affairs: "[The foundation] had been all over the map . . . [It] was involved in lots of things that may or may not have been what this company . . . really has an interest in promoting. What we're doing now at the foundation is to assess what the people at this company would really like for their foundation to do. Our guidelines are really very simple: we want to give to good causes in communities that we serve or have some business connection with." The business connection was important, since "the concept of shareholder value is more on everybody's mind." But it was evident that making the concept operational in the area of charitable giving was proving more difficult than in most areas of company operations. Still, an effort was underway to test its extension, as the same official made clear:

Do you want the foundation to be wholly autonomous or do you want to try to promote the company's overall good by applying the foundation's funds in a way that serve the company's interests? . . . We're actively asking ourselves if our foundation funds can be disbursed on a more rational basis, and whether or not our company's interests can really be served by the foundation . . .

We're deliberating whether or not it makes sense to have a foundation serve our business interests a little more directly . . . We've got this great big goddamned foundation . . . and where do we want it to go?

Support for candidates and elected officials through federal political action committees acquired greater focus as well. The pharmaceutical firm's PAC, with electoral-cycle funding of more than $100,000, concentrated its money on incumbent senators and representatives from its home office region as well as on heads of powerful congressional committees concerned with health matters and drug policies. It was even prepared to contribute to a U.S. senator whose social views it generally considered deplorable but who was about to play a key role on legislation of special interest to the company.

The company had followed a relatively self-interested PAC strategy for some time, but it was preparing to narrow its giving even more. It sought, for instance, ever more vigorous champions for its causes, whatever the adverse effects on other companies, industries, or public policy. If the right politician could be found, the head of the company's PAC (the senior vice-president for public affairs) was prepared to offer unlimited support: "This industry doesn't have its Jesse Helms [U.S. senator from North Carolina], and we should. We have never been able to cultivate somebody who will lie down in front of the tracks for us, as Jesse does for the tobacco industry . . . We've been trying [to find the right senator or representative] but we've only been trying in the past few years. I think it will bear fruit ultimately."

In the meantime, the company had also devised other means for molding the policy process. During the late 1980s, for instance, it set up a one-day site visit and seminar for staff members of congressional committees concerned with drug regulation or health care financing. The several dozen participants in each visit, hosted entirely at company expense, were ushered through a series of meetings with company staff on policy questions related to product development, testing, and marketing. Federal agency officials could not accept such visits at company expense, but congressional staffers were not so inhibited. With nearly a hundred participants, the new program had proven, in the view of the public affairs manager, "enormously successful."

Despite the intangible outcomes of many such efforts, tangible payoffs were evident from time to time. Though episodic, the unambiguous incidents served to reconfirm the utility of political outreach to managers made more skeptical by the culture of alignment. As in other areas of top management decision making, telling events often carried more weight than painstaking analyses or statistical indicators (Mintzberg, 1975). A compelling example could sustain a political course for which other tangible results would never appear.

One such incident could be seen in the near hostile takeover of the Dayton Hudson Corporation, a large retail firm whose generous support of nonprofit organizations was to prove an invaluable political asset in resisting the unwanted advance. In June 1987, the Dart Group Corporation rapidly amassed a large number of Dayton Hudson shares in preparation for a takeover bid. A key weapon in Dayton Hudson's ensuing defensive strategy was to seek state protection from Minnesota, its headquarters and state of incorporation. Unlike a number of states, Minnesota at that time offered no legislative umbrella against hostile takeovers, and the legislature had adjourned for the summer. Persuading the governor and the legislature not only to hold a special session but also to approve an antitakeover law within weeks would require an extraordinary mobilization of the legislative players. More than willing to join the mobilization were the region's nonprofit organizations, long the beneficiaries of Dayton Hudson's generous giving program. Indicative of the company's exceptional level of commitment, its contribution budget was near 5 percent of pretax net income. In simple dollar terms, Dayton Hudson was the state's leading donor to nonprofit organizations. When the region's civic leaders were surveyed in 1981 and again in 1989, they named Dayton Hudson the area's top-rated corporate sponsor (Galaskiewicz, 1990, p. 29).

In response to Dayton Hudson's call for state protection against Dart's advances, nonprofit leaders were quick to join and promote a groundswell of local backing. Within a mere two weeks of its political initiative, the company obtained the statutory protection it needed by nearly unanimous vote of a special session of the legislature called by the governor (Kennedy, 1990). In subsequent defense of his company's giving record against conservative and shareholder challenges, Dayton Hudson's chief executive could persuasively accent his stance of enlightened self-interest (Macke, 1990, p. 11): "Our motives for making donations are not purely altruistic.

Rather, we view them as sound investments in a society that has to cope with illiteracy, poverty, drug abuse and disease. And we believe that they have paid off not only for the communities we serve, but also for our customers, our employees and our shareholders. In fact, quite a number of shareholders—including several major institutional investors—have told me that our charitable contribution policy is one of the reasons they support the company so strongly.''

Fine-Tuning the Networks

Several of the companies we studied elevated the art of involving top managers in community affairs to a science, though this process was generally not a self-conscious outgrowth of disciplined grant making. Giving money and volunteering executives had long been practiced in tandem. If a senior manager agreed to serve on the governing board of a nonprofit organization, both sides understood that regular company contributions would follow. A reverse chronology could evolve as well, if company contributions had come first and had been of sufficient magnitude. As companies tightened their reign on giving, they did the same with executive placement in community networks.

The explicitness of the process was revealed in actions of the pharmaceutical company, when a new senior manager was brought into headquarters from outside the region. As a matter of company policy, the office responsible for corporate giving and community affairs sought to have the newcomer placed on a high-visibility governing board. The director of corporate affairs turned to his counterpart at a nearby university to see if a trusteeship might be soon available. By fortuitous coincidence, a seat was about to become vacant. The university had long enjoyed generous support from the company, and a private luncheon was soon arranged for the new executive to meet the university president. Shortly thereafter, the trustees' nominating committee proposed the executive's name, and he found himself attending a trustee meeting within a year of coming to the corporation. The company initiated a similar plan to place him on the governing board of an area hospital. Two major trusteeships were considered optimal for rooting the new manager—and through him the company—in the local power structure.

Though the community involvement of managers was technically a matter of personal choice, for senior managers it was also a matter of company guidance. Outside directorships and trusteeships of officers were tracked and managed at some firms with the same precision as executive succession.

During the late 1980s, for example, the electrical-products company created an information system for overseeing all senior outside appointments. Most of its some forty senior managers held four to six; the top two officers each carried a score. For the rising manager, such appointments were viewed as part of executive development; for the organization, they were seen as part of company political strategy. All requests for a manager to join an outside board were screened by a vice-president for corporate relations, who was also responsible for managing the outside ramifications in the event of executive turnover.

Since the firm's officers collectively sustained an orchestrated web of outside ties, when an officer retired or otherwise left the firm, the fractured network required restoration. The responsible manager's capacity to make such repairs was put to the test when one of the electrical-product company's two top executives retired without immediate replacement. The two—one the chief executive officer, the other the chief operating officer—had jointly overseen approximately forty outside directorships. The one who remained could not absorb even a fraction of the retiree's outside appointments without giving up many of his own. The decision on which to shed and which to absorb was not a matter of the remaining official's personal preferences. Rather, it was primarily a company decision, taken with detailed forethought on which strands of the outside network were critical and which were dispensable.

Because the heads of the various business units within the electrical-products company had acquired so much additional responsibility as part of the company's devolution of authority, often overseeing divisions with budgets of more than $1 billion, the company was also quietly giving them invitations that in the past would have gone only to the chief executive. The remaining top officer, for example, had decided as part of the consolidation to relinquish his oversight position with the Chamber of Commerce, and the responsible company office had then targeted a new divisional executive for that role. Similarly, as new outside invitations were received by the CEO, they were shunted to the corporate relations office for review. The invitations were then often rerouted to other corporate and divisional managers, especially if they had "holes" in their outside portfolios. It was still left to the manager to decide if he or she had an interest in working with a particular organization, though even here company preference frequently prevailed over personal proclivity. If the manager was prepared to accept the appointment, it would then be company brokered. The agenda was driven by familiar concerns, as the vice-president for corporate relations made clear:

> We've broadened what we mean by shareholder value. In order to be positively perceived not just by the security analysts but by everybody else who might invest in you, and buy from you, you have to broaden your audiences to include security analysts (who we normally get most hung-up about), employees . . . , customers . . . , and the communities in which we live.
>
> If you are positively perceived by your communities, they end up giving you more free PR and advertising than you could pay for. When someone's going to write an article about you, whom do they go to, besides you? They go the analysts [and] they go to community leaders, so [community affairs] makes good business sense . . .
>
> I just know that community perception influences the beta in the equation that says how much of a discount your stock sells at . . . How concrete is beta? It's all perception. That's why it exists—it's a factor to account for the unaccountable.

Political Action for State Protection

Dayton Hudson's enlistment of a governor and a state legislature to ward off an aggressive shareholder was symptomatic of an unacknowledged but profound philosophical reversal. Long opposed in principle to state intervention in the marketplace, large companies faced with a loss of control were not to be inhibited by this concern. The antiregulatory principle seemed to pale by comparison with the higher principles of sheer survival. As the market for corporate control intensified during the late 1980s, many companies inverted their political agendas, from resisting state control to enlisting state protection.

The new call to arms was couched in alarmist rhetoric. Specializing in governance and legislative devices to protect management, a prominent attorney pressed for urgent action in a 1988 note to his clients, many of them large corporations: "The institutional investors—who have gained control of virtually every major company—show no restraint and no regard for the public good. They must be policed" (Lipton, 1988, p. 1). The call did not go unopposed, as the securities industry, large investors, and shareholder advocates mounted a counterattack. The founding chairman of United Shareholders Association, T. Boone Pickens, offered a comparably provocative countercall: "Most Business Roundtable CEOs . . . barricade themselves from stockholders. They take the stockholders' money and use it to lobby against the stockholders' interests . . . We've got to pre-empt state anti-takeover legislation or we'll end up with 50 banana republics in which the most powerful CEO in each state will draft the legislation to fit his particular situation" (Pickens, 1987, p. 17).

Though federal antitakeover statutes had been proposed, the Washington political climate during the 1980s had been largely unfavorable to such protection. Symptomatic of the climate were the unequivocal prescriptions of two senior officials in the Reagan administration: "From all available evidence, we conclude that the market for corporate control works well. There is no market failure that should cause the government to intervene" (Ginsburg and Robinson, 1986, p. 14). Similarly, the president's Council of Economic Advisors wrote in opposing any antitakeover legislation in 1985 that "stockholders as a group will . . . suffer as a result of excessive regulation because it reduces the chance to earn takeover premiums." Abuses were, if anything, on the side of the victims: "Abusive practices in the market for corporate control are limited largely to tactics employed by target managements who, in opposing takeover bids, defeat or deter tender offers at the expense of their shareholders and the economy" (Council of Economic Advisors, 1985).

Companies discovered, however, that the local political process was more malleable. Locally based employers commanded a much greater presence in state capitals than did investment firms, pension funds, or shareholder advocacy groups, few of which could boast any local employees or operations. Until the late 1980s, the mobilization had been slow. Between 1982 and 1987, only five states—Kentucky, Maryland, Missouri, Ohio, and Indiana—passed antitakeover legislation to protect an in-state company from acquisition. Then, in a seminal 1987 ruling, the Supreme Court upheld the Indiana law. A 1982 decision had discouraged such legislation until then, and within two years of the 1987 ruling, thirty-seven states passed antitakeover laws or amended old laws in response to a wave of corporate lobbying. By 1991, forty-one states had adopted some form of antitakeover legislation (Figure 6.3). Only two states with significant concentrations of large corporations—California and Texas—remained without such protection in 1991 (McGurn et al., 1989, and updates through 1991 prepared by the Investor Responsibility Research Center).

State antitakeover legislation generally included a combination of pro-

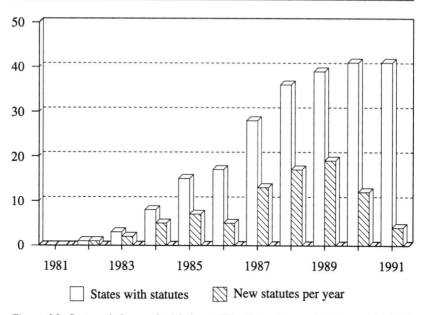

Figure 6.3. State antitakeover legislation, 1981–1991. (Source: McGurn et al., 1989 and updates.)

visions intended to protect incumbent management against an unwanted acquisition. They applied to locally incorporated firms, though in some instances the coverage was extended to companies that held an out-of-state charter but that had a major presence within the state. The most widespread provisions were as follows:

Freeze out. A bidder with a large fraction of a company's shares (for example, 20 percent under New York law) may not combine the soliciting and targeted businesses for several years (five years in New York, adopted by twenty-nine states by 1991).

Director responsibilities. Permits company directors, in deciding whether to accept a tender offer, to consider nonfinancial factors, such as the interests of employees, customers, suppliers, bond holders, and community, as well as the long-term financial interests of the firm and its shareholders (adopted by twenty-eight states).

Control share acquisition. An acquirer of a major block of stock is required to obtain the approval of a majority of the disinterested outstanding shares before it can exercise its voting rights (adopted by twenty-seven states).

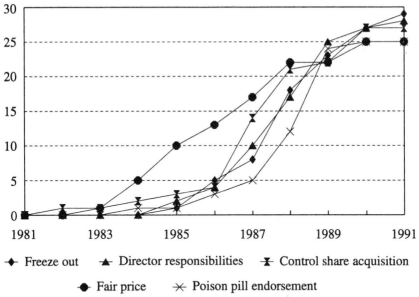

+- Freeze out   -▲- Director responsibilities   -✕- Control share acquisition

-●- Fair price   -✕- Poison pill endorsement

Figure 6.4. Number of state antitakeover provisions, 1981–1991. (Source: McGurn et al., 1989 and updates.)

Fair price. An acquirer is prevented from offering a high share price until control is obtained and then acquiring the remaining shares at a lower price (adopted by twenty-five states).

Poison pill endorsement. Authorizes the use of shareholder rights plans (adopted by twenty-five states).

Other state provisions included restrictions on greenmail, limitations on judicial review of board decisions, protections of employee security and collective bargaining agreements, and requirements for bidder disclosure (McGurn et al., 1989, pp. 5–13). Five or fewer states offered each of the protections in 1984; by 1990, all of the provisions were offered by at least half of the states (Figure 6.4). Local capitals furnished companies with what the national capital would not.

Legislating State Protection

Virtually all state antitakeover provisions were the direct product of political mobilizations led by individual companies and business associations based within the state. Many large firms did not participate, sometimes even quietly opposing the legislation. But other corporations shouldered the campaign, and without their concerted efforts, there would have been no legislation in most cases.

The actions of one of the seven focal companies are illustrative (the company will not be further identified, since some of its actions were a matter of public record). The company initiated the writing of an antitakeover bill, and then shepherded it through the many twists and turns of the local political process. So intensive were the firm's efforts that some press accounts nicknamed the bill after the company.

The company had initially sought state protection for a familiar reason: a major Wall Street firm had been buying large numbers of the company's shares. Company managers inferred that the brokerage firm may have been buying the shares on behalf of a company or group planning a takeover bid. The stock purchases triggered several defensive moves. On the advice of a law firm well known for its innovative antitakeover devices, the company's resistance strategy included the introduction of new legislation in its headquarters' state, which at the time had no antitakeover statutes. Another company had sought an antitakeover measure several years earlier, but at that time the volume and ravages of unwanted acquisitions had been insufficient to attract political attention. The takeover atmosphere now was far more ominous. Several other major companies based in the state were fighting acquisitions, and still other firms worried about their security. Even short of succumbing to a raider, simply being "put into play" was viewed with trepidation. "No matter how successful your company may be," argued an executive vice-president of the company, "once you are targeted by a raider, you are trapped in a system of financial gamesmanship that results in a final sale of the corporation or staggering debt and unavoidable restructuring."

The company enlisted the support of the state's major labor and business associations, including the AFL-CIO, the Chamber of Commerce, and the local equivalents of the National Association of Manufacturers and the Business Roundtable. (The state equivalent of the latter had been earlier formed at the initiative of the company to consider such policy questions as the "regulation of hostile takeovers.") The company readily drew the backing of firms that had been targeted for takeover or that feared becoming targets. Several major securities firms, the Securities Industry Association, and the United Shareholders Association opposed the measure, though because they had little employment base in the state, their voice drew more on economic principle than on real power.

To orchestrate the process, the company retained a political communications organization and two law firms, one known for its antitakeover work, the other for its familiarity with state politics. The company and its allies helped draft the legislation, focusing on freeze-out and fair-price provisions. Supported by a well-mobilized business community and encountering little countermobilization, the bill soon passed with only scant opposition. The company, however, remained on alert. Despite the new state protection, there were continued rumors of the company's targeting for takeover. Though these reports never proved true, they were sufficiently credible to draw press and Wall Street attention. An extended *Business Week* article, for instance, described the company's vulnerability, reviewed the takeover rumors, and cited a relatively high break-up value for the company if it were acquired. As one indication of the rumors' credibility, the company's stock experienced a modest run-up in price when the *Business Week* issue appeared. Wall Street analysts took explicit note. One major brokerage house placed the company on a short-list of likely takeover targets.

Though the recent state law offered substantial protection from unsolicited takeovers, the company sought even stronger safeguards. It again went on the offensive, drafting an amendment to give directors still more discretion in considering unfriendly bids. Directors were to be granted authority, the proposed amendment stated, to consider the interests of employees, the community, and other constituencies in addition to the financial interests of shareholders.

The company renewed its multifaceted campaign to secure the antitakeover amendment's early passage. This round included personal letters from the chief executive to all state senators and the chairmen of a number of other large corporations based in the state. The CEO's message to the elected officials stressed the state's lingering disadvantage: the legislation "would restore [the state's] competitive position in the area of state corporate governance in comparison to neighboring states which have already adopted such a statute." The letters to other company chairmen were similarly customized to touch on their vital concerns: "We are all aware of the serious threat which hostile takeovers present to our corporations . . . It is, therefore, critically important that we are not at a disadvantage in dealing with corporate raiders and unsolicited takeover bids" (company records, late 1980s).

The company's antitakeover amendment campaign was furthered by the organization of a special "action group" of half a dozen chairmen of the state's largest publicly traded firms. Their companies divided the contacts with state legislators, focusing on those in whose constituencies the firms had greatest presence. Ample company money for local elected officials and would-be candidates facilitated the cause. Under state law, unlimited amounts of company funds could be directly donated to candidates and elected officials (in contrast to federal law, which imposes caps on corporate PAC donations and requires that they come entirely from managers' volunteered contributions, not from company coffers). Locally donated political funds offered exceptional flexibility, observed the company's giving director: "The decision-making process can be relatively efficient, not encumbered by a political action committee. Politicians appreciate support, and view that as a vote of confidence in them. I don't think you buy votes, but I think you create an image, because of the contributions, that you are interested in the political process and understand it." When the firm's chief operating officer was scheduled to meet with one of the state's legislative leaders to promote the antitakeover amendment, gift bearing helped set the tenor. By quiet prearrangement, the executive was to bring a company check for $1,500 as a donation to the politician's anticipated gubernatorial campaign. In the name of reestablishing "an even playing field" in a takeover environment which had "shifted far too dramatically in favor of the raider," conversation then turned to a prodding of the legislative leader to bring up the antitakeover amendment for a vote. The company's general counsel even found an opportunity on one of business's oldest lobbying venues: the golf course. In playing a company-arranged round of golf with a key state senator, the firm's attorney quietly pressed the case, reminding the senator of the "cloud that still lingers over" the state's antitakeover defenses. Still another legislative leader was invited, at a private company luncheon with the firm's top management, "to enlist his leadership." Not long thereafter, the antitakeover amendment was called up by the legislative leaders. It passed almost unanimously.

The engagement in the antitakeover initiative brought the company more actively into the local political arena. Having taken such a visible stand on the regulation of takeovers, the company believed it could not soon recede into the background. Doing so, it feared, risked leaving the impression of an unprincipled passing interest in a single act of special pleading. To avoid such an appearance, and in any case because interest had developed in other legislation, the company remained engaged, aided by continuous gifts to local politicians and candidates. In the words of the company's director of public affairs:

The company prior to 1985 dabbled in state political activities. We made modest contributions to candidates, and we were part of trade association lobbies for or against bills. The company's interest in [the antitakeover] issue raised our visibility from very low to very high . . .

You don't go from a low level [of political involvement] to a high level and then drop down, because then . . . if I were a reporter, I'd say, "you people only did that because you wanted to buy that bill" . . . By being so involved in the takeover legislation, we became more involved in [the state capital] and legislation. There are [now] loads of bills and loads of issues to keep us out of trouble.

Still, the original issue remained of concern. Since the firm distributed approximately $75,000 annually to local elected officials and candidates (nearly on a par with its contributions to congressional candidates), the antitakeover issue loomed in the background long after the desired amendment had passed. It was not the only issue, as the company's political giving was also driven by a sense of pragmatism and a preference for winners, a trait it shared with many large firms (Burris, 1987; Mizruchi, 1992; Clawson and Neustadtl, 1989). The firm supported gubernatorial candidates in both the Republican and Democratic primaries, and when a preferred Democratic contestant lost in the late 1980s, the company simply backed his winning opponent anyway. Aside from siding with winners and powerful incumbents, however, the company's political giving was still driven by its antitakeover agenda. It had carefully tracked the role of each legislative member during the state legislature's various votes and actions in passing the original antitakeover legislation and later amendments. This data base provided a continuing guide for identifying the company's friends and enemies. Concluded the company manager who oversaw local political funding: "The number-one issue is the takeover legislation, still, [after] four years . . . If you're not with us, you're against us. If you're with us, we'll help you."

Opting Out of State Protection

Although institutional investors and shareholder advocates could exercise little influence in state legislative corridors, they were in a better position to pressure individual companies to oppose antitakeover legislation within their states. Such efforts were undertaken, though often they were little more than letter-writing campaigns. Anticipating defeat on this front, some investors and shareholder advocates then pressed companies to lobby at least for "opt-out" provisions that would permit them to exempt themselves from the antitakeover measures after the measures had been signed into law.

More vocal investors openly threatened disinvestment from companies coming under antitakeover protection. For instance, such warnings were sounded when Pennsylvania passed stringent antitakeover legislation in 1990. Initiated in response to a hostile bid for Pennsylvania-based Armstrong World Industries, the statute included a provision that would permit the seizure of profits from short-term investors who disposed of their holdings within eighteen months of a failed unwanted takeover. It guaranteed labor and severance contracts in the event that a hostile takeover was successful. And it permitted directors to consider the interests of employees, customers, and communities—and the past conduct of the bidder seeking control—in judging whether to accept a takeover offer. The interests of no single group, not even those of shareholders, were to be considered dominant. In light of these management protections, Fidelity Investments stated, after lobbying against the legislation, that it would now be reluctant to increase its investments in Pennsylvania companies. The director of the New Jersey state public employees pension fund was less equivocal: "I can't see myself buying the stock of any Pennsylvania company coming to market now" (Ronald Machold, quoted in Henriques, 1990). Subsequent study of stock prices of Pennsylvania firms revealed some short-term disinvestment. In several analyses, share prices were estimated to have dropped 1 to 9 percent below what would have been expected if no bill had been passed (Investor Responsibility Research Center, 1991b).

Even without the explicit exercise of such shareholder pressures, companies implicitly acknowledged their potential and quietly sought exemption. One of the seven companies followed this course. The firm had not been averse to protection from unwanted takeovers. No offer to purchase, friendly or otherwise, had ever been received. The company's stock had never been "in play." Yet, as was the case at many firms, the late-1980s takeover climate had sent a message to the executive suite. Management became alarmed, and the company was placed on alert. Anxieties were exacerbated by occasional (though always unsubstantiated) rumors that another major firm in a similar industry might be preparing an unwanted offer. The company had already adopted a poison pill and a classified board for protection against what it considered abusive takeover possibilities.

Carrying primary responsibility for corporate governance affairs, the general counsel found ample reason for these takeover defenses:

> During the eighties there was a lot of concern among a number of us at [the company] because there was a potful of money out there that was being thrown around . . . There was always a rumor that [another company] with $15 billion might go after us.
>
> That's why I was so concerned in the eighties. I didn't want to see [my company] dismembered . . . [The takeover groups would] come in and do these financial deals where people are not really looking at the long-term interests of the shareholders. People bandy that term about, but there really is a long term that I think that institutional investors and shareholders have to look at. If you put us up against the wall in the short term, we're not going to do very well.

The company was headquartered in a state for which one of the nation's most stringent antitakeover statutes had been formulated. The bill included included freeze-out and control-share provisions, an enlargement of director duties to include reference to employee and community interests, a poison pill endorsement, and protection of director decisions from judicial review. The proposed legislation had been catalyzed by hostile pursuit of several state-based corporations. Targeted firms, others that feared becoming targets, and the state's major business associations championed the bill.

Though not immune to takeover threats, the company considered that the proposed state antitakeover legislation went far beyond what it needed. Worse, the company feared that such protections could seriously impair relations with its major investors, many of which equated antitakeover defenses with antishareholder practices. Despite the company's privately held opposition, however, it did not publicly resist the legislation. A number of major corporations with nearby headquarters were lobbying for the protection, and several had pressed the company to join the coalition. One of the firms that had been under attack assiduously cultivated its natural corporate allies, its chairman even appealing directly to this chief executive for assistance. In spite of an internal recommendation to oppose the bill publicly, the CEO forced a noncommittal stand. The local area network of managerial quid pro quos had made the difference: "We have to work with these people," observed the general counsel, "and therefore if they want something and we can get the opt-out, why should we make them look silly in the newspapers? It was just one of those things where we had to take into account the other constituencies in the community.'' In seeking to offend neither shareholders nor corporate brethren, the company's posture at times seemed ambiguous. Some national business journalists even misread the company's signals to connote support for the legislation, listing the company among the bill's prominent backers.

An opt-out provision would furnish the needed finesse. With such a clause, the company would not openly oppose the bill and would thus avoid antagonizing those corporations desperate for state protection. After passage, the company could then decline protection, thereby avoiding a backlash from its major investors. Yet the legislation initially lacked a clause to allow corporations to exempt themselves. On this issue the company openly entered statehouse politics. It pressed for the provision's inclusion, even writing the opt-out amendment language that was finally adopted. The line of attack was laid down by the company's executive vice-president for legal affairs, who had drafted the amendment: ''It's presumptuous on the part of [a main business association] or anybody else to make a judgment on behalf of the board of directors in this area . . . 'Don't you guys sitting in this little room over here [at the statehouse] make that decision for major companies and small companies.' We were very concerned about our institutional investors because obviously they're very upset, and we understand that.'' When the legislation passed, the company immediately exempted itself from coverage. This required a change of the company's charter, which the board readily approved. Some of the company's major investors had written to urge the opt-out, but by then the issue was already moot as far as the company's officers were concerned. The decision, said the general counsel, had been made months before: ''It was an easy decision for us . . . The statute goes far too far. We have been a shareholder-value-driven corporation for many years now . . . [The law] just added to the whole entrenchment-of-management concept that I think is really prevalent today.''

The Accidental Element

Although political action was more disciplined around company goals, it could never be fully aligned. The personal experiences, values, and networks of top management still intruded. Corporate behavior was as socially ''embedded''—to use Mark Granovetter's concept (1985)—in this area as any. Senior managers would often skew company PAC and charitable contributions, for example, toward causes that they personally favored, regardless of the company's organizational stake (Galaskiewicz, 1985; Useem, 1991). Turnover in top management occasioned by the ascendance of a new ownership group or by new shareholder pressures reoriented political action in unique ways. Restructuring's managerial turbulence contributed to a corresponding political turbulence.

The specific changes depended on the particular blend of political values and networks brought by the new managers. This can be seen in the aftermath of the ownership acquisition of one major high-technology firm by an even larger high-technology company in the mid-1980s (as documented in the study by Clawson, Neustadtl, and Scott, 1989). The acquired firm had long operated a political action committee, but the acquiring parent had not. After the merger, the PAC officials of the smaller firm persuaded the new parent that it should establish a PAC. Prior to the merger, the acquired firm's PAC had strongly favored Republican candidates, in part because the chief executive was a strong supporter of Ronald Reagan and had even served as the head of a federal advisory council during the Reagan administration. When the parent set up the new PAC, however, the political skew was far more bipartisan, in part because the parent's chief executive had had earlier Washington experience and now headed a major advisory council of the national Democratic party. Turnover in ownership and top management led to twists in political strategies little determined by company concerns and much related to executive preference.

The one area where a more general change was expected when the new managers were owners or were closely controlled by them was the area of political compromise. It is arguable that owner-managers were more opposed to government regulation and interference in the market than were professional nonowning managers, who tended to be more accepting of bipartisan solutions and joint business-government initiatives. Whatever the argument's plausibility, examination of corporate PAC contributions during the 1982 election revealed, however, that owner-controlled firms were no more likely than management-controlled companies to favor congressional candidates identified as highly conservative (Burris 1987, pp. 734–739).

Weakened Classwide Political Action

Although corporate political strategies were primarily shaped at the company level, business political action was also independently structured by networks and associations transcending companies. Shared directorships, mutual stock ownership, and other forms of intercorporate ties had not been created for the purpose of political mobilization, but they provided a vehicle through which collective initiatives could be mobilized. Firms furnished resources for the collective action, but the level and direction of the action were shaped in ways that transcended individual companies.

The webs of ties among U.S. companies were not nearly so extensive or ownership-based as the intercorporate links found in Japan and elsewhere (Futatsugi 1986, 1990; Gerlach, 1992a, 1992b; Gerlach and Lincoln, 1992; Orru, Biggart, and Hamilton, 1991). Yet most major publicly traded firms were connected to one another through shared directorships and informal executive relationships. Moreover, such interlocks were entwined with informal policy-oriented networks formed around specific policy issues, ranging from energy development to military spending (Mintz and Schwartz, 1985; Mizruchi and Schwartz, 1987; Laumann and Knoke, 1987). The ways that corporations were tied into these networks shaped the level and direction of their political action. The network ties also shaped the intensity and thrust of collective action, as large numbers of firms were jointly mobilized into the political fray.

In an analysis of corporate PAC allocations in the 1980 election, for example, it was found that one element of company network ties with other companies, their shared board directorships, had a strong bearing on how company PACs distributed their funds (Clawson and Neustadtl, 1989). Firms whose directors sat on a diverse array of other major corporate boards were more likely to give to congressional incumbents, many of whom were moderate Democrats, and less prone to support highly conservative challengers. Another study of the 1980 electoral cycle similarly revealed that well-connected companies gave more often to Republican challengers and conservative candidates for Congress (Burris, 1991). Other studies of giving to nonprofit organizations showed that managerial and directorship network ties with other firms and with the nonprofit sector increased the rate of giving and channeled its allocation (Galaskiewicz, 1985). More generally, a range of business political actions were mobilized through such networks, and the actions taken were often at levels and directed in ways that went beyond the immediate market concerns of the firms involved (Useem 1984).

The reemergence of ownership influence on large firms generated two changes in the networks, with contrary effects. One undercut the foundation for classwide business political action; the other reinforced it. The first was a radical change in governing board composition by publicly traded firms that had been taken private. The second was a product of a more gradual change in governing board composition instituted by publicly traded firms that were under pressure from investors to bring on more independent-minded directors.

At large publicly traded firms, the convention had long been to fill their boards with prominent executives of other firms and those who were otherwise well practiced in or connected with the corporate world. The owners of major firms that had been taken private, however, moved in reverse fashion, creating tightly controlled boards whose allegiances were unambiguously and narrowly tied to the new ownership interests. This new cast to corporate governance was a logical extension of owner efforts to wrest control of the firm from professional managers. But there were two fateful organizational consequences. First, the board composition changed, from a majority of outside directors to a majority of directors who were either owner-representatives or top managers selected by the owners. Second, the new directors maintained far fewer directorship links to other corporations outside the ownership group's tightly held corporations. As a result, privatized firms largely exited from the directorship networks that had traditionally linked large companies in common enterprise.

The withdrawal can be illustrated with changes in the board of directors of RJR Nabisco following its 1988 leveraged buyout by Kohlberg Kravis Roberts, the largest conversion of a publicly traded, management-controlled corporation to private ownership during the 1980s and early 1990s. Philip Morris, a firm of similar size and product mix but untouched by buyout pressures, offers a useful comparison.

Philip Morris maintained a board of twenty-one directors in both 1987 and 1989, the years surrounding the buyout year of RJR Nabisco, and its breadth of ties to other major companies also changed little. By contrast, the postbuyout board of RJR Nabisco displayed scant resemblance to its predecessor (Table 6.2). Only three of the original eighteen directors (Vernon Jordan, John Medlin and J. Paul Sticht) carried over. At Philip Morris, only two of the twenty-one directors did not carry over.

Furthermore, of the eighteen RJR Nabisco board members in 1987, prior to the buyout, ten were outside directors, most serving as managers of other major corporations (for example, Monsanto, BellSouth, and Celanese). By contrast, of the thirteen board members in 1989, after the buyout, only three were outside directors. Half of the ten inside directors

Table 6.2. The board of directors of RJR Nabisco, before and after its leveraged buyout in 1988 by Kohlberg Kravis Roberts (KKR).

1987 board of directors (before buyout)		1989 board of directors (after buyout)	
Director	Employment position or affiliation	Director	Employment position or affiliation
William S. Anderson	NCR Corporation	R. Theodore Ammon	KKR
Albert L. Butler, Jr.	Arista Company	Louis V. Gerstner	RJR Nabisco
Robert Carbonell	RJR Nabisco	H. John Grenniaus	RJR Nabisco
John L. Clendenin	BellSouth Corp.	James W. Johnston	RJR Nabisco
Ronald H. Grierson	General Electric	Vernon E. Jordan, Jr.	Law firm partner
John W. Hanley	Monsanto Company	Henry R. Kravis	KKR
Edward A. Horrigan, Jr.	RJR Nabisco	John G. Medlin, Jr.	First Wachovia Co.
Charles E. Hugel	Combustion Engineering	Paul E. Raether	KKR
F. Ross Johnson	RJR Nabisco	Rozanne L. Ridgway	Atlantic Council
Vernon E. Jordan, Jr.	Law firm partner	Clifton S. Robbins	KKR
Juanita M. Kreps	Former U.S. official	J. Paul Sticht	RJR Nabisco (ret.)
Gerald H. Long	RJR Nabisco	Scott M. Stuart	KKR
John D. Macomber	Celanese Corp.	Karl von der Heyden	RJR Nabisco
John G. Medlin, Jr.	First Wachovia Co.		
Andrew G. C. Sage II	Shearson Lehman		
Robert M. Schaeberle	RJR Nabisco		
J. Paul Sticht	RJR Nabisco (ret.)		
James O. Welch, Jr.	RJR Nabisco		

Sources: Standard and Poor's (1989), and information provided by RJR Nabisco.

represented the ownership organization, KKR, and the other half served as senior managers of RJR Nabisco. The picture at Philip Morris moved in the opposite direction: thirteen of the twenty-one directors were outsiders before, fifteen after.

Similarly, the outside directorship connections of the RJR Nabisco board members were sharply reduced following the ownership takeover. Nine of the eighteen RJR Nabisco directors prior to the buyout served on a total of twenty-two boards of other major firms. After the buyout, three of RJR Nabisco's directors served on a total of only nine boards of major firms other than those owned by KKR. The Philip Morris linkages remained virtually unchanged: eleven directors served on a total of twenty other boards before, and the respective figures were eleven and nineteen afterward.

Examination of the nine other largest leveraged buyouts from 1986 to 1988, the peak period for the conversion of publicly traded firms to privately held companies, revealed a similar pattern. The 1986–1988 period included three of the decade's four years in which company-leveraged buyout totals exceeded $20 billion. Taken together, the buyouts of these three years accounted for nearly three-fifths (59.5 percent) of the company buyout value for the decade. The aggregate buyout value of these ten LBOs together totaled $51.2 billion, about half of all buyouts for those three years.

For comparison, I included Philip Morris and nine other firms that were similar to the buyout companies (the LBO and comparison firms are identified in Table 6.3). The comparison companies were matched to the LBO firms by sector and size: within the industry group for each LBO firm, a paired company was selected with the most similar 1986 sales volume.

Characteristics of the board composition of the ten companies before and after the buyouts appear in Table 6.4. As anticipated, the statistics show a pronounced decline in the number of directors, the number of directors serving on outside boards, and the number of publicly listed companies with which directorships are shared. The average board size was nearly cut in half, and linkages to other companies were cut by 80 percent or more.

The magnitude of the change contrasts sharply with that among the comparison firms. Information on their boards was compiled for the same years as for the buyout match (one year prior to the buyout and one year after). The average board size of the comparison firms slightly increased. The outside connections of the comparison boards declined slightly, consistent with an end-of-decade trend among large publicly traded companies. Examining the 500 largest industrial firms, fifty largest commercial banks, twenty-five largest diversified financial companies, and twenty-five largest transportation firms, Davis (1992) found that the average number of directorship ties among these corporations declined from 8.85 in 1986 to 8.43 in 1988, and to 7.22 in 1990. For eight of the ten matched companies in the present study for which information was available in that data set, the average number of ties dropped from 8.0 in 1986 to 7.6 in 1990. Still, the slopes of the matched-company trends were a fraction of those observed for the buyout group.

The withdrawal of RJR Nabisco and other major corporations from shared directorships with other companies weakened the intercorporate networks that served to mobilize and channel corporate political activity in recent years. Shared directorships among corporations generated greater consistency among firms in the allocations of PAC and charitable donations (and, presumably, other forms of political action), and the withdrawal of companies newly under ownership control from this network undermined one component of corporate consensus (Clawson and Neustadtl,

Table 6.3. Ten largest publicly traded company buyouts in 1986–1988, and ten companies matched for size and sector.

LBO company	Buyout year	Approximate price (in billions of dollars)	Sales in 1986 (in billions of dollars)	Product sector[a]	Matched company	Sales in 1986 (in billions of dollars)
RJR Nabisco	1988	24.56	16.60	38	Philip Morris Companies	25.41
Safeway Stores Inc.	1986	4.20	19.65	29	Kroger Co.	17.12
Borg-Warner Corporation	1987	3.80	3.62	19/33	FMC Corp.	3.00
Southland Corporation	1987	3.72	8.62	29	Winn-Dixie Stores	8.58
Owens-Illinois Inc.	1986	3.63	3.71	7	PPG Industries	4.69
Hospital Corp. of America	1988	3.60	4.93	32	Fluor Corporation	4.46
Fort Howard Paper Company	1988	3.57	1.55	24	Louisiana-Pacific	1.51
Burlington Industries	1987	2.13	2.81	36	Interco. Inc.	2.55
Viacom International Inc.	1986	1.82	0.92	26	Dow Jones & Co.	1.14
Supermarkets General Corp.	1987	1.80	5.51	29	Albertson's Inc.	5.38

Sources: Grimm (1989) and various issues of Business Week, Fortune, and Standard and Poor's Register of Corporations.

a. The industry groups are (following a Business Week classification): 7 = building materials; 19 = miscellaneous manufacturing; 24 = paper and forest products; 26 = publishing, radio, and TV broadcasting; 29 = food retailing; 32 = service industries; 33 = special machinery; 36 = textiles and apparel; 38 = tobacco.

Table 6.4. Composition of the board of directors before and after ten large buyouts in 1986–1988, and composition for ten matched companies.

Board composition	Before buyout year[a]	After buyout year[a]
Average number of directors:		
Ten buyout companies	15.1	8.0
Ten matched companies	13.6	13.9
Average number of directors serving on outside boards:		
Ten buyout companies	7.2	1.5
Ten matched companies	6.1	5.8
Average number of outside companies on which directors serve:		
Ten buyout companies	23.8	3.1
Ten matched companies	18.4	17.7

Sources: Standard and Poor's *Register of Corporations, Directors and Executives* (various years); *Who's Who in America* and *Who's Who in Finance and Industry* (various years); company reports and personal communications with company offices.

a. The differences between the "before" and "after" figures for the buyout companies are all statistically significant at the .05 level. The "before" and "after" figures for the matched companies are not significantly different.

1989; Mizruchi, 1992). It also demobilized political action, as the newly private companies focused more on internal financial performance and less on external agendas.

This was at least temporarily evident in the decline of total corporate PAC contributions among the LBO firms just after they were taken private. Overall corporate contributions continued to rise throughout the 1980s, albeit at a slower pace by the end of the decade as the political climate changed and PAC limits were reached. Prior to their purchase, PAC giving among the buyout companies rose more rapidly than among all companies, but it then dropped by nearly a fifth during the 1987–1988 electoral cycle, which came after or during the period in which they were taken private (Figure 6.5). Comparison-firm PAC trends, by contrast, rose steadily throughout the period from 1979 to 1987–1988, though at a slower pace than for all companies. During the 1989–1990 cycle, however, buyout-firm PAC giving rose sharply again. Disaggregated analysis reveals that this was a product of a near-tripling of PAC gifts by RJR Nabisco (while those of Philip Morris rose by only 3 percent).

At the same time, companies remaining publicly traded were pressed

Index of total PAC contributions,
with 1979–1980 contributions set at 100

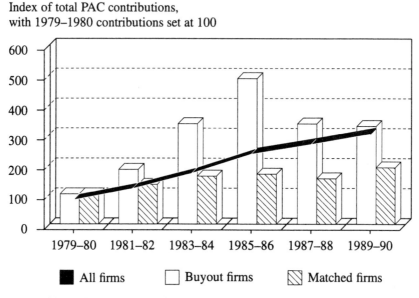

Figure 6.5. PAC contributions of buyout, matched, and all companies, 1979–1990.
(Source: U.S. Federal Election Commission.)

toward less insularity. Institutional investors urged more directors with fewer ties to inside management. Independent directors, the investors theorized, would be more effective in representing shareholder interests and less protective of inside management prerogatives. Acting on the presumption, several public pension funds pressed for more autonomous governing boards. In 1990–1991, the California Public Employees' Retirement System sought to create a roster of independent director candidates for this purpose. Calpers wrote to the directors of companies included in the Standard and Poor's 500 (the 500 publicly traded firms with largest market capitalization), soliciting an array of information about each of them. Protest from individual directors and the Business Roundtable led to a reformulation of the effort, but not to the operating premise: "It has become increasingly clear to us that the most important contribution a shareholder can make is to ensure that the company has the best possible directors, operating in a structure in which the interests of directors and long-term shareholders are aligned" (Calpers, 1990).

In this effort, Calpers joined a long tradition of advocacy for more

Number of directors

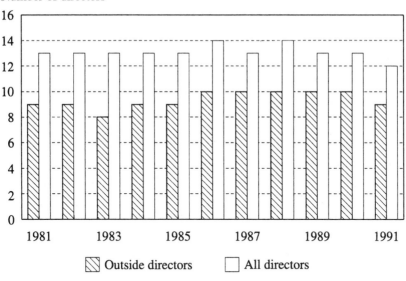

Figure 6.6. Composition of boards of directors, 1981–1991. (Source: Korn/Ferry International, 1991 and earlier years.)

independent boards, much of which was intended not to enlarge share-holder control but to enhance board effectiveness (Lorsch, 1989, pp. 169–193). Whatever the impetus, there were more company boards with outsider majorities in the late 1980s than there were in the early 1970s. A Conference Board survey of 589 large manufacturing firms in 1989 found that 86 percent had elected a majority of outside directors, up from 71 percent of the 851 firms surveyed in 1972 (outsiders were defined as those who were not employees or former employees of the firm; Bacon, 1990, p. 8).

During the 1980s, however, company board composition displayed only modest overall movement toward greater independence. This was evident in an annual survey of board composition by an executive-search firm (the targeted population in 1991 was *Fortune*'s 500 largest industrial firms, 350 of the largest service firms, and 150 smaller companies). At the start of the decade, nine out of thirteen board members on average were outsiders (Figure 6.6). This dropped to eight of thirteen in 1983, but by 1990 it had reached ten of thirteen, and in 1991 nine of twelve.

Conclusion

Most major corporations had had long experience in managing their political and social environment through political action committees, company foundations, executive lobbying, and a host of related techniques. Shareholder-driven organizational alignment altered the thrust of such efforts. As the shareholder revolt altered the ways of organizing company business, it also altered the ways of doing political business. Corporate political strategies were rooted in the firms' organizational foundations, and when the foundations were aligned, so too were the strategies.

During the 1970s, firms found common cause in fighting the newly imposed costs of the expanded forms of social regulation cutting across industry lines. Government intervention was widely blamed for business's declining profit margins. Firms focused their political energies on causes and candidates that promised more free economy and less state restriction (Silk and Vogel, 1976; Himmelstein, 1990). Few managers or owners pointed their fingers at one another.

The extensive deregulation and improved business climate achieved under the Reagan administration, however, defused the issue of government regulation. The problem was redefined in some quarters to be less a matter of excessive government intervention and more a matter of inadequate stockholder vigilance. Yet as shareholders sought to exercise more vigilance, companies were already well versed in the politics of fending off meddlesome critics. As a result, corporate political action acquired a different profile. "Social responsibility" came to be defined in more self-interested terms. Collective business responsibility came to be less well defined. And state regulation came be to enlisted rather than resisted.

Moving Alignment Up

The organizational changes in the seven firms that I observed were undertaken with the concurrence of the companies' boards of directors. The governing bodies had approved the downsizing measures, the incentive plans, and the devolution of responsibilities. They gave their chief executive the backing he needed to transform a vision into reality, to translate organizational principles into operating practices. They stayed with the chief executive when he was challenged from within by disgruntled managers and resistant unions. They backed him when he was challenged from without by angry shareholders and warring raiders.

To management, the board's backing was personally gratifying. It was also essential. Improved alignment of the company's components could not have occurred without board concurrence. With formal authority and responsibility for the company's performance, the directors would have to consent to any significant company redirection. Their agreement was a necessary condition for any corporate restructuring.

That the boards supported their managements through this period of change should draw no special notice. It was a commonplace in the world of senior managers and directors that boards almost always back their managers (Lorsch, 1989). To do otherwise on more than occasional matters was to signal extreme displeasure, an oblique signal to the chief executive to seek his or her fortune elsewhere.

But that the boards reactively rather than proactively embraced the principles of alignment was noteworthy. After all, alignment was intended to enhance shareholder value. According to the theory of the firm, directors had been elected by the shareholders to select managers and strategies to optimize that return. If shareholders were restless over company performance, directors, as their representatives, should be the first to know. If the interests of shareholders were receiving short shrift, directors, as their representatives, should be the first to complain. Yet during the late 1980s and early 1990s, it was management that took the case for alignment to the directors, not directors to management.

Directors' Compliance

Senior managers in the firms I studied almost uniformly expressed satisfaction with the support that they had received from their boards. Some of the executives knew it first-hand as inside directors themselves. Senior managers not on the board knew it from their own presentations to the board and from detailed accounts by the inside directors with whom they shared the executive suite.

Senior management's relations up the organizational chart often stood in pleasant contrast to experiences down the chart. The years of downsizings and other conflict-ridden changes inside the company had taken a toll. It could be seen in a kind of battle weariness among some of those interviewed. They had survived and prospered, while many of their contemporaries had long since been passed over or let go. In some instances, they had been personally responsible for laying off colleagues with whom they had worked closely for years. In other cases, they had directed bitter struggles against their unions. In still other instances, they had won, or sometimes lost, protracted fights over strategic direction. On occasion, the preferred path backfired, as newly empowered divisions went awry. None of the managers, however, reported anything analogous from their years of experience with the board of directors. Board meetings were virtually always civil, the questions courteous, the backing predictable. Although senior managers prepared rigorously for board meetings, the sessions themselves rarely proved unpleasant.

An executive vice-president of the chemical-products company, though not a director himself, attended every bimonthly board meeting to report on his side of the business. He highlighted both the achievements and the problems of the several business units reporting to him, on the premise that boards abhor surprises. Depending on the directors' interest, his short presentations would sometimes expand into two-hour discussions. Though investors carefully tracked the company and managers experienced constant pressure to meet quarterly objectives, in this executive's experience the shareholder pressures were rarely mirrored in board questions or concerns. Rather, aided by acceptable results, management enjoyed unswerving support:

> The company has had three very successful years of performance, so that there have not been major fiscal confrontations that the board had to address. The board's role has been one of support and encouragement and of trying to seek innovation and helping the company grow, without confrontation at all . . .
>
> I'll tell you, I don't think that the board knows a hell of a lot about the details of the company. They really don't throw tough, uncomfortable questions . . . We've not had confrontational issues. We've not had major concerns or disagreements about strategies that we're trying to employ in the company. I think the chairman has kept the board well informed, and obviously he's kept them satisfied . . .
>
> It's not the kind of meeting that I dread going to, not "Oh my god, I'm going to get tough questions" . . . The board is in thoroughly good sync with what we are trying to do.

Even when a recent quarter had proven nearly disastrous, board members still posed no awkward questions.

The board's support, however, was rendered as a largely passive backing. Directors had not led the charge for restructuring. They had not articulated the need to align, nor had they pressed top management to do so. Whatever shareholders small and large may have wanted, directors were not their messengers. Rather, directors offered their support reactively, accepting most of management's agenda and ready to be convinced of the more controversial elements.

At times the directors resisted, but usually due to the pace, not the thrust, of the change. When asked what the board had done to steer management in directions it might not have otherwise pursued, a senior vice-president at the pharmaceutical company responded: "Nothing." The board, he observed, was free to ask any questions, but "there hasn't been any great incentive for them to push. And obviously, because we've done pretty well, there hasn't been a strong questioning of the strategies." When asked why investor pressures, which senior managers constantly experienced, were not conveyed through the board, he answered that the directors "are not in that circle; they're not in that chain."

Similarly, the chief executive who had guided the transportation company through much of its restructuring during the mid-1980s had been ahead of his board for most of it. On taking office, he had been "personally appalled that the shareholders had been so ignored'' by the company, and was dismayed to find so little guidance on this front from the board: ''To the extent that [the directors] understood what was going on, they always approved. They were not very well informed. I briefed them twice [on the sale of a major part of the business]. I was stunned when [my successor] briefed them the third time, and one of them said, 'I'm glad to really finally understand' . . . The board was way behind . . . If anything, I got messages from the board to slow down.'' In one instance, this CEO had given a speech to a meeting of the company's major customers. Not realizing that a reporter was in the room, he spoke frankly of the company's restructuring plans. The firm's intentions to downsize were made clear, including an interest in selling some of its units to any parties who thought they could better manage the business. When several members of the board learned of the comments from press accounts, they reacted angrily to the plans. Nonetheless, subsequently mollified by discussions with the chief executive, they eventually approved.

While the board of the transportation company did not always lag behind the CEO on the pace of his restructuring initiative, it was almost always behind him chronologically. In his view, the directors sometimes seemed to understand even less about the company than the stockholders that they had been elected to represent. The contrast was sharpened, for instance, when he traveled to New York to meet the company's major shareholders: ''[The major shareholders] asked a lot of penetrating questions. In fact, they were more penetrating than the board was. They knew more about what was going on than the board did . . . It's straightforward. The board doesn't control that much because they don't know what's going on. So if the management is doing a bad job, they can't stop them. And if they're doing a good job, they're not very aware of it.''

On occasion, boards did move preemptively. Several directors of the retail-services company, for instance, had prodded management to introduce a stronger incentive system. As described in Chapter 4, they had witnessed its effectiveness in their own companies, and they successfully pressed a new CEO at the retail company to make the annual management bonuses genuinely contingent on performance, not simply on year's end. Yet these were the exceptions to the otherwise recurrent patterns of board support and compliance. The board usually endorsed organizational innovations brought to it in the name of shareholder value. But few such measures were ever initiated by the board.

Even then, senior managers sometimes concluded that their directors' perceptions required refinement. The board, management felt at times, was not sufficiently aware of its shareholder base. In the case of the chemical-products company, several of the directors were seen by management as bringing especially limited sensitivity to shareholder issues by virtue of their employment histories. One director headed a university research laboratory and another a Washington public relations firm. A third had been chair of a European company, and a fourth the head of a federal agency. The company's own former chief executive still served on the board, and he had left the office at a time when the company was still little bothered by shareholder concerns. As a result, the company's current chief executive found it necessary to remind these directors, at times even inform them, of the concerns of "the Street." Investors sought steadily expanding quarterly earnings, the CEO intoned, and that was why he was taking a proposed action. He sought to educate his directors on what their electors wanted.

Representation of Shareholder Interests

The theory of the modern corporate form would have led us to a different forecast of how the board of directors might have acted during this period. In principle, the directors were elected by stockholders to protect and advance their investments. This legally sanctioned arrangement has long been officially presumed to guide the governance of publicly traded firms. Lest the official norm be eroded, companies and senior managers offered frequent reaffirmation. In a 1990 report on corporate governance, the Business Roundtable, an association of chief executives of some 200 large corporations, so reminded an intended audience of senior managers and policy makers: "The board of directors is ultimately accountable to the shareholders for the long-term successful economic performance of the corporation consistent with its underlying public purpose" (Business Roundtable, 1990b). Individual companies often did much the same. ITT Corporation reminded its own shareholders in 1991, for instance, that the "Board of Directors is responsible for establishing broad corporate policies and for overseeing the overall performance of ITT" (ITT Corporation, 1991).

Since directors are elected by and accountable to shareholders, the rising tide of shareholder power and activism should in theory have first been felt in the boardroom. As the stockholders' agents, directors would have been the first to detect the groundswell of discontent among their largest shareholders, if not always among the rank and file. "From an agency perspective," theorized one analyst, "boards can be used as monitoring devices for shareholder interest." When directors in turn effectively communicate what they have monitored, "top executives are more likely to engage in behaviors that are consistent with stockholders' interests" (Eisenhardt, 1989, p. 65). Under the model of shareholder sovereignty, corporate directors could thus have been expected to lead, not lag behind, the winds of change. Instead of simply backing management's proposals brought to them, they might have brought the proposals to management.

Corporate behavior almost never conforms precisely to what theorists have forecast, but rarely has it been at such complete odds. When myth and reality stand in such inverse relation, a fertile ground for explanation is likely to be found in underlying power relations. These are the informal power disparities among the shareholders, directors, and managers— asymmetries that are masked for political necessity by different, sometimes completely contrary, formal portrayals. Analysts from C. Wright Mills (1956) to Henry Mintzberg (1983), from G. William Domhoff (1967) to Jeffrey Pfeffer (1981a), have reminded us that when power is at issue, what is conveyed to be true can sometimes be the opposite of what is true. Their warnings offer useful guidance here.

The reactive rather than preemptive board behavior can be traced in this case to the de facto power relations prevailing among the companies' three major power groups. The official pyramid placed shareholders on top, directors in the middle, and managers below. Yet this de jure picture stood in stark contrast to an inverted power pyramid that actually prevailed at many corporations. Directors had long been influenced more by the concerns of the top management they had selected than by the concerns of the shareholders who had selected them. Put differently, management exercised more influence on the board than did the shareholders, a direct inversion of the presumed flow of influence. This was, after all, the critical decoupling that had furnished the foundation for the managerial revolution a half-century earlier. The official principles of shareholder control of directors and director control of managers were honored more in the breach than in the observance.

Perhaps no single indicator better captured this decoupling of director accountability from shareholder power than the electoral process itself. In principle shareholders voted on directors to represent their interests, but in fact shareholders almost never enjoyed an electoral choice. The disenfranchisement began with the nomination of directors. Most major boards had constituted a nominations committee, often composed entirely of outside directors (though in some cases the full board retained the nomination function). The committee (or board) annually formed a slate of candidates for shareholder approval. In virtually all elections, the committee nominated a number of candidates precisely equal to the number of board openings. Moreover, information about the nominees presented to shareholders was limited to their employment record, their other corporate directorships, and the extent of their company holdings. Information about the nominees' views or their record on matters of special interest to shareholders would virtually never appear.

A 1987 proxy statement by Lockheed Corporation illustrates the options and information presented to shareholders. It was typical of most proxies by large, publicly traded companies. Issued in the calm climate that prevailed several years before the struggle with NL Industries for control of Lockheed's board, the Lockheed proxy contained conventional biographies for the thirteen nominees standing for reelection to the board's thirteen openings. The information was the minimum mandated by the Securities and Exchange Commission: the director's age, principle business experience, first year on the board, and shares held in the firm (Table 7.1). It was from this profile that shareholders were to decide if the nominees would faithfully represent their concerns and interests. All thirteen of the board-nominated candidates were elected to the Lockheed board.

Exceptions to the one-nominee/one-opening norm can help illuminate the power of this convention. They reveal alternatives that are feasible but effectively excluded by an entrenched norm. The offering of more board candidates than openings was a rare electoral event, and was almost always the result of shareholder challenge. In such instances, shareholders received information going well beyond the usual biographical sketches. Investors found that they faced opposing slates whose nominees offered starkly different messages. The 1990 campaign by NL Industries to take over Lockheed included such an alternative slate of director nominees. The board-nominated and alternative slates offered voters distinct alternatives, and ample information reached the voters on how the alternatives differed. The incumbent Lockheed directors standing for reelection, for instance, had recently rejected a measure to adopt confidential shareholding voting, a measure valued by many institutional investors. By contrast, each of the directors proposed by NL Industries had endorsed the introduc-

Table 7.1. Descriptions of director nominees for the board of Lockheed Corporation, company proxy statement, 1987.

Name	Age	Director since	Number of shares	Principal business experience[a]
Roy A. Anderson	66	1971	66,401	Former Lockheed chief executive Director of 6 other companies
Michael Berberian	53	1973	300	Secretary-treasurer, Berberian Brothers
Jack L. Bowers	66	1986	0	CEO of Lockheed subsidiary Director of 1 other company
Joseph P. Downer	64	1976	300	Retired vice-chairman, Atlantic Richfield Co. Director of 1 other company
Houston I. Flournoy	57	1976	300	Professor, University of Southern California Director of 3 other companies
Robert A. Fuhrman	62	1980	65,647	Lockheed chief operating officer Director of 1 other company
James F. Gibbons	55	1985	0	Engineering dean, Stanford University Director of 1 other company
Jack K. Horton	70	1966	1,000	Former CEO of Southern California Edison Co. Director of 4 other companies
Lawrence O. Kitchen	63	1975	77,619	Lockheed chief executive officer Director of 2 other companies
Vincent N. Marafino	56	1980	88,252	Lockheed chief financial officer Director of 3 other companies
J. J. Pinola	61	1983	800	CEO of First Interstate Bancorp Director of 2 other companies
Joseph R. Rensch	64	1978	600	Vice-chairman, Pacific Lighting Corp. Director of 5 other companies
E. Swearingen	68	1978	6,000	CEO, Continental Illinois Corp. Director of 4 other companies

Source: Proxy statement of Lockheed Corporation, March 31, 1987.

a. Descriptions of principal business experience are abbreviated.

tion of secret balloting. The two rosters also differed on the poison pill, on opt-out provisions, and on other governance issues of tangible interest to shareholders. Moreover, in sharp contrast to conventional practice, the nominees' campaign platforms, not just their biographies, were carried to the voters. One newspaper advertisement by NL Industries, partially reproduced in Table 7.2, bared the differences.

Lockheed countered with its own media campaign to reach its investors, asserting that its board would ''continue to make the hard choices we believe will enhance shareholder value.'' It urged its shareholders ''to reelect your board, which is committed to maximizing values for *all* shareholders'' (*New York Times,* March 27, 1990, p. D11). No such information or claims about the official director nominees had been made available to Lockheed shareholders in 1987, let alone an alternative slate.

Such choices and information about them were available to shareholders on only exceptional occasions. By convention—and by contrast—stockholders were without choice or information in virtually all board elections. In choosing to so structure the nominating and voting process, companies had met with scant resistance until the late 1980s. So deeply ingrained was the norm, that disgruntled shareholders knew it was pointless to ask a company to offer a choice.

Table 7.2. Excerpt from an NL Industries' newspaper advertisement for nominees to the board of directors of Lockheed Corporation, 1990.

Lockheed and Shareholder Rights
NL Industries and the Lockheed board take contrasting positions
on several shareholder rights issues.

Here is where the two sides stand:

	NL nominees		Incumbents	
	For	Against	For	Against
Adopt confidential voting	X			X
Opt out of antitakeover law	X			X
Eliminate poison pill	X			X
Prohibit greenmail	X		X	
Forbid golden parachutes	X			X

When you decide whom to support in the election of Lockheed's board of directors, we urge you to ask yourself where you stand.

Source: New York Times (March 27, 1990), p. D7.

Indicative of this learned helplessness, a 1989 study by the Conference Board confirmed the dearth of shareholder initiative. Only seventeen of 589 large firms surveyed, or 3 percent, reported that institutional investors had suggested or requested that they, the investors, play a role in selecting directors. And only a single company said that it had acceded to a demand from a major shareholder to add another outsider to its board (Bacon, 1990, p. 16).

Even when presented with a choice, shareholders were reluctant to break with management. In one widely publicized contest, Robert A. G. Monks, a shareholder activist, sought election in 1991 to the board of Sears, Roebuck and Company. His critical views of shareholder disenfranchisement had already been well publicized through the work of a group he founded, Institutional Shareholder Services, and a book he coauthored, *Power and Accountability* (Monks and Minow, 1991; *Institutional Investor,* the industry's chief trade publication, aptly titled a review, "Shareholders, unite!"). Making himself a dissident Sears nominee through an independent nomination process, Monks campaigned on the promise of considering a break-up of Sears to benefit shareholders, an action vigorously opposed by management. He was estimated to have drawn about 15 percent of the votes cast, including support from several of the large public pension funds (Berg, 1991). But he fell short of the 25 percent needed for election.

Monks' experiment in democratic challenge reconfirmed for the corporate world what the congressional world has long known: the staying power of incumbency is enormous. Without a tradition of genuine democratic experience, voters, when presented with a choice, were seemingly unprepared to face either the ire of incumbent managers or the risk of replacing them. They were further discouraged by federal securities regulations, which dissuaded investors from acting in common. Campaign mobilization by a set of dissident stockholders was difficult at best.

Aligning the Board

Regardless of the extent to which the board of directors might be the captive of management, the logic of alignment pointed nonetheless in the board's direction as well. The idea of ownership-disciplined change carried up as well as down the organizational chart. As in the case of business units and individual managers, the decisions of directors could be better linked to shareholder concerns, and the directors could acquire more power to express those concerns. Moreover, such change would be consonant with, not a challenge to, both business ideology and the theory of the firm. Both already extolled shareholder and board sovereignty, even if its manifest absence never seemed terribly bothersome in the past. Steps to align the board would be consistent with corporate culture and legal tradition, shifting the burden of proof against reform to those who would oppose it.

While many shareholders and managers were uninterested in pressing for reformation of the board, both camps included people who were ready for change. From diverse starting points, they had concluded in common that the corporate governance system was neither impeccable nor immutable. Furthermore, they knew that governance principles were on the side of reform. The board in theory was to serve investor interests, not management prerogatives, and the skew was admittedly too much toward the latter.

Boards of directors were thus to be made more responsive to shareholders, less the captives of tradition. So powerful was the reformist current that proposals emerged to change virtually all major aspects of the governing board: its *election,* its *composition,* and its *compensation.* However, though investors and companies often shared common ground on the general thrust of change, they would choose radically different paths for achieving it. Shareholders more often preferred electoral reform; managers, compensation reform. A fourth area, board *information,* was also favored by management but drew comparatively little interest from investors.

One negotiated effort in 1991 had sought to find common ground in these several areas. A small set of top company and investment managers issued a ''new compact for owners and directors,'' urging that shareholders regularly evaluate the performance of directors, and that directors regularly evaluate the performance of managers. But the common language was unique. On most major matters, the landscape was yet one of conflict, not compromise. (See Working Group on Corporate Governance, 1991. A sampling of calls for reform and resistance can be found in Sherman, 1989; Thompson and Trumble, 1990; Johnson, 1990; National Investor Relations Institute, 1990b; Business Roundtable, 1990b, 1992; Comment, 1990; Grundfest, 1990; Wharton, 1991; Gilson and Kraakman, 1991; Monks and Minow, 1991; Porter, 1992; Regan, 1992a; Roe, 1992; and Pound, 1992. Assessments of relevant research are available in Walsh and Seward, 1990; and in Hoskisson and Turk, 1990.)

Board Election

Among the leading electoral proposals were the adoption of confidential voting and cumulative voting. Both would increase the likelihood that a dissident candidate or slate would stand for election, and win. Investor activists often favored such changes, while managements were opposed. During a twenty-month period in 1989–1990, for instance, activists brought resolutions to shareholder vote over management opposition at eighty-nine firms for confidential voting, and at eighty-four firms for cumulative voting. Proposals for confidential voting drew an average 34 percent of the vote in 1990, and for cumulative voting 21 percent, insufficient to force management's hand but sufficient to persuade some companies to make the changes voluntarily (Table 2.6).

Since the voting process was subject to federal regulation, shareholder activists also pressed for regulatory reform. Several large public pension funds and the United Shareholders Association sought to make it easier for antimanagement nominees to run for the board and communicate their campaign to other shareholders (Calpers, 1989; United Shareholders Association, 1990). Companies and their associations generally opposed any electoral reform. In a 1990 survey of 130 companies listed on the New York Stock Exchange, four-fifths (81 percent) concurred that "the present structure of the board of directors provide[s] sufficient means for effective communication with institutional investors" (National Investor Relations Institute, 1990a).

When the SEC published a set of proposed proxy rule changes in 1991, companies mobilized to preserve long-standing practice. The SEC proposals included provisions that would (1) permit institutional investors to confer with one another concerning a company's governance issues without first filing a proxy statement, (2) allow "disinterested parties" (for example, the United Shareholders Association and proxy advisory groups) to communicate with shareholders without a similar filing, and (3) permit investors to acquire a company's list of its shareholders (U.S. Securities and Exchange Commission, 1991). Many corporations moved to defeat all of the proposed changes. Their Washington associations spearheaded the opposition through an ad hoc lobbying body, the Proxy Working Group. It included representatives of major corporations, the National Association of Manufacturers, the Business Roundtable, the American Society of Corporate Secretaries, and the National Investor Relations Institute. The rule changes, warned the president of one of the group's constituencies, "will enable the investor activists to target a greater number of companies in the future" (Thompson, 1991). "The Commission," he charged in a formal comment to the SEC, "is responding to aggressive ideas and initiatives of some of these same institutions [that had supported hostile takeovers] who want to dominate the process of governing America's corporations—especially the proxy process" (Hodges and Thompson, 1991). Alignment was to be moved up, but for most company managers, reform of the voting process was not to be a vehicle. The SEC, however, did relax its investor communication rules in 1992.

Board Composition

Managements were more sympathetic to reform in the composition of the board of directors. Leading proposals, most coming from outside management, included an increase in the ratio of outsiders to insiders, expansion in the number of outsiders fully independent of management, election of directors more responsive to shareholder interests, and separation of the position of board chair from that of the chief executive (in 1989 they were fused in three out of four large companies; Bacon, 1990, p. 37). Related changes included limiting the nominations and other key committees to outside directors, and equipping boards with better means, such as independent staffs and shareholder advisory committees, for exercising oversight.

Drawing a chapter from contemporary debates over national electoral reform, one analyst even found merit in setting terms for directors. A ten-year tenure limit, for instance, would force turnover in five of General Motors' directors in 1991 and six of Sears, Roebuck, ensuring at least new personnel if not a pronounced change in generic composition. The rationale: "By pruning some deadwood—and even active, constructive board members whose creative thinking days may have passed—term limits on directors could push companies to do better" (Barnard, 1991a, 1991b). While large shareholders were urged to foster charter changes, such amendments would not be received as friendly by either managements or directors.

Companies made modest movements to increase outsider presence during the 1980s (Figure 6.6). Whether the proportion of outside directors on a board generally affected a company's policies or performance remained an open question. Affirmative instances abounded: had it not been for the independent actions of outside directors on the CBS board in September 1986, the reigning CEO would probably have retained his job, the company could have remained in publishing, and entire floors of its headquarters building would not have acquired their ghostly cast by early 1987.

Systematic assessment of large cross-sections of firms, however, yielded ambiguous evidence. Various studies reported that board outsiderness modestly increased company performance, decreased performance, or engendered no change (see, for instance, Barnard, 1991b, p. 1169; Faulk and Co., 1991). Other studies report outsiderness to have had no bearing on whether a company adopted such antitakeover defenses as a poison pill, but positive bearing on the adoption of golden parachutes (Davis, 1992; Wade, O'Reilly, and Chandratat, 1990; Singh and Harianto, 1989; Cochran et al., 1985). At the least, more outsiders diminished the likelihood that shareholder suits would charge the board with breach of fiduciary responsibilities (Kesner and Johnson, 1990).

As in other areas of corporate change and policy debate, however, such evidence was generally little known by either advocates or opponents. Even had it been known, it would probably not have had more than marginal bearing on action in this area, which was largely dominated by senior management preferences. Indicative of the importance of the latter, board composition could sometimes dramatically change on the heels of management change. The board of the chemical-products company, for instance, had more inside than outside directors during the 1960s, but by 1990 and several regimes later, only two insiders remained. The most relevant technical studies appeared well after the transformation, and even after the change they were still largely unknown to those who had brought it about.

Aside from a certain openness to altering the balance of inside and outside directors, however, managements were generally reluctant to press for or accept proposed reforms. On one change favored by some investors—to include board representatives from special shareholder groups, such as large institutional holders—managements closed ranks in almost total opposition. In a 1990 survey of 130 large companies, only seven were even mildly sympathetic to a proposal to elect a member of the board that had been nominated by institutional investors (National Investor Relations Institute, 1990a).

A 1989 study of 589 large companies by the Conference Board also revealed hesitancy on the other side. Half of the companies (54 percent) already included, in their proxy statement or annual report, descriptions of procedures by which shareholders could recommend a candidate for the board. The invitation by ITT Corporation, for instance, read: "The Nominating Committee will consider recommendations for director nominees that are submitted by shareholders in writing to the Secretary of ITT" (ITT Corporation, 1991). But only 17 percent of the companies received at least one such recommendation, and on average they received only two. Just 4 percent of the companies placed a shareholder-recommended nominee in official nomination, and only a single candidate won election (Bacon, 1990, p. 16). ITT's statement drew a larger than average flow of nominees, but all were considered frivolous, the list being topped by a shareholder who proposed his spouse.

The electrical-products company would not rule out the possibility of an investor-sponsored director. But the pragmatic problems of implementation seemed intractable. Even the identification of suitable candidates seemed problematic. The investor field was viewed as so diverse that no fund manager was likely to be found who would be sufficiently catholic to play a representative role. The general counsel carried special responsibility for board governance and composition, and though sympathetic to the call for investor directors, he remained stymied on how to address it:

> I want to make sure we're at the cutting edge of this kind of thing . . . But I'm not quite there yet; I'm not quite sure because there are so many different institutional investors. There are insurance companies, and defined-benefit plans, and private corporations, and defined-contribution plans, and state plans. Everybody talks about institutional investors in a generic way, but they're very diverse . . .
>
> I'm not afraid of the institutional investors, but who would they put on the board? . . . Right now I would be willing to look at it, but I would want to make sure that it happened in the right way . . . [Institutional investors] have issues they have to sort out if they really want to be on the board.

Even more to the point was what was left off the agenda. The company worried about the pragmatic problems of selecting a suitable investor representative to serve on the board. What remained unthinkable, however, was the alternative of allowing the investment community to identify and nominate its own representatives. Shareholder-initiated nominees, it seemed, would violate an unstated management maxim of relinquishing as little control as possible.

In some instances, senior managers were moving to recompose their board, but in directions not necessarily responsive to investor concerns. The board of one of the seven companies, for example, was viewed by some insiders as populated with too many "ex's." It included three ex-CEOs and two soon-to-be ex-CEOs. With several academics, consultants, and other professionals also occupying space on the board, room remained for a single reigning CEO from outside. Some companies had a policy of requiring CEOs to offer their resignation from a board when they stepped down as active manager of their own company. The board would then have the prerogative of deciding whether to renominate them. This firm did not maintain such a policy, to the regret of one of its officers: "It's a [board] profile that I don't like, to be perfectly blunt about it. I think we have to have active CEOs at work on the board . . . After you depart the company, you lose a little bit." A newly appointed chief executive was determined to alter the cast of this board. Among his priorities was the addition of a CEO with international experience. To this end, one of his senior colleagues had researched the field, seeking to identify prospective director candidates among chief executives or soon-to-be CEOs of major European industrial firms, such as Germany's BMW. A short-list of twelve candidates had even been prepared, but here the board itself seemed to balk, not quite ready to welcome a newcomer into the club. The directors preferred candidates from among those that they already personally knew from other boards, a world that to date had included virtually no Europeans. And if European managers generally remained beyond this glass wall, investor representatives were surely outside it.

Board Compensation

Managements were most sympathetic to proposed changes in board *compensation,* the area that attracted least investor interest. Senior managers had pushed contingent compensation through their own ranks, and they were naturally drawn to similar measures for the board. The leading initiative here was to compensate directors less through a flat annual fee, as was customary, and more through stock options and kindred payments that linked directors' income to company performance.

Programs at General Electric and Exxon were typical of those adopted by many large companies: outside directors received options or direct grants of 1,500 shares per year. For senior managers, this meant working with the familiar. One advocate, a director of two companies where he had arranged to be paid in shares rather than cash, offered the simple rationale: ''As my stake in both companies grew, there was no need to remind myself that as an independent outside director, I had been elected by the shareholders to represent their interests'' (Neff, 1990). As testimony to the special appeal of this initiative to management, the practice spread substantially during the late 1980s. A survey of large companies in 1990 revealed that 25.4 percent compensated outside directors with stock options, up from 3.1 percent in 1985, the most rapid spread of any of eleven forms of director compensation (Table 7.3).

The logic according to which contingent compensation moved up the organization as well as down was illustrated in the work of a CEO-appointed task force to revise the compensation system at the electrical-products firm. Its primary recommendation was to build a ''culture of empowerment'' in which managers would think and act like owners. Compensation was seen as a convenient and powerful instrument for creating that culture. If senior managers were compensated like owners, the company might internally achieve what Kohlberg Kravis Roberts and other leveraged buyout firms had created externally. Instead of LBOs, the company sought to generate LBIs, ''leveraged buy-ins.''

The task force urged downward urgency. ''Change in compensation and measurement can have a significant impact on financial performance,'' asserted the final report in 1990, ''but only in the context of a major change in the way we manage the people resources of the company.'' Those changes were to include greater teamwork, empowerment, and communication. Headquarters and each business unit were pressed to push

Table 7.3. Percent of large companies using stock options to compensate outside directors, 1983–1990.

Year	Percent with stock options	Number of firms surveyed
1983	1.5	603
1984	1.1	633
1985	3.1	592
1986	8.2	532
1987	8.8	504
1988	15.7	458
1989	23.9	426
1990	25.4	352

Source: Korn/Ferry International (1991 and earlier years).

the changes as far down the organizational chart as they could go. The task force found little in need of change at the executive level, the area where compensation and alignment had already been extensively developed. At the board level, however, the task force saw ample room for change. Its recommendation was cut from the same cloth, formally urging that the company "consider paying directors' retainers in stock (phantom or restricted)" (company document, 1990).

Board Information

A natural corollary of increased contingency in directors' compensation was increased information with which to make informed decisions. If directors were to be more responsible for the firm's performance, they would require better data for rendering judgments. Like contingent compensation, managements found comfort in this area of reform, since it was a matter of extending up the reporting hierarchy what had already been extended down. To some investors, the problem was not so much the amount of information as the source of information, which was almost entirely from management. Concluded the chief executive of the $44 billion College Retirement Equities Fund: "I believe that the way information is obtained by most corporate boards is one of their greatest weaknesses" (Wharton, 1991, p. 138).

The size of the communication gap between shareholders and directors was evident when Calpers reported its displeasure with the performance of American Express in 1991 to its chief executive, James D. Robinson III. Calpers sent copies of its complaining letter to all members of the board of directors via American Express's New York headquarters. Recognizing none of the directors' names when the letters arrived, the headquarters mailroom considered the letter undeliverable and returned them to the sender (Dobrzynski, 1992).

As part of the transportation company's restructuring strategy, senior managers had deliberately increased the flow of information to their board. This was partly to persuade the board to support the management-initiated changes, and partly to empower the board to initiate its own changes as well. In the words of the firm's vice-president for human resources:

Even with the board now it has changed. The president takes the board meetings and presents a great deal of information to the board members about what the company is all about. That didn't happen in the old days. The board meetings were very quick, very formal, and 'Let's get the resolutions approved and be done with it.'

Now, we'll spend two hours at every one of the board meetings talking about what's going on in the marketplace, what kind of pricing things are going on, how operations are proceeding, and the finance and labor relations areas. So they get a great deal more information than they did before.

By way of example, the transportation company's director of strategic planning had completed a competitive analysis in 1990 demonstrating that the firm still faced a cost disadvantage of 6 to 16 percent in its core business areas. In contrast to past practice, management reviewed the analysis in detail with the directors. To the board it came as significant and compelling news. With the new information in hand, the board was quick to back management's resolve to "face the hard facts," initiate a new round of cost cutting, and pull funding from noncore areas.

The electrical-products company adopted a similar policy of meticulously informing its directors. According to the general counsel: "Our board is very well prepared. We hear from our board members who sit on other boards that there is no other board where they sit where they get the advance information that we do. We really prepare them. We do an agenda, we send out information in advance. If there's anything in the newspapers where they might not have heard about it, we advise them by letter or fax. We really spoon-feed them." When antitakeover legislation affecting the firm was wending its way through one state legislature, the company, via letter and board-meeting briefings, frequently updated the directors on the bill's status and the company's lobbying strategy. "They were fully advised," declared the general counsel. "We don't give any surprises."

The electrical-products management also had a policy of apprising the board of major decisions it was about to take. To facilitate the process, the company introduced, prior to the regular board meeting, a separate executive session in which the chief executive involved the directors in the firm's immediate strategic issues. The company's three-year strategic plan was annually reviewed with the directors, and the operations of the company's fifteen business units were discussed in detail on a rotating basis every third year. The directors became well informed, even if they were still not fully invited to apply the information. "We don't ask them to make the decision," said the general counsel, "but they're aware of it. They understand what we're going to be buying, what we're selling, why we're doing it. Looking at the three-year plan—they have complete knowledge of what's going on."

Moving Alignment Out

Remolding managerial forms and the accompanying culture required enormous energy. It was also markedly risky, but when it seemed to work, its authors felt the pride of invention. Some felt a zealousness of spirit as well. They were ready to confess their formerly misguided ways. And they were ready to tell the world about their new organizational designs. Conversion was the mother of the proselyte.

Among the confessional themes were an admittedly erroneous lack of respect for the depth of shareholder' grievances and an unresponsiveness to them. Daniel Tellep, the Lockheed chief executive who successfully resisted the bitter proxy fight in which a near majority of shareholders had sided with NL Industries, took his place among the chastened: "We sailed into that 1990 proxy contest naively thinking we were in harmony with the majority of our shareholders," he said. "During the six-week proxy contest, we learned more about our institutional shareholders than we had in the previous 10 years . . . We at Lockheed intend to continue on the path of interaction and dialogue as a route to genuine progress on issues of mutual concern. I think the institutions learned from our proxy experience. I know Lockheed did" (Tellep, 1991, pp. 41–43). If fellow managers were not also ready to recognize their errant ways, read the confessional, similar fates could lie in store.

Now on a new path, the managerial converts were sometimes ready to convert other institutions. Moreover, though the organizational innovations were developed in the name of improved performance for company shareholders, some innovations were viewed as generically applicable to any large organization, public or nonprofit, with or without shareholders.

Company efforts to move alignment out, not just up, can be seen in one executive's advice to the United Way. The United Way was the nation's premier community-based, federated fund-driving effort. With chapters in virtually all major American metropolitan areas, the United Way provided support for thousands of nonprofit social service agencies throughout the country. Corporate opinion loomed large, since corporate funding was large. Approximately three-quarters of the United Way's funds were raised through voluntary contributions from companies and their employees. The corporate advice-giving occasion was a 1991 national conference of United Way volunteer leaders. The proselytizer was the chief executive of a firm that was then well into a round of organizational tightening and redirection.

John Akers, the chief executive of IBM, sought to "sell" the volunteers an "agenda for change." The course and rationale were drawn from his own restructuring experience. Beginning in 1986, IBM had redeployed more than 15,000 of its 237,000 employees into new positions, moving many from engineering and technical positions into customer sales and service; had decentralized its administrative structure, granting many units more autonomy; and had shed some 30,000 employees through voluntary severance incentives. With decision-making responsibility more fully vested in the separate business units, IBM's "fundamental redefinition" of itself by 1991 was intended to transform headquarters into a kind of holding company for the largely autonomous operating units (Markoff, 1991; Carroll, 1991; Cohen, 1992). Akers proposed five leading organizational recommendations for the United Way, modeled explicitly on changes recently instituted at IBM (Akers, 1991a, pp. 7–11):

Incentive management. An incentive system should be adopted, urged IBM's chief executive, that allocates national funds to "top performing individual United Ways."

Customer focus. Akers recommended an extension of donor choice in which individual givers, the United Way's "customers," exercised greater influence on the use of their gifts. "Today the IBM company is trying increasingly to become 'driven by the market' . . . I think exactly the same thing applies to United Way."

Cost reduction. Budget tightening was essential. "Over the last five years we have reduced the population of IBM by 50,000 people," "eliminated over 70,000 staff positions," "cut 8,000 managerial jobs," and "removed as many as three layers of management." Though not explicitly expected to make layoffs, United Way was expected to "hold the line on its budget" and "implement efficiency measures at the local level."

Quality improvement. Service delivery should be enhanced, Akers recommended. "If American business is working hard to improve the quality of its processes and its products and its support of customers, then why not the United Way?"

Committed volunteers. The United Way's volunteer ranks needed expansion. "Half of the 200,000 employees we have in the United States volunteer up to five hours a week, and I'm very confident that we can increase that percentage. As a corporation, every year we're adding to our volunteer activities," and so too could the United Way.

It seemed that the IBM way would be a good model for the United Way, and the for-profit sector was not reluctant to so inform the nonprofit sector. When a spending scandal forced the United Way's president to resign in 1992, he was replaced by an IBM executive.

IBM's chief executive proffered similar advice to public education. "Business employees are constantly measured, trained and retrained," Akers argued, "and it makes no sense to exempt education from this worthy principle" (Akers, 1991b). Accordingly, schools should adopt higher standards of accountability, create stronger means of assessment, face greater market competition, and give greater authority to teachers and principals (Akers, 1991b). Atlantic Richfield, RJR Nabisco, and Honeywell joined in the advice giving, coupling their grant making with explicit efforts to improve school management (Bailey, 1992).

More commonly, however, the consequences of alignment were felt not so much through explicit exhortation, but more through implicit impact on other organizations that worked with, depended upon, or supplied the restructured firms. This was probably nowhere more evident than in the employment market for new managers and professionals seeking to enter careers in large firms. As managers acquired more responsibility, accountability, and flexibility, a premium was placed on the capacities of entry-level managers to work in settings requiring greater self-direction and adaptability.

Colleges and universities, the source of the next generation of managers, received an array of market signals to this effect from recruiters. Research studies focusing on industrial change further articulated the signals. A university-based commission on productivity in manufacturing, for instance, concluded in 1989 that educational programs engendering greater breadth in skills and work flexibility were required to service emerging industrial forms (Dertouzos et al., 1989). Another late-1980s investigation found widespread company interest in hiring broadly educated, though also practically oriented, college graduates (Useem, 1989).

Yet the recruitment messages stemming from this corporate change registered partially at best on educational providers. Colleges and universities still tended to follow their own organizational logics. Even business schools, more attuned than most to the changing employment market for managers and professionals, heard the message imperfectly. A study of company managers and management-school faculty and administrators during the mid-1980s, for example, revealed widespread campus misperceptions of company recruiting priorities. The company managers were asked whether their firm preferred to recruit newly graduated business majors who (a) were well prepared to perform on the first job but whose preparation for major responsibilities later on was uncertain, or (b) were well prepared for later leadership but whose preparedness for the first job was uncertain. Two out of three company managers reported that their organizations preferred to recruit business graduates with the second combination of qualities. But some two-thirds of the business-school faculty and administrators believed that companies were more likely to seek the first combination (Porter and McKibbin, 1988, pp. 106–109).

Through managerial exhortation and market process, the alignment agenda went beyond company boundaries, though the message was not always well heeded. Still, nonprofit organizations and public institutions were pressed to change, and since their prosperities were so often intertwined with corporate generosity, the pressures could not be entirely ignored. If companies increasingly insisted that recipients of their donations apply more discipline to their own organizations, recipients were in a weakened position to say no. Adding teeth to its calls for managerial reform in the nonprofit sector, for instance, IBM initiated a $24-million grant program in 1991 in which gifts to colleges and universities were tied to demonstrated efforts to improve their own management. The program was intended, the company announced, to "encourage" a college or university to "apply TQM [total quality management] to the operation of the institution itself and to propagate TQM to other colleges and universities." If responsive to the call, institutions could receive as much as $3 million in cash and equipment. "Responsiveness" was defined by IBM to include a commitment to implement TQM concepts in areas ranging from finance and admissions to instruction and research "to achieve improvements in customer satisfaction" (International Business Machines, 1991).

IBM also joined forces with American Express, Ford Motor Company, Motorola, Procter and Gamble, and Xerox to urge that all colleges and universities tighten their organization. In an open letter to higher education, chief executives of the six companies asserted that "companies and institutions of higher education *must* accelerate the application of total quality management on our campuses if our education system and economy are to maintain and enhance global positions" (Robinson et al., 1991). If these companies could restructure and streamline their own operations, then so too could other organizations.

Conclusion

The organizational logic of ownership-disciplined alignment offered seemingly straightforward guidance. The governance structure, like all parts of the corporation, came under scrutiny that sought to determine if its decisions and design were consistent with investor interests. If not, the decision criteria and design arrangements were open to reconfiguration.

Unlike the rest of the firm, however, the board occupied uniquely high ground. All other units reported to top management, and formal and informal control were never at issue, since they displayed only minor divergence. But in the case of the board, they diverged far more. Indeed, they were nearly inverse, with directors holding formal authority over managers and managers exercising informal control over directors. Management had long ago taken de facto control of the board, and while seeking better alignment of its governing body, management was not about to abdicate effective control, even if organizational theory and shareholder activists said it should.

As a result, most of the governance changes advocated or resisted by management were inversely correlated with those advocated or resisted by major investors. Investors wanted an open electoral process; managers preferred an incentivized compensation scheme. Investors pressed for regulatory and governance reform giving dissident nominees a better chance; managers pressed for more stock and information in the hands of directors. Investors would not be mollified by better-compensated and better-informed directors; managers would be horrified by the prospect of openly elected directors. Only on the underlying premises did the contending parties find common ground. Both shared the organizational theorist's diagnosis: the key to control of the company was control of the board.

As a venue if not the fulcrum for the continuing struggle over company control, corporate governance in the early 1990s remained a little-explored frontier. Tactical skirmishes over specific antitakeover provisions slowly gave way to strategic struggles over general governance. Conflicts over poison pills and opt-out provisions lost intensity. In their place were intensified conflicts over who served on the board, how they got there, and what authority they wielded over management on behalf of shareholders.

To the extent that directors acquired more of an upper hand, however, an old set of problems would reappear in new guise. Just as management found it difficult to know precisely what its diverse shareholder base wanted from the company, newly empowered directors would face the same difficulty. And they would face it with a smaller toolbox. With no full-time staff, no investor relations specialists, and no time to meet with shareholders, directors would not necessarily be much better at representing shareholder interests than management. A subsequent frontier for organizational change was thus likely to be the enhancement of communication and control between empowered directors and their ultimate source of empowerment.

EIGHT

The Paradoxes of
Management and Ownership

The senior managers I interviewed presided over multi-billion-dollar enterprises. At their headquarters, the signposts of authority were everywhere. Lavish offices, ready helipads, and tight security announced that the executive suites must be centers of great power.

The deliberately constructed ambience of authority was not misleading. It was here that the careers and security of thousands of employees would be determined. It was here that local communities would have their fates decided, with the opening or closing of a plant. It was here that thousands of investors would see their wealth accumulate, or maybe dissipate. The lifetime fortunes of hundreds of thousands individuals depended on the foresight of just several individuals who daily reported to work in the executive suite. Within such offices, those presiding over a $10-billion company would spend an average $40 million per day. With the stakes so vast, wrong decisions could be catastrophic, right decisions historic.

Yet omnipotence was rarely felt to be a characteristic of the executive suite. Instead, senior managers complained of a host of limitations on their powers. They found they could do little to bolster a market in long-term decline. They found it difficult to unfreeze staffing patterns frozen by decades of experience. And they found they were captives of the system in which they had succeeded. Once in power, they sometimes felt they could do little more than play the hand already dealt.

Such perceptions confirm an analysis by Jeffrey Pfeffer (1978, 1981b) of the limitations on organizational leadership. Top-management actions in most firms, he reasoned, were highly constrained by market and organizational forces. The rise and fall of general economic conditions, the growth or decline of specific economic sectors, and even a company's size were more determining of company earnings than were the people who passed through the executive suite. In empirical confirmation of the argument, other analysts found that variations in company earnings were, as predicted, far more a product of those conditions than turnover in the chief executiveship (Lieberson and O'Connor, 1972; Weiner and Mahoney, 1981; Thomas, 1988).

Given the context of such perceptions and analyses, however, three apparent paradoxes in the relationship between owners and managers emerged in the course of this study. The seeming contradictions pointed to an ironic implication of ownership-disciplined alignment for corporate leadership: management power over the work process decreased as stockholder power over the management process increased.

The Paradox of Executive Power

If the chief executive is constrained by the firm's market and history, the first paradox emanated from the starkly contrary perceptions by senior managers who worked closely with the chief executive. In the seven companies studied, most senior managers had weekly contact with the CEO, and many spoke with him daily. They had witnessed him in action in board meetings, management committees, strategic reviews, and crisis moments. They had seen him worry about new products, fret on takeover rumors, and agonize over senior appointments. Despite this extensive working contact, none of his colleagues could confirm anything even approaching the image of a CEO trapped by office traditions and market trends. On the contrary, the image was of organizational dominance, a commanding presence, a unique crafting of the company's destiny. This assessment did not come from the awe-struck. It came from seasoned senior managers who themselves had long worked in the corridors of power. In private they often found fault with the CEO's style and actions. But they never conveyed disrespect in public or private for the power he wielded.

At the chemical-products company, the chief executive had been in office for a number of years. His appointment had capped a long climb through the firm's various divisions, and he knew its people and products intimately. To those at a distance, he sometimes loomed larger than life. Even among those with whom he worked every day, his authority was considered extraordinary. In the words of one who had daily contact, the vice-president for strategic planning: "Everything I'm describing here is heavily influenced by the [CEO's] style, personality, and desire. He's a born-again analyst. He *loves* it, absolutely enjoys it personally. At the strategy board meetings that are held quarterly, . . . it's really a direct dialogue between the manager and the chief who has done his home-work . . . He is strategically and tactically involved with them from quarter to quarter." Another senior associate, the chief financial officer, underscored this: "I frankly am astounded at how much influence the chief executive has . . . There is absolutely no question that the tone is totally set by the CEO. His personality is what the company is." At the special-equipment company, the CEO's style was more collegial, less commanding, and he had built a strong senior management team. But even the power of the team was seen as the CEO's broader incarnation, an extension of his will. When asked to identify the factors accounting for the company's lean and decentralized operating style (recall that headquarters staff had been reduced from 300 to thirty), the CEO's colleagues pointed to him and his team, not to market trends and certainly not to tradition. Even discounting for the occasional personification of inanimate forces, the commentary's consistency and fixity here and at the other companies lent the diagnosis a compelling quality.

The chief executives faced important constraints, but the latitude within seemed great. And even the constraints themselves did not always prove immutable. Though six of seven CEOs were products of their company systems, and steeped in their hoary ways, all nonetheless mustered the strength to break with many of the traditions. They could and did shed faltering divisions, dismiss associates, confront unions, relinquish author-ity, and otherwise shatter long-standing shibboleths. Chief executives would find it difficult to have more influence on the bottom line than did the trends of the markets in which they worked. But in organizing the work flow within the firm, their powers loomed large to all who received a paycheck.

The power of chief executives to affect organizational decisions, as reported by corporate denizens, is thus not inconsistent with their relative weakness in shaping overall performance, as reported by academic re-searchers (Hambrick, 1988). Marginal differences loom large at the micro level. Just as politicians often attribute great power to newspaper editors, even though their editorials have little macro influence on electoral prefer-ences, managers ascribe great power to chief executives, even though their actions have little macro impact on industry demand. But both are right, for editors and executives do have an effect on the smaller decisions, and these are the only decisions typically on the table.

The Paradox of Preemptive Executive Action

Top management's independent capacity to shape events was starkly evident in the restructuring exercise. But herein lay the second paradox: two of the firms, the electrical-products and the special-machinery companies, had initiated their ownership-disciplined actions in the early 1980s, well before the "market for corporate control" came to resemble an amalgam of a Chicago futures exchange and a Vermont town meeting. These firms had not been pressed by takeover threats or investor revolts, for none had yet occurred.

Despite the absence of external demands, however, the senior managements had launched their companies on profound reshapings. They were undertaken in the name of enhanced shareholder wealth long before stockholders were clamoring for such. Other companies would come to similar conclusions in response to rising takeover and investor pressures. But the actions of two of the firms were clearly preemptive. They were initiated in part to avert shareholder unrest, but above all because top management had decided it was simply the right action to take.

At the electrical-products company, several strategic planners had first introduced the concept of managing for shareholder value into the company in 1981. Drawing on ideas gleaned from conferences and consultants, these "idea champions" initially circulated their notion informally among the senior ranks. The planners recognized that the concept, a largely untested theory, was fraught with uncertain implications for company operations. Still, it found fertile ground, for the company had long professed (though until then modestly implemented) the principles of decentralization. The company's analytic bent was drawn in any case to an encompassing framework. "This was like Newton's second law," recalled the chief architect of the program. It offered a compelling logic, a comprehensive management ideology. A sense emerged among the strategists that "you have to be crazy not to follow it."

Yet it remained for top management to embrace and implement the concept. The conditions proved auspicious: a relatively new chief executive was at the same moment searching for a vehicle to promote a program of change to improve earnings. When briefed on the new concept, the CEO reportedly snapped, "That's it, let's do it." Shortly thereafter he assembled the company's top 300 managers, all of whom carried significant profit-and-loss responsibilities, for a two-day development seminar. With a presentation entitled "The Stock Market is Rational," the company's chief financial officer, already a convert, urged the gathered managers to assess their strategic options with a new yardstick: the creation of the highest stock market value for the company.

With the chief executive and chief financial officers fully behind the concept and operating managers informed about it, headquarters staff moved to implement it. The staff revised everything from accounting procedures and balance sheets to compensation schemes and divisional authority in the process. In recognition of the defining power of language, a new term was coined to label the concept. In the company's special lexicon, the term came to define both the company's generic objectives and its decision-making criteria. The term was used to announce what the company stood for, and it was used to guide strategic planning to get there.

The special-machinery company followed much the same course. Its mini-revolution also came during the early 1980s, pushed by the chief executive before he had seen value-based planning in operation elsewhere. The other five companies commenced their actions later, though by the late 1980s all programs were in full swing. When IBM, General Motors, and other major companies announced similar changes in the early 1990s, ample precedent was by then available so that firms could safely embrace the main ideas. IBM, for instance, announced in 1991 that authority was being devolved to operating divisions and that headquarters was being reduced to the status of a holding company (Carroll, 1991). By then, such actions had already been thoroughly field-tested, as many companies, including those studied here, had been operating in this way for years.

Though much of the restructuring described in this account was driven by the heightened takeover and investor pressures of the latter half of the 1980s and the early 1990s, some of it preceded the mobilization. Whether or not they had foreseen what was to come, two company managements had preemptively acted. They had broken with one of the greatest conventions of all, the short-term horizon.

The Paradox of Internal Ownership

The first paradox pointed to the inconsistency between the relative power-lessness sometimes attributed to top management and the widely shared belief among corporate denizens that their chief executive wielded extraordinary power. In at least the area of organizational redesign, the denizens were right. It was the committed CEO who had initiated the change. To be sure, it was not an "executive" action taken by fiat, for other factors were clearly catalytic. But it was an action that belied any image of a CEO constrained by circumstances.

Oddly, however, the catalytic factors for several of the early-acting companies did not include exceptional shareholder pressure. That was the irony of the second paradox: management launched the ownership alignment before the owners themselves were demanding it. Together, these developments led to a third paradox: executive implementation of the ownership-disciplined organizational measures had the effect of diminishing the power of the executive.

The organizational logic of focusing on shareholder value had pushed decision-making authority down the hierarchy. Just as the Protestant ethic shaped early capitalist institutions, the alignment ethic contained implications that were to be fully revealed only in practice. One of the most important, that of managerial ownership, was first manifest in the expansion of performance-based compensation focused on measures of shareholder return. But the concept also meant that divisional and unit managers should come to feel and act like owners themselves. This would be a simple but appealing means of ensuring that managerial and shareholder interests were aligned. Its elegance lay in the fact that it required minimal administrative oversight. If the right people were selected to manage, and if they were structurally conditioned to act like genuine owners rather than their imperfect agents, headquarters should have less to do and shareholders more to show.

Because of its early start on restructuring, the electrical-products company had moved farther than any on this front. Others had not reached as deeply into their operations and may never do so, but the experience of the electrical-products firm illustrates how far the concept's logic can be carried. When shareholder-value planning was first introduced in the early 1980s, the concept had included an emphasis on "empowerment." By 1989, and several CEOs later, the concept had evolved to "ownership."

The company was even toying with the idea of taking the ownership concept literally. Borrowing a chapter from the strategy of leveraged buyouts, strategic planners were examining whether business units could be put through a "leveraged buy-in" (LBI). Here, a business unit's top five to twenty managers would be invited to own up to 10 percent of its assets. If their stewardship proved successful, they could retire with far more personal wealth that their salaries would have ever permitted. Conversely, if their decisions proved inept, they could also lose everything. In short, they would face the same risks and gains as owner-entrepreneurs, the structural equivalence of full ownership. The holding system of Kohlberg Kravis Roberts was even studied with an eye to replicating its scheme of financial oversight without administrative interference.

At a 1990 meeting of top management, company planners proposed key recommendations for pushing further down the same road. One course was to more deliberately build a culture in which managers would come to function like owners. A second was to adjust the compensation system to more precisely enforce the feeling of ownership, with each business unit given almost complete latitude to develop its own mix of specific criteria. Beyond this, planners stressed the long march downward. As the director of strategic planning at the electrical-products company said, "We can change the compensation piece and that will help matters—but only if connected to an empowerment culture where people see that their actions influence the business, [that] they actually can act as owners, and when they do act as owners, it makes a difference." To the heads of the operating units, the message was to apply the concepts within: "Inside the business unit, you should work very aggressively on an empowerment culture, empowerment in the sense of getting people to think and act like owners. And then you should also address your compensation system accordingly." Empowerment should be taken "all the way down to the shop floor, the empowerment of the work area. It really is a unique behavioral phenomenon . . . [In] doing so, you really take advantage of the capability, the creativeness, the innovativeness of a large group of people. You unleash all that power . . . When the people believe that they are owning their job, that they own the results, that they own the whatever, . . . they actually want to come to work . . . With the ownership thing, you both unleash the power and you heighten the motivation. My god, it's almost like a geometric outcome." For those employees who survive the accompanying downsizing, the world of work should be more appealing: "To get from point A to point B, where point A is the given structures that are hierarchical and bureaucratic and point B is a totally empowered workforce, you are going to have a collapsing of levels and an expansion of spans of control, and you have to reduce the numbers of managers, unfortunately. But when you do get [to point B], those managers are going to be having a lot of fun, they are operating in a different mode ... There has got to be less stress on an individual in an empowered world than an unempowered world.''

Though not entirely zero-sum, extending ownership down meant retracting control from the top. "When you empower somebody, somebody else is losing,'' observed one senior manager. "If some person goes up in power, somebody else goes down.'' In the name of shareholder value, senior managers willingly relinquished the power, though some, as noted in Chapter 3, found it easier to do so in words than behavior. Still, they recognized the trade-off of less control for better results. And of course they intensified financial control by focusing more on business-unit performance and caring less how their managers achieved it.

The chief executives had broken an iron cage of organizational tradition. Yet in the very process of exercising their power to reshape and revitalize, they had diminished that power. As ownership was extended downward, less was retained upward.

In 1991 the Soviet president, Mikhail Gorbachev, made his office superfluous by empowering the Soviet republics. Some company managements moved in much the same direction. For them, however, there would be no lowering of the flag, no final dissolution. Corporate headquarters never quite so fully unleashed its business units. It would remain the arbiter, the banker, the protector of shareholder interests. But autocratic bosses and centralized bureaucracies were less the dominating model. Although they were still more prevalent than sometimes admitted, their perpetuation had become a cause for chagrin.

Ideology for Action

Aspects of these organizational changes had appeared before, driven by factors only marginally related to alignment concerns. The decentralization of decision making and the empowerment of employees, for example, have been introduced over many decades for many reasons, ranging from the stimulation of worker productivity to the inspiration of product innovation (Levine and Tyson, 1990; Kanter, 1983). Now these concepts were introduced because they were seen as facilitating improved company performance for owners, whatever the value for productivity, innovation, or any other purpose. Similarly, executive salaries had been tied to firm performance, and performance-based compensation is known to affect later performance (Ehrenberg, 1990; Abowd, 1990). Now, however, the criteria for executive performance were more explicitly tied to shareholder value, more extensively applied to the compensation package, and more widely extended to managers.

Business leaders had long made reference to shareholder sovereignty, and such rhetoric was hardly new. Since the rise of the joint-stock company, ownership supremacy had been one of the enduring mantras of corporate life, a preeminent tenet of American capitalism. Less commonly, however, did executives seek to comprehend and act on the tenet. Nodding reference, and sometimes deference, was made to the demons of Wall Street. But this was usually near the outer edge of specific managerial attention. As seen from the executive suite, the absence of detailed concern was as it should be. Fractures between managerial and shareholder interests were believed to be hairline at most.

With the collective mobilization of shareholders, investor interests could no longer be taken for granted. Nor were they still conceived as virtually synonymous with managerial preferences. A belief emerged that understanding the differences required direct dialogue with, and careful reading of, owners' concerns. Equally important was a belief that conflicts stemming from diverging interests should be resolved more often in favor of owners, less often in favor of managers. A third belief was that the role of managers should be transformed as well. Though they had been imperfect investors' agents in the past, senior managers were now to become more responsive to their principals. In the framing of the chief financial officer for the special-equipment company, they were to become more genuine agents: "We work for the shareholders. We think we can increase stock value by increasing our earnings. And earnings over a long period of time ought to drive stock price." To this end, there would be no better discipline than to transform the managers into owners, or at least their structural equivalent.

Underpinning and sustaining these managerial beliefs was the conviction that the varied alignment actions significantly contributed to shareholder return. If the actions had not been taken, it was generally believed, investors would have less to show for their holdings. Like many convictions, this assessment was rooted as much in shared perception as in empirical foundation. Despite the lack of an explicitly factual basis, or perhaps because of its absence, the conviction became a kind of doctrine, an abiding confidence that what was being done was the right thing to have done.

This managerial mindset was reinforced by plausible impact evidence. But it was little more than plausible. Establishing strict cause-and-effect relations was beyond what most managers considered either necessary or within their means to produce. Impressionistic assessments, however, were both necessary and widely generated. Confirming stories and myths, the usual vehicles of corporate cultures, furnished compelling testimony.

Since the electrical-products company had initiated its emphasis on shareholder value earlier than most, managers had time to build a grounded confidence not only in the intrinsic virtues but also in the impact on firm performance. The pervasiveness of the belief was evident in managerial conceptions of executive compensation at the electrical-products company. When senior managers were asked if the new compensation system was working as intended, they expressed great conviction, sometimes pointing to the company's strong performance, at other times to line managers who now worked more intensively and better understood company objectives.

Never questioned was the confounding influence of a host of other potentially causative factors. During one visit to the company, for example, I met with seven senior managers to report preliminary results from the present study. I alluded to several recently published multivariate analyses of large sets of firms that demonstrated the impact of contingent compensation on company performance, net of other factors. On learning of the research, two of the managers who had been centrally involved in redesigning the compensation system immediately sought copies of the journal articles. As they had hoped, the research findings confirmed the performance consequences of what they were doing. Yet the research had not been necessary for them to initiate the changes, nor was it now needed to sustain them.

Still, though the extent to which actions taken in the name of investors actually enhanced shareholder value was beyond rigorous proof, companies were not shy about asserting causality. Illustrating the tenor of the typical claim was an appraisal by the chief operating officer of the electrical-products company at a 1988 meeting of the firm's top management: "Shareholder value is the one quantitative measure of success that applies to *all* publicly owned businesses. Applying *value* concepts encourages management discipline and the making of sometimes painful decisions that might not otherwise occur . . . The proof is in the experience: Until the third quarter of 1987 and October 19, we outperformed all of the publicly held companies on the market.''

Similar causal claims appear in a document circulated among the electrical-product company's top planning circles in 1991. Reproduced in Figure 8.1 (slightly modified to conceal the company's identity), the graph pointedly showed that the introduction of the shareholder-value program was followed by a period in which the company's total shareholder return (stock price plus dividends) rose sharply to outperform that of the Standard and Poor's 500. The stock market crash of October 19, 1987, brought that period to a close, but the shareholder-value program was widely credited for the company's resurgence during the mid-1980s. Whether true or not, this was believed to be so.

Taken together, the several beliefs constituted a world view, a general guide to action whatever the specific decision. As a systemic way of viewing the company, the belief system was akin to what Reinhard Bendix

Index of total shareholder return,
with 1970 return set at 100,
relative to Standard and Poor's 500

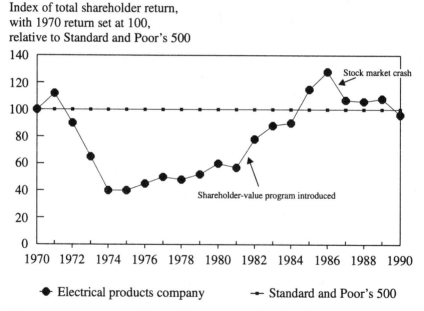

Figure 8.1. Introduction of shareholder program and stock performance of electrical-products firm, 1970–1990. (Source: Company records, 1991.)

(1963) would class as "managerial ideologies." These comprehensive sets of beliefs can seem natural and even eternal to their adherents. Yet they are historically conditioned, decisively shaped by an era's events and the organizational constraints confronting managers. The historical variant described here might be termed the managerial ideology of shareholder value, a natural reflection of the investor power that emerged during the 1980s. The ideology provided a guide for better managing the firm's relations with its shareholders, increasingly a "strategic contingency" for many companies.

Distinctive managerial ideologies dominated earlier eras, as shown in the analysis of Neil Fligstein (1990). Their rise and fall paralleled the rise and fall of other strategic contingencies. The formation of large-scale industrial enterprise in the early part of the century had given rise to an overarching stress on manufacturing. Its mastery was key to company prosperity and career mobility. In later decades, as many manufacturing issues were successfully resolved, managerial attention turned first to market share, bringing sales and marketing ideologies to the fore. Then, Fligstein demonstrates, managerial focus turned to growth and profits, and financial ideologies took hold. These financial conceptions, Fligstein and Markowitz (1992) report, moved companies during the early 1980s toward a host of financial restructurings, such as stock repurchases and divestitures. Eventually, as the present analysis suggests, an ideology of shareholder value came to coexist with them all.

Managerial Action and Short-Term Gain

The ideology of shareholder value meant that top management was able to improve company wealth in the near term through specific actions. When investors pressed for managements to act, they assumed their decisions would make a difference. When they pressed for managements to change, they made a similar assumption. Managers of course agreed: their major actions would, they assumed, have significant bearing on shareholder return.

It is instructive to examine the research literature on whether discrete management actions and, occasionally, management turnovers could have immediate impact on stock price, a major component of shareholder value. Such studies generally focused on "abnormal returns," movements in a stock's price that departed from what would have otherwise been expected, given the company's recent share price history and that of the industry and stock market at a whole. Many investigators concentrated on periods of some thirty to forty trading days before and after an announced change, though some focused on just one or two days and some well beyond forty. The appropriate period depended in part on the type of company: larger firms, for instance, generated longer market reactions to their earnings announcements (Defeo, 1986).

Market response to a General Motors action in early 1992 illustrates the nearly instantaneous reaction that can come on the heels of a company action. Moved by a $4.45 billion corporate loss in 1991, the outside directors of General Motors intervened in unusual fashion. They did not dismiss the chief executive, Robert Stempel, who had assumed the post just twenty months earlier, but their actions were the next closest thing: they removed Stempel from chair of the board's powerful executive committee; they demoted his president and his chief financial officer, both long-time allies; and they installed a chief operating officer. (In late 1992 they would finally force Stempel's resignation as well.) Since several large institutional investors had been pressing for board action to stanch the losses, the board's action should have been expected to lift the share price. Reaction by the trustee of the New York State and Local Retirement Systems, a public pension with large GM holdings, was symptomatic of how many investors felt: "It's like opening a window and letting in fresh air" (Regan, 1992b). The day after the board's announcement, a day on which the Dow Jones Industrial Average dropped by sixty-two points, GM stock rose by 3.4 percent (Treece, 1992; White and Ingrassia, 1992; Levin, 1992a, 1992b; Smith and White, 1992; Lohr, 1992).

Senior managers at the seven focal companies were generally well aware of their own stock movements, and they reported an intuitive feel for how their own actions had affected prices in the past. They expressed little if any awareness, however, of any of the many academic studies on the subject. Still, an examination of the studies is useful, since their findings offer guidance on the extent to which management and board actions could improve a company's market worth. Most of the research did not directly address shareholder value. Investigations typically focused on a single component, with neither dividends nor longer-term effects appearing in most analyses. The studies are nonetheless instructive, for they confirm that certain company actions do make a short-term difference in a company's market valuation.

Much of the research focuses on five areas of management and board discretion: human-resource policies, mergers and acquisitions, organizational design, top-management turnover, and company governance. Small but measurable changes in a firm's share price were reported by many of the more recent studies, our focus here (references to earlier studies can generally be found in the works cited, and assessments of other research can be found in Black, 1992b).

Human-resource policies. Both collective bargaining and failure to reach agreement can have an impact on stock price. In a study of two-tier wage agreements negotiated during the early 1980s, Thomas and Kleiner (1992) found that these innovative provisions, in which new hires were compensated at a lower rate than existing employees for essentially the same work, led to above-average returns of 2 to 4 percent during a ten- to twelve-week period following their announcement. Conversely, failure to reach agreement and an ensuing strike can have a negative impact on investor attitudes. In an analysis of strike data for 1962–1982, Becker and Olson (1986) report below-average returns of about 4 percent, mostly coming in the wake of the strike rather than in anticipation of it. Other management actions affecting large numbers of employees have no consistent effects on stock prices, according to a study by Abowd, Milkovich, and Hannon (1990) of nearly 650 such announcements by 256 companies in 1980 and 1987. Focusing on changes in compensation, staffing, plant closings, and related events significant enough to warrant *Wall Street Journal* coverage, they found abnormally high price swings in the immediate aftermath of plant shutdowns and permanent staff reductions, but neither positive nor negative net effects. However, other research reveals positive and negative market reactions to company layoffs depending on the context. In a study of 194 announced layoffs by large firms during the period 1979 to 1987, Worrell, Davidson, and Sharma (1991) report negative effects when the reductions are attributed to financial reasons but positive effects when they are attributed to restructuring.

Mergers and acquisitions. Abnormal returns following mergers and acquisitions drew extensive research attention. Studies often found positive abnormal impacts on the stock of acquisition targets, smaller or mixed impacts on acquirers, and modestly negative or no impacts on unsuccessful bidders. Effects were contingent on such factors as the type of takeover and the period in which it was executed: acquirers gained more from tender offers than from mergers, for example, and they gained more during the 1960s than the 1980s (Jensen and Ruback, 1983; Jarrell, Brickley, and Netter, 1988; Bradley, Desai, and Kim, 1988).

Organizational redesign. Significant organizational changes can have a bearing as well. Koh and Venkatraman (1991) examined 175 joint ventures launched by 239 firms in the information technology sector between 1972 and 1986. They reported that when such ventures were focused on the same products and markets as their parents, abnormal returns were positive by some 1 percent on two days surrounding the joint-venture announcement. But the results also contained a cautionary twist: joint ventures that focused on new products and new markets unrelated to those of the parents generated no abnormal returns, indicating that managerial actions in even a highly circumscribed area such as joint venturing may make a difference under only restricted conditions. This study also confirmed an important but rarely tested assumption that abnormal returns forecasted future performance reasonably well: a strong correlation (0.39) was found between the immediate movement in share price and later assessments of the joint ventures' successes by senior managers who oversaw them. Related studies report positive market reactions to new research and development projects, major capital expenditures, and joint ventures (Woodridge and Snow, 1990), and positive reactions to increased company focus on fewer lines of business (Comment and Jarrell, 1992).

Top-management turnover. Changes in the executive suite can affect short-term movements in stock prices as well, but again only under specific conditions. Examining turnover in the positions of president and chairman among some 2,500 companies listed on the New York and American Stock Exchanges in 1978 and 1979, Reinganum (1985) found a positive impact during a five-day trading period at the time of the announcement. If an outsider was named as a replacement, positive abnormal returns averaged more than 1.4 percent, whereas an internal replacement led to virtually no change. Detailed study of the results, however, revealed that positive effects were largely confined to smaller firms. In a study of 477 events of CEO succession at large companies from 1971 to 1985, however, Lubatkin and his associates (1989) found positive effects as high as 7 percent when a well-performing company appointed a new chief executive from the outside. And Friedman and Singh (1989), in a late-1980s analysis of the last CEO succession at 235 large companies, reported favorable market reactions to board-initiated replacements of CEOs, though primarily when presuccession company performance had been poor.

Company governance. As should be expected from the earlier discussions of takeover defenses (Chapters 2 and 5), company actions to make hostile acquisition more difficult could also make stockholders more hostile. Researchers reported negative abnormal returns when companies adopted poison pills (Ryngaert, 1988; Malatesta and Walkling, 1988), reduced or eliminated cumulative voting (Bhagat and Brickley, 1984), or issued special classes or blocks of stock which served to deter unwanted takeovers (Partch, 1987; Dann and DeAngelo, 1988; Jensen and Warner, 1988). Similarly, companies subjected to protection under new state anti-takeover statutes experienced abnormal price declines (Jarrell, Brickley, and Netter, 1988). And, conversely, companies that appointed a new outside director, presumably lessening the likelihood of management entrenchment, experienced abnormal price increases (Rosenstein and Wyatt, 1990).

Management behavior during crisis response also shaped shareholder reactions. In the aftermath of accidents, such as Union Carbide's 1984 chemical disaster at Bhopal, India, and scandals, such as the discovery of Lockheed's 1975 bribery payments abroad, some managements reacted defensively, others with accommodation. Marcus and Goodman (1991), drawing on fifteen major accidents, scandals, and related incidents between 1969 and 1984, found negative shareholder reactions when managements were accommodating after accidents but positive responses when they were accommodating after scandals.

These are the knowns. When a company took such actions, its value to its shareholders was enhanced—or damaged, in the case of strikes and takeover defenses—at least for the moment. Though academic studies rarely entered into such decisions, they corroborated what managers, and occasionally directors, believed from their own less systematic but more experienced appraisals.

The unknowns, however, overshadowed the knowns. Neither research investigations nor practical experience could confirm that comprehensive company programs to enhance a company's worth to its owners would actually do so. When firms decentralized operations, reduced headquarters staff, expanded incentive compensation, and tightened management selection, rarely were the actions framed to achieve abnormal market returns within two to twenty or even 200 days. They were usually framed instead to achieve returns over two or three or more years, sometimes many more. And they were intended to generate enduring value, an accumulation of cash payouts and market worth. But on this terrain, the footing remained unstable. The ideology of shareholder value offered guidance where research and practical experience could not.

Systemic Alignment

A defining characteristic of managerial ideologies is that they are comprehensively applied to virtually all phases of business. By this criterion, ownership-disciplined alignment certainly qualified. Repeated efforts were made to convert the general rhetoric of ownership value into decision-making criteria that explicitly stressed returns to owners. In taking decisions, whether to establish a business unit, acquire a company, change a compensation system, add a product, or approve a strategic plan, the operational criteria made more explicit reference to stockholder return than in the past. Rather than expecting results from alterations in single organizational components, the emphasis on ownership-disciplined alignment led to wholesale redesign of the organization, akin to the wholesale architectural changes that are oftentimes the precursors of successful technological innovation (Henderson and Clark, 1990).

A cumulative and thus more far-reaching impact of this kind of systemic change was expected from other research indicating that organizational change limited to single components often results in limited impact at best (Kochan and Useem, 1992). Simultaneous changes in many organizational components are mutually reinforcing, while isolated changes in single components are often undermined. The introduction of new information technologies, for example, unless there is a concomitant opening of the organization and empowering of workforce users, is found to leave the new systems' potential largely unrealized (Scott Morton, 1991). According to other research, the introduction of employee stock ownership plans can significantly increase a firm's productivity, but only when the plans are accompanied by employee involvement in company decision making (Conte and Svejnar, 1990). New technologies in auto manufacturing, reports still another investigation, realize their potential only when integrated with innovative human-resource policies stressing workforce skill, motivation, and flexibility (MacDuffie and Krafcik, 1992).

The company-wide application of ownership-disciplined alignment was thus on the mark. Starting with the chief executive, alignment was pushed through the many offices and operations of the firm. Applications were far from complete. Yet the principles were made explicit, and management assumed that the promoted changes would take hold sooner or later. Moreover, the process was viewed as irreversible. As operating units acquired more power to control their operations and line managers more power to determine their human-resource policies, it seemed that there could be no turning back. Once power was distributed, repossession would prove arduous.

Systemic alignment connoted change not only throughout the organization but beyond it as well. The proponents of shareholder value and its organizational implications brought a zeal to their initiatives that knew no bounds. As true believers, they pressed other organizations to embrace the new-found wisdom. Whether these were firms with which they traded, colleges from which they hired, or charitable organizations to which they gave, newly aligned companies expected their organizational fields to come to resemble themselves.

This exporting of the new design principles furnished an unusual driver for the process of organizational imitation. As chronicled by Paul DiMaggio and Walter Powell (1983), organizations often mimic one another to reduce risk and uncertainty. The imitation process is typically one in which the imitator seeks to copy the innovator. Companies thus frequently adjust their managerial compensation levels by reviewing what their leading competitors are paying (using data readily provided by consulting firms). Similarly, many companies adopted the multidivisional form after their executives had seen it in operation among other successful companies in the industry or among firms for which they served as outside director (Fligstein, 1985; Palmer et al., 1987, 1989). In the case of alignment, however, the imitation process was reversed. Instead, the exemplars often took the initiative, seeking to have others copy them. It was not a holy cause, but it was carried as a just cause, since it was seen as offering a superior path to results. Traditional company resistance to anything "not invented here" encountered an insistent message that it was "already proven there."

For later adopters, however, the payoffs may not have been the same. The benefits were likely to shift from an accent on the positive to avoidance of the negative. This can be anticipated from company experience with other organizational innovations. Initial adopters of computer-based information systems, for instance, often found early advantage, while later adopters found only that they had finally shed competitive disadvantage (Scott Morton, 1991). Whatever the impact of the changes described here on the early adopters, a belated absence among other companies may come to be a significant liability. For investors and analysts, the absence of a focus on shareholder wealth and its alignment corollaries could come to signify an antiquated management.

Investor Capitalism

As shareholding concentrated and companies changed, the social organization of American business acquired new fabric. Fresh ways of doing business were laid over the old. The old still dominated, as managerial capitalism was by no means in eclipse. Michael Jensen's "eclipse of the public corporation" remained more a normative image than a factual condition (Jensen, 1989). Professional management's grip on power, early foreseen by Adolph Berle and Gardiner Means and later confirmed by Alfred Chandler, remained intact.

Yet alongside the operating principles of managerial capitalism appeared a new set of operating principles associated with what might be termed investor capitalism. Management retained much control over a company's fate, but no longer could it claim complete control. When, under the persistent prodding of institutional investors, the directors of General Motors Corporation forced the chief executive in 1992 to step down from his chairmanship of the executive committee and to replace two of his top executives, the *Wall Street Journal* saw the end of unfettered management rule: "He became the first GM chief executive in more than 70 years to lose control of his board" (White and Ingrassia, 1992, p. 1). Later, the chief executive would lose his position as well. But the loss of complete control was rarely the same as the loss of all control. Professional managers listened more attentively, yet they usually remained at the helm.

Without displacing managerial capitalism, investor capitalism nonetheless came to coexist with it. Its relative salience at any given company depended on the balance of power between investors and managers, which greatly varied from company to company (in ways that Zald's early analysis of board powers would have readily anticipated; Zald, 1969). Yet transcending the firm-to-firm variation was a general gain of investor power, and a corresponding loss of executive power. And with that came the spread and acceptance of the new management practices I have grouped under the rubric ownership-disciplined alignment. Some were intended to produce greater shareholder value; others were designed to thwart greater shareholder influence. But all could be traced to the altered owner-manager relations under the rule of investor capitalism.

The process by which the investor-related principles were developed and then embedded in company practices was a mix of immediate problem solving and subsequent solution sharing, as theorists of institutions would have us anticipate (Powell and DiMaggio, 1991). This could be seen, for instance, in the evolution of the poison pill, one of the most effective and widespread antitakeover devices invented during the 1980s. In 1983, no Fortune 500 company had a poison pill; by the end of the decade, nearly two-thirds had adopted a pill. The first Fortune 500 firm (Crown Zellerbach) approved a poison pill in July 1984, and another twenty-one firms adopted pills within sixteen months, a majority in response to hostile takeover bids or rumors. The process of concrete problem solving was then readily evident. Later, it was far less so. Only five of the remaining 268 pill adoptions through July 1989, were in response to unfriendly bids or anticipated bids. The later determinants, reports Gerald Davis (1991a), included such predictable factors as company size—smaller companies were more vulnerable to takeovers and thus more likely to adopt such measures (though poor financial performers, also more vulnerable, were no more likely to do so). But a critical driver was also the network of shared directors among the Fortune 500 firms. If a nonpill company held a common directorship with others companies that had already adopted a pill, it was far more likely to do so itself. If I had sought to predict which companies would adopt a shareholder rights plan, I would have started with a company's organizational and financial characteristics. Yet I could have offered a far more precise forecast if I had also taken into account the company's embeddedness in the network of interlocking directorships. That network was responsible for the spread of other "best practices," and it was clearly at work here, too (Granovetter, 1985; Mintz and Schwartz, 1985; Mizruchi, 1982; Pennings, 1980; Davis and Powell, 1992).

As the principles of investor capitalism acquired greater salience, they challenged not only the tenets of managerial capitalism, but two other sets of operating principles as well, those of "family" capitalism and those of "institutional" capitalism. Though managerial precepts in most large companies had largely supplanted family rules dating back to the companies' founding, remnants of family influence remained at some. Also, as top managers of major companies had come to work with one another through shared directorships and associations such as the Business Roundtable, still another set of principles emerged during the 1960s and early 1970s. These rules stressed classwide criteria in company decision making, considerations that sometimes placed the concerns of the business community ahead of the interests of specific firms. This set of institutional principles came into coexistence with, but likewise never displaced, either managerial capitalism or the remnants of family capitalism (Useem, 1984, pp. 172–196).

The principles of investor capitalism promised to do much the same. Families still dominated some major companies; professional managers were strongly in control at many others; and the top managers of most constituted an informal community whose culture and influence transcended a simple aggregation of their constituent firms. But parallel with all of the above came this still-new logic. If family capitalism emphasized kinship bonds, managerial capitalism stressed professional performance, and institutional capitalism pressed classwide advantage, then investor capitalism emphasized stockholder gain. It ushered in an additional set of guidelines for judging company decisions, designing company organization, and evaluating results.

A paradox here concerned the baseline for evaluating the gain. Despite the common charge that managers shorn of ownership oversight would perform less well, extensive research over several decades generally indicated that professional managers were probably no less effective than their family-owner predecessors. A typical research strategy had been to compare the performance of management-controlled and owner-controlled companies. Owner-controlled firms included those still dominated by founding families, the most typical form, though other forms of ownership control were also in evidence. Systematic comparison of their financial performance indicated that the management-controlled firms had usually not done notably worse. An early stocktaking of these studies led one reviewer to conclude that the managerial revolution should be consigned to the category of "pseudofact" (Zeitlin, 1974). Later evaluation of additional studies by another scholar led to much the same assessment: "[The] triumph of management control in many large corporations has not left them in the hands of neutral technocrats. The control groups of these organizations seem as devoted to profitable growth as are the leaders of entrepreneurial and owner-dominated companies, past and present" (Herman, 1981, pp. 112–113). Still later review found some evidence of faltering performance among management-controlled companies: "If any pattern is discernible in the findings, it is that management-controlled companies tend to be somewhat less profitable than corporations with a concentrated outside ownership group, as Berle and Means might have predicted" (Scherer, 1989, p. 58). Yet even this assessment closed on an ambiguous note: "ownership structure can make a difference but [one is] uncertain what difference it makes" (p. 62).

Although other studies reported differences between owner-dominated and manager-dominated firms in related areas, ranging from decentralization to charitable giving (Palmer et al., 1987, 1989; Atkinson and Galaskie-wicz, 1988), consistent evidence on pronounced financial divergence prior to the mid-1980s was thus not forthcoming. Measurement strategies could have been responsible in part. The studies' performance measures rarely focused on return to shareholders, concentrating instead on traditional financial criteria such as rates of return on assets, and it is possible that a more nuanced study of investor returns would have revealed more of a difference. Yet that was arguably unlikely, for managers in management-controlled firms were often directed and constrained by incentives not unlike those facing the original owners. Some studies reported that they were even more so: companies with declining fortunes were found in one study to dismiss a chief executive more quickly if they were management-controlled than if they were owner-controlled (Allen, 1981).

If the performance of the firm before a management takeover from the founding owners was set as the baseline for comparison, then the new shareholder activism could expect to achieve little. Yet the shareholder agenda was not restorationist. Few if any calls were heard from institutional investors to bring back the founding entrepreneurs, their descendants, or those still responsible for the family fortunes. And the agenda was not, with the exception of a limited number of specialty buyout firms, to place the new owners directly in charge (Crawford, 1987). The hallmark of investor capitalism was ownership influence, not control.

The fact that companies in decades past performed no worse under professional managers than comparable firms still under owner control, however, did little in the late 1980s and early 1990s to dampen investor demand. What counted here was investor belief that many companies could do better than in their immediate past, however that might compare to the distant past. Company performance was compared to an inferred potential, not an ancient record. And what gave special voice to investor belief was the freshly realized power of their concentrating holdings. Investors wanted more value than professional managers had been yielding them, and they wanted it soon. The managerial revolution was thus not reversed. Investor capitalism instead brought forward a new set of owners, shorn of any family or company loyalties. They simply demanded more than they had been receiving under the unchallenged rule of managerial capitalism.

The intensification of investor demands on companies, however, may have reduced the influence of companies upon one another. Imitation is too valuable and costless a strategy to be abandoned. Yet as management was pressed to devote more attention to shareholders, less attention may have gone to other companies. We have already seen that the network of shared directorships, one informal communication channel across companies, weakened during the late 1980s and early 1990s. We have also seen that the communication channel between senior managers and their investors, by contrast, strengthened. And much of the message from the investors was for the company to enhance efficiencies, even at the expense of abandoning widely accepted management practices. As a result, company designs and policies may have acquired greater diversity, more customized by investor insistence and less constrained by management convention. At the risk of confusing terminologies, institutional investing can be said to reduce institutional imitation.

This decline of what Paul DiMaggio and Walter Powell (1983) termed organizational "isomorphism" within the management community, however, may be accompanied by the rise of isomorphism within the investor community. Investor adoption of fund indexing, for instance, generated behavioral similarity among fund managers that was unheard of within the corporate world. Other evidence also pointed toward the pursuit of security in numbers. Drawing on extensive interviews with fund managers, Conley and O'Barr, for instance, described a "preoccupation with . . . displacing responsibility," with seeking to shift final responsibility for investment decisions away from identifiable individuals. Cloning investment strategies of other prominent funds was one way to do so; so, too, was simply delegating investment decisions directly to those funds (Conley and O'Barr, 1992; O'Barr and Conley, 1992).

Institutional investors faced their own uncertainties, and in groping for ways to reduce risk here, they may be no less prone to imitation than companies when they had faced their uncertain futures. Moreover, the growing scale of the holdings and the consequent expansion of exposure was likely only to intensify these isomorphic tendencies. A decline of managerial imitation among companies may thus be accompanied by increased investment imitation among shareholders.

Counterpoints

The interpretations I set forth here should be seen as inductive propositions. They did not guide the research at its outset. They instead emerged in the course of discussions, observations, and review of documents within the seven companies. I chose them over other interpretations because they appeared to offer more parsimony, more consistency, more predictability. Still, they are propositions: tentative in generalization, subject to revision.

In choosing to focus more intensively on a limited set of companies, albeit from diverse sectors, I compromised sample representativeness at an early stage. Gathering information directly from key participants had necessitated such a focus. Yet short of an insider look at a far larger cross-section of major American corporations, I cannot be sure how widely my results applied. Still, the common threads running through the seven company experiences suggested more than seven unique reactions.

To sharpen the propositional nature of the interpretations, let us consider four counterarguments. The first is that the observed organizational changes may have been driven by a host of forces other than shareholder power or anticipation of it. The second is that the changes implied improved organizational performance, but they did not confirm it. The third is that the changes may have been more passing than enduring, little more than a temporary surge of investor influence. The fourth is that the institutional pressures and management responses were too general to guide specific actions.

Observed organizational changes may have been driven by factors other than shareholder power. We know that some of the reconfigurations enjoyed impetus from several quarters. The observed changes, as a result, may have been "overdetermined": even without the rise of shareholder power, it can be argued, they were likely to have occurred. Investor demands were not among a manager's primary concerns.

The seemingly secondary salience of shareholder interests was evident, for instance, in company responses when the firms were surveyed on why they had downsized their workforces. A cross-sectional sample of companies with fifty or more employees by the U.S. General Accounting Office (1987), for instance, asked the firms to identify the leading factors behind their decisions to close plants or reduce their workforces. The three leading factors were product demand (cited by 60 percent), increased competition (56 percent), and labor costs (45 percent). A Conference Board survey of 512 large companies in 1985 asked firms to identify the reasons for closing a facility during the prior three years. Among the 210 companies that had done so, the primary factor was deemed to be changed company markets, increased domestic or foreign competition, and production or process obsolescence (Berenbeim, 1986). A 1991 survey of 406 major companies asked human-resource directors to identify the reasons behind company decisions to close operations, sell business units, and take other downsizing measures during the previous five years. The three leading factors here were lack of profitability, cost containment, and inadequate productivity (Useem, 1993). Neither responding to institutional investors nor building shareholder worth was among the expressed concerns in any of these surveys.

Managers of the seven focal companies alluded to still other sources of inspiration for the changes their companies had implemented. These sources ranged from the total quality movement to changing workforce demography. A few managers even implicitly emphasized change for its own sake: familiar with Douglas McGregor's distinction between "theory X" and "theory Y" (managing employees by directives versus managing by objectives), they saw decentralization as an overdue company recognition of what McGregor had foreseen more than three decades earlier (McGregor, 1960).

Moreover, other companies appeared to have undertaken changes parallel to those described here, but apparently for unrelated reasons. ABB Asea Brown Boveri, a European manufacturing company with 240,000 employees worldwide, operated through some fifty "business areas" and local organizations. Like the seven focal companies, ABB had moved considerable authority into those profit centers. It reduced its Zurich headquarters staff of 1,600 professionals in 1988 to just 100 three years later. These changes were the product of an emergent ABB "logic" for managing an array of production sites and sales systems across a host of national settings. By all outward appearances, shareholders played little role in shaping these familiar features of restructuring (Taylor, 1991).

The observed organizational changes implied improved organizational performance, but they did not confirm it. Senior managers certainly believed in the efficacy of the changes they had engineered. Yet whether the dispersion of responsibility or expansion of variable compensation yielded the intended results remained an open question. So, too, was the extent to which intermediate outcomes, such as customer relations, product quality, and worker productivity, were improved as well. Studies of specific elements had yielded suggestive findings. Hill and Snell (1989), for instance, reported that companies with more concentrated ownership structures displayed higher productivity levels. Golden (1992) found that business units with more control over strategic decisions also displayed better performance. Oswald and Jahera (1991) observed that firms with higher levels of inside ownership showed higher stock returns. And Pearce and

Zahra (1991) reported that companies with more empowered boards also had better performance records. Such findings pointed in the right direction, but the impact of specific components could not necessarily be combined and extrapolated to infer an encompassing impact of the interlinked forms of change described here.

A related challenge concerned potentially adverse consequences for other company stakeholders. If shareholder power increased, it presumably did so not only relative to management but also at the expense of employees, suppliers, bond holders, creditors, local communities, and other groups. In areas where these constituencies shared common ground with shareholders, alignment promised gains for all. In areas such as employee payroll and dividend policies, however, investor gains could spell losses for most (Kreiner and Bhambri, 1991). The unanswered question here was at the heart of much of the era's public debate over hostile takeovers, financial restructuring, and "short-termism." A national commission on business competitiveness, for instance, concluded a 1992 report with a plaintive query: we still needed to know "the degree to which management's goals of creating shareholder wealth and advancing the interests of stakeholders (including workers, suppliers and communities) conflict or harmonize with each other" (Competitiveness Policy Council, 1992, p. 31).

Observed organizational changes are more passing than enduring. Commercial banks, organized labor, and incumbent managements had been weakened during the late 1980s and early 1990s, and the resulting power vacuum opened the way for investor leverage. But those conditions, suggests this counterargument, may prove more cyclical than secular. Commercial banks could again come to play the central role they had played in earlier business development. The labor movement might likewise find new muscle, forcing higher wages at the expense of lower dividends. And managements themselves might secure even stronger barriers to investor interference, restoring a dominance they had so long enjoyed.

The institutional pressures and management responses identified here were too general to determine specific actions. Major investors pressed for enhanced shareholder value. Major companies responded by moving authority down and incentives up. According to this counterargument, such actions and reactions were too generic to determine specific actions. Shareholders sought better returns, but given their manifest absence of managerial experience, they were in no position to render advice on how to achieve them. Executives devolved authority, but after doing so, they were no longer in a position to provide specific guidance.

The first counterargument, which claims alternative drivers of change, is undoubtedly partially correct. The concept of total quality management, simultaneously emergent during the late 1980s and early 1990s, moved companies in some of the same directions as described here; so, too, did globalization. Yet at the same time, these alternative sources could not account for many of observed components of change. They could not, for instance, explain why measures of shareholder value were increasingly used to evaluate executive performance and business plans. Nor could they account for why companies sought to build a culture stressing investor wealth. Nor were they able to account for why promotion criteria were broadened to include contribution to company value. The alternative sources added fuel to the ownership-disciplined alignment, but they did not entirely drive it.

The second counterargument, relating to organizational performance, is largely correct. While managerial ideology attributed great efficacy to the changes induced, causal effects on company performance—above all, shareholder value—were far from proven. This was, however, no impediment to change. Executives required no scientific proof before moving ahead. They had ample faith in where they were going. Yet although they believed, it remained to be seen if their actions yielded the right results. It also remained to be seen if the wealth of other company constituencies rose or fell with that of investors.

The third counterargument, stressing cyclical change, is potentially correct. The rise of investor influence on management was partially a function of the fall of labor and other claimants. If the latter's influence were restored, shareholders might find their own wings clipped once again. On the other hand, the continuing concentration of company assets among a relatively small set of institutions was likely to impede full retreat. Their capacities for individual and collective action only intensified with time. The investment funds themselves, however, could face transformation. Were pension funds, for instance, to give more voice to their own beneficiaries, their definition of shareholder value could take on new meaning. Companies with exemplary employment records, for instance, might be defined as a better value than those which disregarded their human resources.

The fourth argument, which asserts generic guidance, is correct. Because institutions spread their holdings among many companies, they had limited capacity to learn the businesses in which they invested. Though some investors overstepped the line, most respected the convention that specific advice was sure to be misinformed. They were not shy, however, about general advice on company performance. Similarly, as company executives more carefully selected their top operating managers and then gave them more operating authority, they were also reluctant to press for specific decisions. They were not reluctant, by contrast, to appraise those decisions. And what differed in both cases were the criteria for appraisal.

Conclusion

The wave of corporate restructuring during the late 1980s and early 1990s left a lasting imprint on the internal world of many companies. Animating much of the change was an accelerating reassertion of ownership power, both outside and inside the organization. Shareholders gained more leverage over company decisions, sometimes in spite of opposition by top managements, at other times with their concurrence. Line managers gained more ownership over their product and performance as a result of top-management action.

This challenge to the managerial revolution came with a novel twist. Ownership power was resurgent, but not from the original founder-entrepreneurs. They had long since hedged their risks and dispersed their wealth (with exceptions, as noted by Allen, 1987). The new exercise of ownership muscle came instead from major institutional investors, takeover specialists, and financial professionals. It was they who led the opening of markets for corporate control during the late 1980s and early 1990s, intensifying ownership pressure on, if far short of control over, many firms. Changes in organizational structure were driven somewhat less by management strategy, which had long been the orthodoxy, and more by stockholder stratagems. And in the process, a new kind of managerial-ownership was created within the organization.

The revolt gave greater primacy to an organizational logic stressing shareholder value. Other principles were not replaced, but their relative primacy was diminished. The ascendance of ownership-disciplined alignment recast company design and decision making. The emergent forms varied from firm to firm, but woven through the diversity were common threads. The shared strands included devolution of authority from a centralized group into operating business units; contraction of headquarters managers and staff functions; heightened stress on management succession; expanded use of performance-based compensation; and creation of mechanisms for internal ownership. At the same time, companies learned to resist and realign their own shareholders. They also learned to turn public policy to their own advantage. And some experimented with reformation of their board and governance principles as well.

Internal ownership moved operating power downward in the company. Yet while relinquishing some power to better manage on the inside, top management simultaneously sought to enhance its power to manage the outside. Top managers had long dominated their board and shareholders, virtually without challenge. But that era, too, was coming to a close, as investors pressed managements in ways unthinkable a decade earlier. To reassert its powers, management invented a host of antitakeover devices, reconstituted its shareholder base, and sought protection through state legislation.

Shareholders were not to be easily deterred, and they adopted still other devices to pressure management, from proxy challenges to SEC reform. Whatever the outcome of the many skirmishes, secular trends ensured that the power struggle would continue. The concentration of growing proportions of shareholding in relatively few large institutional investor hands showed few signs of abating in the early 1990s, and certainly no signs of reversing. While outwardly resisting direct shareholder pressures, companies were thus likely to push ownership-disciplined alignment even more pervasively down the organization, and perhaps even up to the governing bodies. And they were likely to press it more intensively on public agencies, nonprofit organizations, and the other institutions that had reason to do business with business.

Appendixes

References

Index

A Note on
Compiling Information

My primary source of information was the restructuring experiences of the seven corporations. Supplementary sources ranged from interviews with executives elsewhere who were familiar with restructuring experiences, to informal dialogues with current executives and direct observation of professional gatherings of managers. Initially, I compiled information on a broad set of issues generally associated with corporate restructuring. Soon, however, the compilation efforts acquired far greater focus. The guiding concern came to be to characterize and understand the set of bundled changes grouped here under the concept of alignment.

Gathering information from inside the seven companies, and above all from their senior managers, proved indispensable. I became familiar with media reports, stock reports, and self-reports on each of the corporations. Given their size and prominence, all of the companies garnered extensive public coverage. And as publicly traded firms, all generated numerous reports for the public. But the story that emerged from discussions with the senior managers proved more complex and interesting than the one that could be gleaned from any public record. Indeed, most of my initial working hypotheses were soon discarded as the interviews came to reveal a set of largely unanticipated developments. As a result, what is chronicled here is less an exercise in deductive theory confirmation, and more an exercise in inductive model development.

Gaining access to the senior tiers of the seven companies was essential, and high-level entrée had opened the first doors. In six of the seven cases, the president of the sponsoring organization, the National Planning Association, contacted senior managers of corporations whose cooperation I sought for the study. He asked executives who represented their company to the association to arrange for me to have access to a range of senior managers within their company. Generally this proved straightforward, and in most cases I was soon passing through headquarters security on the way to an early-morning appointment with the executive who served as liaison for the study. This was typically followed by back-to-back, tape-recorded interviews with five to fifteen of his senior colleagues throughout the day or days that followed. Virtually all of the managers invited further discussion, and most provided a range of specific documents and records upon request. Since the documents and records were generally proprietary and some were considered highly sensitive, access to such materials was most often obtained only during a second or later visit to the company.

In one instance, however, initial access to the firm proved exceptionally arduous. An executive had agreed to serve as liaison for his company, and I sought to make an appointment to see him. For several months he was almost constantly out of the office on special assignment. During one period, he was leaving the country at the start of every workweek, returning to the United States only for weekend sojourns. His secretary politely reported that he would try to get back to me, but it became evident that most nonessential business was on hold. After several months of no response, an intermediary well known to the executive placed several calls to his office, even faxing a query when the executive failed to return the calls. Discrete questions to the executive's associates confirmed that the unresponsiveness simply reflected time constraints rather than any reversal of commitment to the study. Finally, in an act of creative desperation, his secretary suggested an early-morning call to an unlisted car-telephone number while her boss commuted to the office. Shorn of all organizational buffers, the executive was reached finally, and within days he had opened his organization to the project.

In a number of instances, companies provided relatively free access to files on specific issues related to this study. One senior public affairs manager, for example, was scheduled to participate in a charity tennis tournament, an event viewed as a natural extension of his work life, since the governor and other political and corporate notables were among the contestants. He arranged for me to use his office for the day, making available a filing cabinet of correspondence, memoranda, plans, and other documents related to the company's successful effort to secure antitake-over legislation in the state. In another case, the company's chief administrative officer walked me to a cabinet containing internal memos and other documents outlining the firm's plans for defeating a shareholder proxy resolution that would have weakened management and strengthened investors in the event of an unwanted takeover bid. In a third instance, I was seated in the room of an absent executive and provided with the company's performance-related compensation plan for senior management. In still another case, I was able to review the strategic plans of a number of the corporation's operating business units.

Among several additional steps used to sharpen the study's findings was a presentation of preliminary results to the headquarters staff of one of the companies. A four-hour seminar with seven managers, four of whom had been interviewed for the study, provided helpful affirmation and refinement of the study's thrust, especially in two areas. One area concerned an explanation for why the firm had focused relatively early on shareholder value. Having played important roles in its early development, the managers knew the events well. But as group discussions often do, the collective insight from pooled experience added invaluable nuance to the account. The second area concerned the next phases of the company's decade-long process of restructuring. Several of the participants stressed the need to extend the logic of organizational alignment already set in motion. The group identified several areas especially ripe for targeting, including the company's industrial relations and management of nonexempt employees, neither of which had been previously mentioned.

Other sources provided additional context on organizational restructuring. These included interviews that I conducted in 1988 with a number of managers with three other corporations as part of a study of turbulence in managerial and professional employment (Doeringer et al., 1991, pp. 156–178). The corporations comprised a manufacturing and service company; a maker of office equipment; and a large manufacturer of information systems. The revenues of each exceeded $10 billion. Like the seven firms focused on here, none had undergone a change in ownership but all had experienced intensified shareholder pressure. I also interviewed approximately twenty-five individuals who were directly familiar with the issues of ownership and restructuring. These individuals included two senior partners of a firm specializing in financing and managing leveraged buyouts of other companies; an individual who had served as the chief financial officer of a large transportation company that had unsuccessfully resisted purchase by a well-known takeover specialist; the former chief executive of a company that had successfully resisted acquisition when he and his family had repurchased a large block of outstanding shares; and the former chief executive of a company that had undergone extensive restructuring in response to Wall Street pressures.

Information came through still other avenues. Visits to the Washington offices of several of the major associations concerned with shareholder relations and corporate governance (for example, the Investor Responsibility Research Center) yielded a great deal of data. I conducted interviews with representatives of other organizations and groups involved in these issues (for example, Institutional Shareholder Services). And visits to meetings of several groups, including those of the Investor Relations Association and the National Investor Relations Institute, were extremely helpful. Business at such gatherings was not always strictly business. One of the business meetings, held in 1990 at New York's Waldorf Astoria hotel and attended by hundreds of investor relations specialists and fund managers, drew fresh insight on the ways of Wall Street from a talk by Tom Wolfe, author of *The Bonfire of the Vanities*.

Finally, moving through company corridors and around executive offices was a source of unscheduled opportunities as well. As I traveled between appointments on the executive floor of the electrical-products company, for example, I encountered a manager whom I had interviewed earlier in the day. He was accompanied by an instantly recognizable colleague, to whom I was introduced. It was the company's chief executive, and I found an unexpected moment to ask about the view from the top. In another instance, I obtained access to company files on the firm's strategy for defeating a shareholder proposal. As I perused the files in an open reception area surrounded by the offices of the firm's top management, two senior officers stopped by for lengthy informal conversations, an unanticipated extension of earlier discussions.

Even the most minor moments sometimes proved revealing. I had completed an interview with the president of the special-machinery company and was about to start an interview with the vice-president for marketing. While we were obtaining coffee from an executive kitchenette, the president walked in for a cup as well. He served himself, and changed the filter in the coffee machine. He had earlier described a radical reduction in his central-office staff, resulting in an extremely lean headquarters. Following several minutes of banter, he left the room quipping, "You can say that the *real* secret of our success is that I make the coffee."

A number of events are briefly described to illustrate key elements of organizational change, and in building these accounts I have sought to draw upon information from at least several sources. In one incident of crisis management, for instance, I witnessed an edge of the crisis directly, obtained company documents on it, and subsequently interviewed several managers about it. All three sources proved useful in reconstructing the event. More generally, I checked key points by consulting at least several managers and documents when possible. New issues that emerged spontaneously in early interviews were often explicitly raised in later interviews.

I have also sought to let the managers frequently speak for themselves. Their own words help describe important nuances of the organizational world which they inhabited and helped create. The texture of their world is captured in ways that other kinds of evidence would miss.

While each manager's experience and each company's practice contain unique elements, the objective has been to extract the generic patterns. In selecting materials for reporting here, I preferred experiences and practices that found parallels or equivalents in at least several corporations, and that were confirmed by a number of managers and documentary sources. Construction of the organizational portrait is thus built on an integrated and cross-checked use of information from many documents, observations, and interviews. I have also drawn upon other studies for corroborating evidence, and to suggest where the observed patterns were finding more widespread application. My goal has been to extract the most salient and widely reported forms of organizational alignment.

All information collected from inside the companies was treated as confidential. This was a condition required to ensure both company access and managerial candor. The acquired information is presented in such a fashion that neither managers nor companies can be identified. This necessitated occasional slight modification of specific figures or references. But all such changes were minor and were made in ways that preserved general meaning. Male pronouns are used throughout to protect the identity of the three female managers who were among those interviewed. Following a convention developed by two analysts who reported extensive interviews with investment managers, I have edited fragmentary statements and corrected minor grammatical errors in presenting directly quoted material, to ensure clarity of expression (O'Barr and Conley, 1992). Otherwise the managers are speaking for themselves in unaltered form, transcribed directly from the audio recordings of the interviews.

This entry into the world of managers carried recognized hazards. For example, managers are traditionally suspicious when asked what they and their organization do. A billiards expert, argued Milton Friedman, may be superb at the game but would be a poor source on Newtonian mechanics. The poolroom player must have intuitive mastery of the laws of physics. Yet mastery does not depend on articulating the laws. To understand the laws, so the argument goes, one must observe the ball movement, not ask the ball mover. Extended to the managerial setting, this hazard might be termed, "They know not why they do." By virtue of company size, time constraints, and hidden pressures, a manager may knowledgeably act but imperfectly understand why (Blinder, 1991; Shiller, 1991; Gordon, 1991).

A second hazard related to the ever-present danger of "going native," of uncritically accepting a paradigm that one had initially intended to appraise critically. Relying not on cold statistics but warm contact, the itinerant interviewer may insidiously be drawn into subject of inquiry. Max Weber's call for *Verstehen,* for understanding the world of those under study, carried the attendant risk that the observer might come to understand it too well.

Both dangers appeared as I entered the seven executive suites. The first danger was perhaps most starkly seen in the differing interpretations that managers sometimes rendered of the same event. The accounts were never as discrepant as when first-marriage husbands and wives sometimes report different numbers of children to Census Bureau interviewers. But managers did differ on fundamentals from time to time, implying bounded rationality for at least one and sometimes all of the insiders.

The second danger was also present from the moment of arrival. Management offices were richly furnished and sometimes given to magnificent views. On occasion, interviews would conclude with an invitation to the executive dining room or a private club. And even a one-time visitor was often received with exquisite courtesy and privileged treatment. On arriving with coat and briefcase for an early-morning interview, I would sometimes find both waiting at the outer office of the last manager on the day's schedule, along with a company car for return to the airport.

Guarding against both dangers, however, went with the territory. I recognized, of course, that managerial perceptions were often limited and sometimes biased. This necessitated a cross-checking of information with multiple sources, sifting through the extensive recorded interviews for consistent threads, returning for follow-up discussions to resolve inconsistencies, and scheduling additional interviews to flesh out inadequate descriptions. It also required a skeptical eye. Though there was little incentive for the managers to distort reality, they were presumably as subject as anybody to misinterpreting the events that swirled around them.

Guarding against going native required fewer preventive measures. Anthropologists are sometimes granted titular status in tribal groups, often an honorary kinship position making clear their local acceptance. Though I might have gladly embraced the title of honorary chief research officer to facilitate access, no such offers were forthcoming. Nor were there any tests of loyalty, as when William Foote Whyte was asked to join in fraudulent voting practices during his sojourn in Italian Boston's "street corner society" (Whyte, 1955). Aside from needing to be presentable enough to walk the executive floor without immediate suspicion, I was a well-defined outsider without titles or tests and was not targeted for assimilation.

A third danger stemmed from the fact that managerial perceptions and interpretations were in part socially constructed. That is, they were not only a mapping of the organization in which the managers resided but also a product of the circles in which the managers traveled. By the late 1980s, for instance, extolling shareholder value had acquired a fashionable aura, much as diversification had during the 1960s. Managers who had neither contact with major investors nor direct responsibility for producing value had nonetheless become highly conversant in its importance. As in any bounded group, business cant came and went (Byrne, 1986), and this was certainly one of the dominant ideologies of the era.

Yet it was also evident that shareholder value carried numerous operational implications. While some managers were not in a position to so operate, many were, and they carried shareholder-related criteria into their performance reviews, planning cycles, and organizational redesigns. Moreover, the rising rhetoric of shareholder value was rooted in the rising power of institutional wealth. This rhetoric was thus both socially rooted and socially constructed, necessitating special efforts to identify the organizational roots and operational implications.

The known hazards of direct questioning of managers can never be fully overcome, but certain facets of organizational life might also never be understood otherwise. Information from annual company reports and proxy statements constitutes an invaluable data base. Though the information seldom goes much beyond minimum reporting requirements set forward by stock exchanges and the U.S. Securities and Exchange Commission, rich inferences on managerial motives and organizational behavior in limited areas can nonetheless be made from such data; I draw frequently on such information in this book. But data bearing on other issues, from the chains of managerial reasoning to the process of executive succession, are largely absent from such records. On these questions, direct contact with the companies and their managers could have no substitute.

Still, the skeptic is encouraged to take a company tour similar to the one I describe here. Replication is invited, both to challenge and expand my account. Many field studies are essential if we are to learn how and why American companies undertook their wrenching changes of the past decade.

Tables Related to the
Rise of Shareholder Power

Table A.1. Announced corporate mergers and acquisitions, 1970–1990.

	Mergers and acquisitions			Total value (in billions of dollars)[a]	
Year	Number among all companies	Number among publicly traded companies	Publicly traded as percent of all companies	All companies	Publicly traded companies
1970	5,152	n.a.	n.a.	16.4	n.a.
1975	2,297	130	n.a.	12.5	n.a.
1980	1,889	173	9.2	44.3	n.a.
1981	2,395	168	7.0	82.6	56.6
1982	2,346	180	7.7	53.7	31.5
1983	2,533	190	7.5	73.1	39.5
1984	2,543	211	8.3	122.2	82.7
1985	3,001	336	11.2	179.8	116.7
1986	3,336	386	11.6	173.1	89.9
1987	2,032	286	14.1	163.7	85.9
1988	2,258	462	20.5	246.9	156.1
1989	2,366	328	13.9	221.1	121.9
1990	2,074	185	8.9	108.2	48.2

Sources: Grimm (1989 and earlier years); Merrill Lynch (1990, 1991).

a. Value figures are based on acquisitions and mergers for which a purchase price was disclosed: approximately a third to a half of all announced transactions and approximately 90 percent of transactions involving publicly traded companies.

Table A.2. Divisional and company buyout activity, 1980–1990.

	Division buyouts		Company buyouts				Division and company buyouts value as percent of all equity value
Year	Number	Value (in millions of dollars)	Number	Number as percent of all public takeovers	Value (in millions of dollars)	Value as percent of all public takeovers	
1980	47	363	13	7.5	967	n.a.	0.01
1981	83	484	17	10.1	2,339	4.1	0.19
1982	115	1,361	31	17.2	2,837	9.0	0.24
1983	139	2,499	36	19.0	7,145	18.1	0.48
1984	122	3,833	57	27.0	10,806	13.1	0.72
1985	132	5,005	76	22.6	24,140	20.7	1.13
1986	144	9,542	76	19.7	20,232	22.5	1.01
1987	90	5,957	47	16.4	22,057	25.7	0.98
1988	89	8,521	125	26.9	60,920	39.0	2.21
1989	91	4,049	80	24.4	18,515	15.2	0.59
1990	63	2,115	20	10.8	3,539	7.3	n.a.

Sources: Grimm (1989 and earlier years); Merrill Lynch (1990, 1991); Securities Industry Association (1991).

Table A.3. Market value of the assets of the ten largest corporate and public pension funds, 1990.

Market value (in billions of dollars)	Corporate employee benefit fund	Market value (in billions of dollars)[a]	Public pension fund
39.1	AT&T	56.5	California Public Employees' Retirement System
36.3	General Motors Corp.	45.2	New York State and Local Retirement System
28.9	General Electric Co.	39.0	New York City Retirement Systems
21.9	IBM	30.9	California State Teachers' Retirement System
20.8	Ford Motor Company	26.7	New York State Teachers' Retirement System
18.5	Du Pont	24.8	Teacher Retirement System of Texas
14.4	Nynex	21.1	Ohio Public Employees Retirement System
14.1	Bell Atlantic Corp.	20.3	State of Wisconsin Investment Board
14.1	BellSouth Corp.	19.3	Florida State Teachers' Retirement System
13.3	Ameritech	19.1	State Teachers Retirement System of Ohio

Source: Institutional Investor (1991).
a. Market value is generally as of September 30, 1990.

Table A.4. Estimated value of stockholdings held by institutional investors, 1949–1985.

Holdings	1949	1955	1960	1965	1970	1975	1980	1985–1986
All public stocks—Series 1:								
Market value (in billions of dollars)	—	73.0	112.7	204.9	266.8	313.4	519.9	1327.2
Percent of total holdings	—	23.0	26.8	28.6	31.1	36.9	33.1	42.7
Public stocks—Series 2:								
Market value (in billions of dollars)	—	—	—	113	177	251	461	899
Percent of total holdings	—	—	—	15.8	20.6	29.6	29.3	34.8
Stocks on New York Stock Exchange:								
Market value (in billions of dollars)	10.1	31.1	52.9	114.4	166.4	241.7	440.2	—
Percent of total holdings	13.2	15.0	17.2	21.3	26.1	35.3	35.4	—

Sources: Brancato and Gaughan (1988) for the upper and lower panels: the upper panel is from studies by the Securities and Exchange Commission, and the final figures are for 1986 rather than 1985; the lower panel is from the New York Stock Exchange; the 1986 figures were independently compiled by Brancato and Gaughan (1988) from a range of sources. Securities Industry Association (1990) for the middle panel (derived from the Federal Reserve Flow of Funds Account).

Table A.5. Largest institutional investors in a special-machinery company and a retail services company, 1990.

Special-machinery company		Retail services company	
Institutional investor	Percent of shares held	Institutional investor	Percent of shares held
Investment company	4.0	Investment company	2.1
Investment company	2.3	Commercial bank trust	2.0
Investment company	2.2	Commercial bank trust	2.0
Investment company	2.2	Investment trust	1.8
Investment company	2.2	Public pension fund	1.5
Insurance company	2.1	Public pension fund	1.4
Commercial bank trust	2.0	Public pension fund	1.1
Investment company	1.8	Public pension fund	0.9
Commercial bank trust	1.6	Commercial bank trust	0.9
Commercial bank trust	1.5	Investment company	0.8
Top ten	21.7		14.3
All institutional investors	63.5		51.9

Sources: Company records (1990); and Disclosure Inc. (on-line information).

Table A.6. Top shareholders of electrical-products company, 1984–1990.

	Percent held[a]						
	1990	1989	1988	1987	1986	1985	1984
Ten largest shareholders (in 1990):							
Investment company	1.8	0.02	[0]	[0]	[0]	[0]	[0]
Commercial bank trust	1.6	1.5	1.1	0.9	0.9	[0.6]	[0.4]
Investment company	1.6	1.9	[0.5]	[0]	[0]	[0]	[0]
Commercial bank trust	1.5	1.5	1.6	1.6	1.6	1.1	[0.6]
Commercial bank trust	1.4	1.3	1.0	[0.7]	1.2	1.0	1.2
Investment company	1.3	1.2	1.0	1.2	1.1	1.2	1.3
Investment company	1.1	0.9	1.0	0.9	[0.4]	[0.3]	[0]
Public pension fund	1.0	1.1	1.0	1.0	1.0	0.8	1.4
Public pension fund	1.0	[0.6]	[0.1]	[0.04]	[0]	[0]	[0]
Investment company	1.0	[0.9]	0.8	0.8	[0.7]	[0.4]	[0.1]
Total number of institutions	481	675	678	632	540	496	400
Other shareholders among top ten in at least one year, 1984–1989:							
Investment company		1.7					
Investment company		1.4	2.4	1.8			
Public pension fund		1.0		0.9	0.9	0.8	
Public pension fund			0.8	0.8			
Investment company			0.8				
Investment company				1.5		0.9	
Investment company					1.3		
Company pension fund					1.1	1.0	1.2
Investment company					1.0		
Investment company					0.9		
Insurance company						1.6	1.5
Investment company						1.0	1.0
Commercial bank trust						0.7	
Investment company							1.1
Commercial bank trust							1.0
Investment company							0.9
Investment company							0.9

Source: Company records (1990).

a. Bracketed figures signify that the investor was not among the largest ten for a given year prior to 1990.

Table A.7. Percent of 358 shareholder proposals voted or pending during first half of 1990, by primary institutional sponsor.

Primary sponsor	Percent of proposals
United Shareholders Association (USA)	10.6
New York City employee retirement funds[a]	8.1
California employee retirement funds[b]	4.5
College Retirement Equities Fund	2.8
Union pension funds[c]	2.8
Other state retirement funds[d]	2.0
All institutions and USA	30.8

Source: Investor Responsibility Research Center, *Corporate Governance Bulletin* (May–June 1990), pp. 79–88.

a. New York City Employees' Retirement System, Fire Department Pension Fund, Police Department Pension Fund, and Teachers' Retirement System.

b. California Public Employees' Retirement System and State Teachers' Retirement System.

c. Pension funds affiliated with International Brotherhood of Electrical Workers, United Brotherhood of Electrical Workers, United Brotherhood of Carpenters and Joiners of America, and United Paperworkers.

d. State of Connecticut Retirement and Trust Funds, State of Wisconsin Investment Board, and Florida Board of Administration.

References

Abowd, John M. 1990. "Does Performance-Based Managerial Compensation Affect Corporate Performance?" *Industrial and Labor Relations Review* 43: 52S–73S.

———, George T. Milkovich, and John M. Hannon. 1990. "The Effects of Human Resource Management Decisions on Shareholder Value." *Industrial and Labor Relations Review* 43: 203S–216S.

Akers, John F. 1991a. Keynote Address, 1991 United Way Volunteer Leaders Conference, May 6. Washington, D.C.: United Way of America.

——— 1991b. "Let's Go to Work on Education." *Wall Street Journal* (March 20): A22.

Aldrich, Howard. 1979. *Organizations and Environments*. Englewood Cliffs, N.J.: Prentice-Hall.

——— and Jeffrey Pfeffer. 1976. "Environments of Organizations." *Annual Review of Sociology* 2: 79–105.

Allen, Michael Patrick. 1981. "Managerial Power and Tenure in the Large Corporation." *Social Forces* 60: 482–494.

——— 1987. *The Founding Fortunes*. New York: E. P. Dutton.

American Association of Fund-Raising Counsel. 1988. *Giving USA*. New York: AAFRC Trust for Philanthropy.

Atkinson, Lisa, and Joseph Galaskiewicz. 1988. "Stock Ownership and Company Contributions to Charity." *Administrative Science Quarterly* 33: 82–100.

Auerbach, Alan, ed. 1988. *Corporate Takeovers: Causes and Consequences*. Chicago: University of Chicago Press.

Autry, Ret, and Mark M. Colodny. 1990. "The Fortune 500: Hanging Tough in a Rough Year." *Fortune* 121 (April 23): 338–345.

Bacon, Jeremy. 1990. *Membership and Organization of Corporate Boards*. New York: Conference Board.

Bailey, Anne Lowrey. 1992. "Corporations' New Social Advocacy." *Chronicle of Philanthropy* (April 7): 6–7, 10.

Baker, G. P. 1990. "Pay-for-Performance for Middle Managers: Causes and Consequences." *Journal of Applied Corporate Finance* 3: 50–61.

Barnard, Jayne. 1991a. "Reducing Tenure in the Boardroom." *New York Times* (December 22): F11.

——— 1991b. "Institutional Investors and the New Corporate Governance." *North Carolina Law Review* 69: 1135–1187.

Bartlett, Sarah. 1991a. *The Money Machine: How KKR Manufactured Power and Profits.* New York: Warner Books.

——— 1991b. "Big Funds Pressing for Voice in Management of Companies." *New York Times* (February 23): 1ff.

Becker, Brian E., and Craig A. Olson. 1986. "The Impact of Strikes on Shareholder Equity." *Industrial and Labor Relations Review* 39: 425–438.

Beer, Michael, Russell A. Eisenstat, and Bert Spector. 1990. *The Critical Path to Corporate Renewal.* Boston: Harvard Business School Press.

Bendix, Reinhard. 1963. *Work and Authority in Industry: Ideologies of Management in the Course of Industrialization.* New York: Harper and Row.

Berenbeim, Ronald E. 1986. *Company Programs to Ease the Impact of Shutdowns.* New York: Conference Board.

Berg, Eric N. 1991. "Dissident Sears Holder Fails to Win Board Seat." *New York Times* (May 10): D1.

Berger, Lance. 1991. "Trends and Issues for the 1990s: Creating a Viable Framework for Compensation Design." In Milton L. Rock and Lance A. Berger, eds., *The Compensation Handbook,* 3rd ed. New York: McGraw-Hill.

Berle, Adolph, Jr., and Gardiner C. Means. 1967. *The Modern Corporation and Private Property.* Reprint. New York: Harcourt, Brace and World.

Bhagat, Sanjai, and James A. Brickley. 1984. "Cumulative Voting: The Value of Minority Shareholder Voting Rights." *Journal of Law and Economics* 27: 339–365.

Biersach, Jeffrey W. 1990. *Voting by Institutional Investors on Corporate Governance Issues in the 1990 Proxy Season.* Washington, D.C.: Investor Responsibility Research Center.

Biggart, Nicole Woolsey. 1991. "Explaining Asian Economic Organization: Toward a Weberian Institutional Perspective." *Theory and Society* 20: 199–232.

Black, Bernard S. 1990. "The Legal and Historical Contingency of Shareholder Passivity." *Michigan Law Review* 89: 520–608.

——— 1992a. "Agents Watching Agents: The Promise of Institutional Investor Voice." *UCLA Law Review* 39: 812–893.

——— 1992b. "The Value of Institutional Investor Monitoring: The Empirical Evidence." *UCLA Law Review* 39: 896–939.

Blinder, Alan S. 1991. "Why Are Prices Sticky? Preliminary Results from an Interview Study." *American Economic Review* 81 (2): 89–96.

Blumenthal, Karen, and Rich Wartzman. 1991. "Simmons Quits at Lockheed with a Loss of $42 Million." *Wall Street Journal* (March 19): A3, A10.

Boyer, Peter J. 1988. *Who Killed CBS?* New York: Random House.

Bradley, Michael, Arnand Desai, and E. Han Kim. 1988. "Synergistic Gains from Corporate Acquisitions and their Division between the Stockholders of Targets and Acquiring Firms." *Journal of Financial Economics* 21: 3–40.

Brancato, Carolyn, and Patrick A. Gaughan. 1988. *The Growth of Institutional Investors in U.S. Capital Markets.* New York: Columbia University Institutional Investor Project.

—— 1990. *The Growth of Institutional Investors, Updated Data: 1981–1988.* New York: Columbia University Institutional Investor Project.

Brickley, James A., Ronald C. Lease, and Clifford W. Smith, Jr. 1988. "Ownership Structure and Voting on Antitakeover Amendments." *Journal of Financial Economics* 20: 267–291.

Buono, Anthony F., and James L. Bowditch. 1989. *The Human Side of Mergers and Acquisitions: Managing Collisions between People, Cultures, and Organizations.* San Francisco: Jossey-Bass.

Burris, Val. 1987. "The Political Partisanship of American Business: A Study of Corporate Political Action Committees." *American Sociological Review* 52: 732–744.

—— 1989. Special reanalysis of data described in Burris, 1987 (above). Unpublished.

—— 1991. "Director Interlocks and the Political Behavior of Corporations and the Corporate Elite." *Social Science Quarterly* 72: 537–551.

Burrough, Bryan, and John Helyar. 1990. *Barbarians at the Gate: The Fall of RJR Nabisco.* New York: Harper and Row.

Burt, Ronald S. 1983. *Corporate Profits and Cooptation: Networks of Market Constraints and Directorate Ties in the American Economy.* New York: Academic Press.

Business Roundtable. 1990a. Letter of December 17, 1990, to U.S. Securities and Exchange Commission. New York: Business Roundtable.

—— 1990b. *Corporate Governance and American Competitiveness.* New York: Business Roundtable.

—— 1992. *Executive Compensation/Share Ownership.* New York: Business Roundtable.

Business Week. 1990. "The Business Week Top 1000." Annual Special Issue, *Business Week.*

—— 1991. "The Business Week Top 1000." Annual Special Issue, *Business Week.*

Byrne, John A. 1986. "Business Fads: What's In—What's Out: Executives Latch on to Any Idea that Looks Like a Quick Fix." *Business Week* (January 20): 52–61.

California Public Employees' Retirement System (Calpers). 1989. Letter of November 3, 1989, to U.S. Securities and Exchange Commission. Sacramento: California Public Employees' Retirement System.

—— 1990. Letter of November 21, 1990, to directors of the Standard and Poor's 500 companies. Sacramento: California Public Employees' Retirement System.

Campbell, John L., and Leon N. Lindberg. 1991. "The Evolution of Governance Regimes." In John Campbell, J. Rogers Hollingsworth, and Leon Lindberg, eds., *Governance in the American Economy.* New York: Cambridge University Press.

Carroll, Paul B. 1991. "IBM to Split Up Mainframe Unit in Restructuring." *Wall Street Journal* (December 5): A6.

Chaganti, Rajeswararao, and Fariborz Damanpour. 1991. "Institutional Onwership, Capital Structure, and Firm Performance." *Strategic Management Journal* 12: 479–491.

Chandler, Alfred D., Jr. 1977. *The Visible Hand: The Managerial Revolution in American Business.* Cambridge, Mass.: Harvard University Press.

Clawson, Dan, and Alan Neustadtl. 1989. "Interlocks, PACs, and Corporate Conservatism." *American Journal of Sociology* 94: 749–773.

———— and Denise Scott. 1989. Interviews conducted for research project on corporate political action committees. Reported in Clawson, Neustadtl, and Scott, 1992 (below).

———— 1992. *Money Talks: Corporate PACs and Political Influence.* New York: Basic Books.

Cochran, Philip L., Robert A. Wood, and Thomas B. Jones. 1985. "The Composition of Boards of Directors and Incidence of Golden Parachutes." *Academy of Management Journal* 28: 664–671.

Coffee, John C., Louis Lowenstein, and Susan Rose-Ackerman, eds. 1988. *Knights, Raiders, and Targets: The Impact of the Hostile Takeover.* New York: Oxford University Press.

Cohen, David K., and Michael S. Garet. 1975. "Reforming Educational Policy with Applied Social Research." *Harvard Educational Review* 45: 17–43.

Cohen, Roger. 1992. "The Very Model of Efficiency: Aesa Leaves Mark on I.B.M. Overhaul." *New York Times* (March 2): D1.

College Retirement Equities Fund (CREF). 1990. Letter of November 8, 1990, to U.S. Securities and Exchange Commission. New York: College Retirement Equities Fund.

Comment, Robert. 1990. "Wimpy Directors Likely Result of Proxy Reform." *Wall Street Journal* (December 4): A18.

———— and Gregg A. Jarrell. 1992. "Corporate Focus and Stock Returns." Rochester, N.Y.: Bradley Policy Research Center, University of Rochester.

Competitiveness Policy Council. 1992. *Building a Competitive America: First Annual Report to the President and Congress.* Washington, D.C.: Competitiveness Policy Council.

Conley, John M., and William M. O'Barr. 1992. "The Culture of Capital: An Anthroplogical Investigation of Institutional Investment." *North Carolina Law Review* 70: 823–847.

Conte, Michael A., and Jan Svejnar. 1990. "The Performance Effects of Employee Ownership Plans." In Alan S. Blinder, ed., *Paying for Productivity: A Look at the Evidence.* Washington, D.C.: Brookings Institution.

Cook, Frederic W., and Matthew P. Ward. 1991. "The Emerging Role of the Management Investor in Corporate Restructurings." In Fred K. Foulkes, ed., *Executive Compensation: A Strategic Guide for the 1990s.* Boston: Harvard Business School Press.

Coperland, Tom, Tim Koller, and Jack Murrin. 1990. *Valuation: Measuring and Managing the Value of Companies.* New York: Wiley.

Council for Aid to Education. 1991. *Corporate Support of Education.* New York: Council for Aid to Education.

Council of Economic Advisors. 1985. *Annual Report.* Washington: Council of Economic Advisors.

Council of Institutional Investors. 1990. "Council of Institutional Investors." Washington, D.C.: Council of Institutional Investors.

Crawford, Edward K. 1987. *What Management Should Know about Leveraged Buyouts.* New York: Wiley, 1987.

Crystal, Graef S. 1991a. "Selecting and Valuing Short- and Long-Term Compensation." In Fred K. Foulkes, ed., *Executive Compensation: A Strategic Guide for the 1990s.* Boston: Harvard Business School Press.

———— 1991b. *In Search of Excess: The Overcompensation of American Executives.* New York: Norton.

Cyert, Richard M., and James G. March. 1963. *A Behavioral Theory of the Firm.* Englewood Cliffs, N.J.: Prentice-Hall.

Dann, D. L., and Harry DeAngelo. 1988. "Corporate Financial Policy and Corporate Control: A Study of Defensive Adjustment in Asset and Ownership Structure." *Journal of Financial Economics* 20: 87–128.

Davis, Gerald F. 1991a. "Agents without Principles? The Spread of the Poison Pill through the Intercorporate Network." *Administrative Science Quarterly* 36: 583–613.

———— 1991b. Data provided from to the author by Davis from Davis, 1991a (above).

———— 1992. "Corporate Governance and the Interlock Network: The Diffusion of Innovations in Takeover Defense." Unpublished manuscript, Northwestern University.

———— and Walter W. Powell. 1992. "Organization-Environment Relations." In Marvin Dunnette, ed., *The Handbook of Industrial and Organizational Psychology.* Palo Alto, Calif.: Consulting Psychologists Press.

Davis, Gerald F., and Suzanne K. Stout. 1992. "Organization Theory and the Market for Corporate Control: A Dynamic Analysis of the Characteristics of Large Takeover Targets, 1980–1990." *Administrative Science Quarterly* 37: 605–633.

Davis, L. J. 1991. "When A.T.&T. Plays Hardball." *New York Times Magazine,* part 2 (June 9): 14ff.

Defeo, Victor J. 1986. "An Empirical Investigation of the Speed of the Market Reaction to Earnings Announcements." *Journal of Accounting Research* 24: 349–363.

Dertouzos, Michael, Richard K. Lester, and Robert M. Solow. 1989. *Made in America: Regaining the Competitive Edge.* Cambridge, Mass.: MIT Press.

DiMaggio, Paul, and Walter Powell. 1983. "The Iron Case Revisited: Institutional Isomorphism and Collective Rationality in Organizational Fields." *American Sociological Review* 48: 147–160.

Dobrzynski, Judith H. 1992. "Calpers Is Ready to Roar, but Will CEOs Listen?" *Business Week* (March 30): 44–45.

Doeringer, Peter B., Kathleen Christensen, Patricia Flynn, Douglas T. Hall, Harry C. Katz, Jeffrey H. Keefe, Christopher Ruhm, Andrew Sum, and Michael Useem. 1991. *Turbulence in the American Workplace.* New York: Oxford University Press.

Domhoff, G. William. 1967. *Who Rules America.* Englewood Cliffs, N.J.: Prentice-Hall.

Donaldson, Gordon, and Jay W. Lorsch. 1983. *Decision Making at the Top: The Shaping of Strategic Direction.* New York: Basic Books.

Drucker, Peter F. 1976. *The Unseen Revolution: How Pension Fund Socialism Came to America.* New York: Harper and Row.

—— 1991. "Reckoning with the Pension Fund Revolution." *Harvard Business Review* (March–April): 106–109, 111.

Easterwood, John C., Anju Seth, and Ronald F. Singer. 1989. "The Impact of LBOs on Strategic Direction." *California Management Review* 32: 30–43.

Ehrenberg, Ronald G. 1990. "Introduction: Do Compensation Policies Matter?" *Industrial and Labor Relations Review* 43: 3S–12S.

Eisenhardt, Kathleen M. 1989. "Agency Theory: An Assessment and Review." *Academy of Management Review* 14: 57–74.

Etzioni, Amitai. 1968. *The Active Society: A Theory of Societal and Political Processes.* New York: Free Press.

Faludi, Susan C. 1990. "The Reckoning: Safeway LBO Yields Vast Profits but Exacts a Heavy Human Toll." *Wall Street Journal* (May 16): 1ff.

Fama, Eugene. 1980. "Agency Problems and Theory of the Firm." *Journal of Political Economy* 88: 288–306.

Faulk and Co. 1991. "Research Report on Shareholder Returns and Independent Directors." Atlanta, Ga.: Faulk and Co.

Fligstein, Neil. 1985. "The Spread of the Multidivisional Form." *American Sociological Review* 50: 377–391.

—— 1990. *The Transformation of Corporate Control.* Cambridge, Mass.: Harvard University Press.

—— and Kenneth Dauber. 1989. "Structural Change in Corporate Organization." *Annual Review of Sociology* 15: 73–96.

Fligstein, Neil, and Linda Markowitz. 1992. "The Finance Conception of the Corporation and the Causes of the Financial Reorganization of Large American Corporations, 1979–87." Paper presented at a conference on "Efficiency and Ownership: The Future of the Corporation," sponsored by University of California, Davis, May 1992.

Foulkes, Fred K., ed. *Executive Compensation: A Strategic Guide for the 1990s.* Boston: Harvard Business School Press.

Freeman, R. Edward, and David L. Reed. 1983. "Stockholders and Stakeholders: A New Perspective on Corporate Governance." *California Management Review* 25 (Spring): 88–106.

French, Kenneth, and James M. Poterba. 1991. "Investor Diversification and International Equity Markets." *American Economic Review* 81: 222–226.

Friedman, Stewart D., and Harbir Singh. 1989. "CEO Succession and Stockholder Reaction: The Influence of Organizational Context and Event Content." *Academy of Management Journal* 32: 718–744.

Futatsugi, Yusako. 1986. *Japanese Enterprise Groups.* Trans. Anthony Kaufmann. Kobe: Kobe University, School of Business Administration. Originally published in Japanese by Toyo Keizai Shinposha, Tokyo, 1976.

—— 1990. "What Share Cross-Holdings Mean for Corporate Management." *Economic Eye* 11 (1): 17–19.

Galaskiewicz, Joseph. 1985. *Social Organization of an Urban Grants Economy: A Study of Business Philanthropy and Nonprofit Organizations.* New York: Academic Press.

————— 1990. *Corporate-Nonprofit Linkages in Minneapolis–St. Paul: Findings from a Longitudinal Study, 1980–1988.* Minneapolis: Department of Sociology, University of Minnesota.

Galbraith, Craig S., and Gregory B. Merrill. 1991. "The Effect of Compensation Program and Structure on SBU Competitive Strategy: A Study of Technology-Intensive Firms." *Strategic Management Journal* 12: 353–370.

Garrison, Sharon H. 1990. *The Financial Impact of Corporate Events on Corporate Stakeholders.* Westport, Conn.: Greenwood Press.

Geeraerts, Guy. 1984. "The Effect of Ownership on the Organization Structure in Small Firms," *Administrative Science Quarterly* 29: 232–237.

Georgeson and Co. 1987. "1987 Poison Pill Rescission Proposals—What Did It All Mean?" *The Georgeson Report* (second quarter). New York: Georgeson and Co.

————— 1991. "USA 'Target 50' Shareholder Proposals for 1991." New York: Georgeson and Co.

Gerlach, Michael L. 1992a. "The Japanese Corporate Network: A Blockmodel Approach." *Administrative Science Quarterly* 37: 105–139.

————— 1992b. *Alliance Capitalism: The Social Organization of Japanese Business.* Berkeley, Calif.: University of California Press.

————— and James R. Lincoln. 1992. "The Organization of Business Networks in the U.S. and Japan." In Robert Eccles and Nitin Nohria, eds., *Networks and Organization Theory.* Boston: Harvard Business School Press.

Gibbons, Robert, and Kevin J. Murphy. 1990. "Relative Performance Evaluation for Chief Executive Officers." *Industrial and Labor Relations Review* 43: 30S–51S.

Gilson, Ronald J., and Reinier Kraakman. 1991. "Reinventing the Outside Director: An Agenda for Institutional Investors." *Stanford Law Review* 43: 863–906.

Ginsburg, Douglas H., and John F. Robinson. 1986. "The Case against Federal Intervention in the Market for Corporate Control." *Brookings Review* (Winter–Spring): 9–14.

Glasberg, Davita Silfen. 1989. *The Power of Collective Purse Strings.* Berkeley, Calif.: University of California Press.

Golbe, Devra L., and Lawrence J. White. 1988. "A Time-Series Analysis of Mergers and Acquisitions in the U.S. Economy." In Alan Auerbach, ed., *Corporate Takeovers: Causes and Consequences.* Chicago: University of Chicago Press.

Golden, Brian R. 1992. "SBU Strategy and Performance: The Moderating Effects of the Corporate-SBU Relationship." *Strategic Management Journal* 13: 145–158.

Gordon, Robert Aaron, and James Edwin Howell. 1959. *Higher Education for Business.* New York: Columbia University Press.

Gordon, Robert J. 1991. "Discussion on 'Why Are Prices Sticky?'" *American Economic Review* 81 (2): 98–100.

Granovetter, Mark. 1985. "Economic Action and Social Structure: The Problem of Embeddedness." *American Journal of Sociology* 91: 481–510.

Grant, Linda. 1992. "GM Shuffle May be Watershed in Reining in CEOs." *Los Angeles Times* (April 13): D1–D2.

Graves, Samuel B. 1988. "Institutional Ownership and Corporate R&D in the Computer Industry." *Academy of Management Journal* 31: 417–428.

Greenwich Associates. 1990. *Getting Down to Business: Institutional Investors 1990.* Greenwich, Conn.: Greenwich Associates.

Greer, C. R., D. L. Jackson, and J. Fiorito. 1989. "Adapting Human Resource Planning in a Changing Environment." *Human Resource Management* 28: 105–123.

Grimm, W. T., and Co. 1989. *Mergerstat Review 1988.* Chicago: W. T. Grimm and Co.

Grundfest, Joseph A. 1990. "Just Vote No or Just Don't Vote." Paper presented to a meeting of the Council of Institutional Investors, November 1990.

Hall, Bronwyn H. 1988. "The Effect of Takeover Activity on Corporate Research and Development." In Alan Auerbach, ed., *Corporate Takeovers: Causes and Consequences.* Chicago: University of Chicago Press.

Hambrick, Donald C., ed. 1988. *The Executive Effect: Concepts and Methods for Studying Top Managers.* Greenwich, Conn.: JAI Press.

Handler, Edward, and John R. Mulkern. 1982. *Business in Politics.* Lexington, Mass.: Lexington Books.

Hanson, Dale M. 1990. Letter to J. Peter Grace, December 6, 1990. Sacramento: California Public Employees' Retirement System.

Hayes, Thomas C. 1991. "Lockheed Fends Off Simmons." *Wall Street Journal* (March 19): D1, D8.

Hay Group. 1991. "Executive Compensation: The Results of an Opinion Survey." Philadelphia: Hay Group.

Henderson, Rebecca M., and Kim Clark. 1990. "Architectural Innovation: The Reconfiguration of Existing Product Technologies and the Failure of Established Firms." *Administrative Science Quarterly* 35: 9–30.

Henriques, Diana B. 1990. "A Paradoxical Anti-Takeover Bill." *New York Times* (April 8): 15.

Herman, Edward S. 1981. *Corporate Control, Corporate Power.* New York: Cambridge University Press.

Hewitt Associates. 1991. Compensation data privately provided. Lincolnshire, Ill.: Hewitt Associates.

Hicks, Jonathan P. 1990. "Icahn Seen Failing in USX Vote." *New York Times* (May 8): D1–D2.

——— 1991. "Split Stock Approved for USX." *New York Times* (May 7): D1, D5.

Hill, Charles W. L., and Scott A. Snell. 1989. "Effects of Ownership Structure and Control on Corporate Productivity." *Academy of Management Journal* 32: 25–46.

Himmelstein, Jerome L. 1990. *To the Right: The Transformation of American Conservatism.* Berkeley: University of California Press.

Hodges, Cheryl D., and Louis M. Thompson. 1991. Letter to Jonathan M. Katz, Secretary, U.S. Securities and Exchange Commission, September 23. Washington, D.C.: National Investor Relations Institute.

Hoskisson, Robert E., and Thomas A. Turk. 1990. "Corporate Restructuring: Governance and Control Limits of the Internal Capital Market." *Academy of Management Review* 15: 459–477.

Hyman, Jeffrey S. 1991. "Long-Term Incentives." In Milton L. Rock and Lance A. Berger, eds., *The Compensation Handbook,* 3rd ed. New York: McGraw-Hill.

Icahn, Carl. 1988. "Icahn on Icahn." *Fortune* 29 (February): 54–58.

Institutional Investor. 1991. "The 1991 Pensions Directory." *Institutional Investor* 25 (January): 153–192.

International Business Machines. 1991. "An IBM Total Quality Managment (TQM) Competition for Colleges and Universities in the USA." Stamford, Conn.: International Business Machines.

Investor Responsibility Research Center. 1985–, various issues. *Corporate Governance Bulletin.* Washington, D.C.: Investor Responsibility Research Center.

——— 1989, various monthly issues. *Voting Results.* Washington, D.C.: Investor Responsibility Research Center.

——— 1990, various monthly issues. *Voting Results.* Washington, D.C.: Investor Responsibility Research Center.

——— 1990a. *Corporate Governance Bulletin* 7, no. 3 (May–June). Washington, D.C.: Investor Responsibility Research Center.

——— 1990b. *Corporate Governance Bulletin* 7, no. 6 (November–December). Washington, D.C.: Investor Responsibility Research Center.

——— 1991a. *Voting Results 1990.* Washington, D.C.: Investor Responsibility Research Center.

——— 1991b. "State Takeover Laws: Pennsylvania." Washington, D.C.: Investor Responsibility Research Center.

ITT Corporation. 1991. Notice of Annual Meeting and Proxy Statement. New York: ITT Corporation.

——— 1992. Notice of Annual Meeting and Proxy Statement. New York: ITT Corporation.

Jackall, Robert. 1983. "Moral Mazes: Bureaucracy and Managerial Work." *Harvard Business Review* 61 (September–October): 118–130.

——— 1988. *Moral Mazes: The World of Corporate Managers.* New York: Oxford University Press.

Jacobs, David. 1974. "Dependency and Vulnerability: An Exchange Approach to the Control of Organizations." *Administrative Science Quarterly* 19: 45–59.

Jacobs, Michael T. 1991. *The Causes and Cures of Our Short-Term Myopia.* Boston: Harvard Business School Press.

Jarrell, Gregg A., James A. Brickley, and Jeffrey M. Netter. 1988. "The Market for Corporate Control: The Empirical Evidence since 1980." *Journal of Economic Perspectives* 2: 49–68.

Jensen, Michael C. 1989. "Eclipse of the Public Corporation." *Harvard Business Review* 67 (September–October): 61–74.

——— and William H. Meckling. 1976. "Theory of the Firm: Management Behavior, Agency Costs, and Ownership Structure." *Journal of Financial Economics* 3: 305–360.

Jensen, Michael C., and Kevin J. Murphy. 1990. "CEO Incentives—It's Not How Much You Pay, But How." *Harvard Business Review* 68 (May–June): 138–153.

Jensen, Michael C., and Richard S. Ruback. 1983. "The Market for Corporate Control." *Journal of Financial Economics* 11: 5–50.

Jensen, Michael C., and Jerold B. Warner. 1988. "The Distribution of Power among

Corporate Managers, Shareholders, and Directors.'' *Journal of Financial Economics* 20: 3–24.

Johnson, Elmer W. 1990. ''An Insider's Call for Outside Direction.'' *Harvard Business Review* 68 (March–April): 3–8.

Kahn, Lawrence M., and Peter D. Sherer. 1990. ''Contingent Pay and Managerial Performance.'' *Industrial and Labor Relations Review* 43: 107S-120S.

Kanter, Rosabeth Moss. 1977. *Men and Women of the Corporation.* New York: Basic Books.

——— 1983. *The Change Masters: Innovation for Productivity in the American Corporation.* New York: Simon and Schuster.

Kaplan, Steven N., and Jeremy C. Stein. 1992. ''The Evolution of Buyout Pricing and Financial Structure.'' Paper presented at a conference on ''Efficiency and Ownership: The Future of the Corporation,'' sponsored by University of California, Davis, May 1992.

Kennedy, Robert G. 1990. ''Dayton Hudson Corporation: Conscience and Control.'' Boston: Harvard Business School Case Series.

Kerr, Steven. ''On the Folly of Rewarding A While Hoping for B.'' *Academy of Management Journal* 18: 769–783.

Kerr, Jeffrey, and Richard A. Bettis. 1987. ''Board of Directors, Top Management Compensation, and Shareholder Returns.'' *Academy of Management Journal* 30: 645–664.

Kesner, Idalene F., and Roy B. Johnson. 1990. ''An Investigation of the Relationship between Board Composition and Stockholder Suits.'' *Strategic Management Journal* 11: 327–336.

Kidder, Robert. 1990. Quoted in ''CEO Roundtable on Corporate Structure and Management Incentives.'' *Journal of Applied Corporate Finance* 3 (Fall): 7–35.

Kimberly, John R., and Robert E. Quinn, eds. 1984. *Managing Organizational Transitions.* Homewood, Ill.: Irwin.

Kochan, Thomas A., and Michael Useem, eds. 1992. *Transforming Organizations.* New York: Oxford University Press.

Koh, Jeongsuk, and N. Venkatraman. 1991. ''Joint Venture Formations and Stock Market Reactions: An Assessment in the Information Technology Sector.'' *Academy of Management Review* 34: 869–892.

Kohlberg Kravis Roberts and Co. 1989. ''Presentation on Leveraged Buy-Outs.'' New York: Kohlberg Kravis Roberts.

Korn/Ferry International. 1991. *Board of Directors: Eighteenth Annual Study, 1991.* New York: Korn/Ferry International.

Kotter, John P. 1982. *The General Managers.* New York: Free Press.

Kotz, David M., 1978. *Bank Control of Large Corporations in the United States.* Berkeley, Calif.: University of California Press.

Krasnow, Lauren G. 1989. *Voting by Institutional Investors on Corporate Governance Issues in the 1989 Proxy Season.* Washington, D.C.: Investor Responsibility Research Center.

Kreiner, Peter, and Arvind Bhambri. 1991. ''Influence and Information in Organization-Stakeholder Relationships.'' In James E. Post, ed., *Research in Corporate Social Performance and Policy,* vol. 12. Greenwich, Conn.: JAI Press.

Larner, Robert J. 1970. *Management Control and the Large Corporation.* New York: Dunellen Publishing Company.

Laumann, Edward O., and David Knoke. 1987. *The Organizational State: Social Choice in National Policy Domains.* Madison: University of Wisconsin Press.

Leonard, Jonathan S. 1990. "Executive Pay and Firm Performance." *Industrial and Labor Relations Review* 43: 13S–29S.

Levin, Doron P. 1992a. "Top G.M. Executives Took Pay Cut in '91." *New York Times* (April 14): D1.

—— 1992b. "President Is Demoted at G.M." *New York Times* (April 7): D1.

Levine, David L., and Laura D'Andrea Tyson. 1990. "Participation, Productivity, and the Firm's Environment." In Alan S. Blinder, ed., *Paying for Productivity: A Look at the Evidence.* Washington, D.C.: Brookings Institution.

Levine, David O. 1986. *The American College and the Culture of Aspiration, 1915–1940.* Ithaca: Cornell University Press, 1986.

Lichtenberg, Frank R., and Donald Siegel. 1989. "The Effect of Takeovers on the Employment and Wages of Central-Office and Other Personnel." Cambridge, Mass.: National Bureau of Economic Research.

Lieberson, Stanley, and James F. O'Connor. 1972. "Leadership and Organizational Performance: A Study of Large Corporations." *American Sociological Review* 37: 117–130.

Lipset, Seymour Martin, and William Schneider. 1983. *The Confidence Gap: Business, Labor, and Government in the Public Mind.* New York: Free Press.

Lipton, Michael. 1988. "Is This the End of Takeovers?" New York: Wachtell, Lipton, Rosen, and Katz.

Lockheed Corporation. 1991. "Promises Made, Promises Kept." Advertisement appearing in *Wall Street Journal* (January 31): A13.

Lohr, Steve. 1992. "Shake-Up Is a Sign Rubber-Stamp Days Have Ended at G.M." *New York Times* (April 8): 1.

Long, William F., and David J. Ravenscraft. 1991. "The Record of LBO Performance." In Arnold W. Sametz, ed., *The Battle for Corporate Control.* Homewood, Ill.: Business One Irwin.

Lorsch, Jay W. 1989. *Pawns or Potentates: The Reality of America's Corporate Boards.* Boston: Harvard Business School Press.

Lowenstein, Louis. 1991. *Sense and Nonsense in Corporate Finance.* Reading, Mass.: Addison-Wesley.

Lubatkin, Michael H., Kae H. Chung, Ronald C. Rogers, and James E. Owens. 1989. "Stockholder Reactions to CEO Changes in Large Corporations." *Academy of Management Journal* 32: 47–68.

MacDuffie, John Paul, and John Krafcik. 1992. "Integrating Technology and Human Resources for High Performance Manufacturing: Evidence from the International Auto Industry." In Thomas Kochan and Michael Useem, eds., *Transforming Organizations.* New York: Oxford University Press.

Machold, Roland M. 1988. "The American Corporation and the Institutional Investor: Are There Lessons from Abroad? A Domestic Perspective." *Columbia Law Review* 1988 (3): 751–764.

Macke, Kenneth A. 1990. "Philanthropic Giving as a Business Tactic . . . With Some Attendant Risks." *New York Times* (December 30): Business Section, 11.

Mahoney, William F. 1990. "Recession Can Provide Extraordinary Opportunity for Investor Relations Practice." *Investor Relations Update* (November): 1–7.

———— 1991a. *Investor Relations: The Professional's Guide to Financial Marketing and Communications.* New York: New York Institute of Finance, and Simon and Schuster.

———— 1991b. "Survey: How Companies View Investor Activism, Interest in Governance." *Investor Relations Update* (January): 8–9.

———— 1991c. "Grappling with the Growing Complexities of Investor Relations." *Investor Relations Update* (June): 1–3.

Malatesta, Paul H., and Ralph A. Walkling. 1988. "Poison Pill Securities: Stockholder Wealth, Profitability, and Ownership Structure." *Journal of Financial Economics* 20: 347–376.

Marcus, Alfred A., and Robert S. Goodman. 1991. "Victims and Shareholders: The Dilemmas of Presenting Corporate Policy during a Crisis." *Academy of Management Review* 34: 281–305.

Markoff, John. 1991. "At I.B.M., Refocusing Yet Again." *New York Times* (November 25): D1, D4.

Matasar, Ann B. 1986. *Corporate PACs and Federal Campaign Financing Laws.* Westport, Conn.: Quorum Books.

McGregor, Douglas M. 1960. *The Human Side of Enterprise.* New York: McGraw-Hill.

McGuire, Jean B., Alison Sundgren, and Thomas Schneeweis. 1988. "Corporate Social Responsibility and Firm Financial Performance." *Academy of Management Journal* 31: 854–872.

McGurn, Patrick S., Sharon Pamepinto, and Adam B. Spector. 1989. *State Antitakeover Laws.* Washington, D.C.: Investor Responsibility Research Center.

McMurray, Scott. 1991. "Du Pont Launches Sweeping Program to Boost Earnings." *Wall Street Journal* (December 5): A6.

Merrill Lynch Business Brokerage and Valuation. 1990. *Mergerstat Review, 1989.* Schaumburg, Ill.: Merrill Lynch Business Brokerage and Valuation.

———— 1991. *Mergerstat Review, 1990.* Schaumburg, Ill.: Merrill Lynch Business Brokerage and Valuation.

Meyer, Marshall W., and Lynne C. Zucker. 1989. *Permanently Failing Organizations.* Newbury Park, Calif.: Sage Publications.

Mills, C. Wright. 1956. *The Power Elite.* New York: Oxford University Press.

Mintz, Beth, and Michael Schwartz. 1985. *The Power Structure of American Business.* Chicago: University of Chicago Press, 1985.

Mintzberg, Henry. 1975. "The Manager's Job: Folklore and Fact." *Harvard Business Review* 53 (July–August): 49–61.

———— 1973. *The Nature of Managerial Work.* New York: Harper and Row.

———— 1983. *Power in and around Organizations.* Englewood Cliffs, N.J.: Prentice-Hall.

Mizruchi, Mark S., 1982. *The American Corporate Network, 1904–1974.* Beverly Hills, Calif.: Sage Publications.

———— 1992. *The Structure of Corporate Political Action.* Cambridge, Mass.: Harvard University Press.

———— and Michael Schwartz, eds. 1987. *Intercorporate Relations: The Structural Analysis of Business.* New York: Cambridge University Press.

Monks, Robert A. G., and Nell Minow. 1991. *Power and Accountability.* New York: Harper Business.

Nadler, David A. 1977. "Concepts for the Management of Organizational Change." In R. Hackman, E. Lawler, and L. Porter, eds., *Perspectives on Behavior in Organizations.* New York: McGraw-Hill.

—— and Michael L. Tushman. 1988. *Strategic Organization Design.* Glenview, Ill.: Scott, Foresman.

Napier, Nancy K. 1989. "Mergers and Acquisitions, Human Resource Issues and Outcomes: A Review and Suggested Typology." *Journal of Management Studies* 26: 271–289.

National Academy of Engineering, Committee on Time Horizons and Technology Investments. 1992. *Time Horizons and Technology Investments.* Washington, D.C.: National Academy of Engineering.

National Investor Relations Institute. 1985. *Emerging Trends in Investor Relations.* Washington, D.C.: National Investor Relations Institute.

—— 1989. *Emerging Trends in Investor Relations.* 2nd ed. Washington, D.C.: National Investor Relations Institute.

—— 1990a. Results of the 1990 Corporate Governance Survey. Washington, D.C.: National Investor Relations Institute.

—— 1990b. "Position Statement on Corporate Governance." Washington, D.C.: National Investor Relations Institute.

NCR. 1991. "A Question for NCR Shareholders." *New York Times* (March 11): D3, advertisement.

Neff, Thomas J. 1990. "Shareholder Muscle Cutting into Corporate Fat." *Wall Street Journal* (March 25): A10.

New York Stock Exchange. 1991. *Fact Book.* New York: New York Stock Exchange.

O'Barr, William M., and John M. Conley. 1992. *Fortune and Folly: The Wealth and Power of Institutional Investing.* Homewood, Ill.: Business One Irwin.

O'Bryne, Stephen F. 1991. "Linking Management Performance Incentives to Shareholder Wealth." *Journal of Corporate Accounting and Finance* (Autumn): 91–99.

Orru, Marco, Nicole Woolsey Biggart, and Gary G. Hamilton. 1991. "Organizational Isomorphism in East Asia." In Walter W. Powell and Paul DiMaggio, eds., *The New Institutionalism in Organizational Analysis.* Chicago: University of Chicago Press.

Oswald, Sharon L., and John S. Jahera, Jr. 1991. "The Influence of Ownership on Performance: An Empirical Study." *Strategic Management Journal* 12: 321–326.

Palmer, Donald, Roger Friedland, P. Deveraux Jennings, and Melanie Powers. 1987. "The Economics and Politics of Structure: The Multidivisional Form and the Large U.S. Corporation." *Administrative Science Quarterly* 32: 25–48.

Palmer, Donald, Deveraux Jennings, and Xueguang Zhou. 1989. "From Corporate Strategies to Institutional Prescriptions: Adoption of Multidivisional Form, 1962–1968." San Francisco: Annual Meeting of American Sociological Association, unpublished.

Partch, M. Megan. 1987. "The Creation of a Class of Limited Voting Common Stock and Shareholders' Wealth." *Journal of Financial Economics* 18: 313–339.

Pearce, John A., II, and Shaker A. Zahra. 1991. "The Relative Power of CEOs and Boards of Directors: Associations with Corporate Performance." *Strategic Management Journal* 12: 135–153.

Pennings, Johannes S. 1980. *The Interlocking Directorates.* San Francisco: Jossey-Bass.

Perrow, Charles. 1986. *Complex Organizations: A Critical Essay.* 3rd ed. New York: Random House.

Peters, Thomas J., and Robert H. Waterman, Jr. 1982. *In Search of Excellence: Lessons from America's Best-Run Companies.* New York: Harper and Row.

Pettigrew, Andrew, and Richard Whipp. 1991. *Managing Change for Competitive Success.* Oxford: Blackwell Publishers.

Pfeffer, Jeffrey. 1978. "The Ambiguity of Leadership." In Morgan W. McCall, Jr., and Michael M. Lombardo, eds., *Leadership: Where Else Can We Go?* Durham, N.C.: Duke University Press.

——— 1981a. *Power in Organizations.* Marshfield, Mass.: Pitman.

——— 1981b. "Management as Symbolic Action: The Creation and Maintenance of Organizational Paradigms." In L. L. Cummings and Barry M. Staw, eds., *Research in Organizational Behavior,* vol. 3. Greenwich, Conn.: JAI Press.

——— and Gerald Salancik. 1978. *The External Control of Organizations: A Resource Dependence Perspective.* New York: Harper and Row.

Pickens, T. Boone. 1987. "Corporate Restructuring: Its Effect on American Business." Transcript of conference, October 27. Atlanta: Emory University School of Business Administration.

Pierson, Frank C. 1959. *The Education of American Businessmen: A Study of University-College Programs in Business Administration.* New York: McGraw-Hill.

Porter, Lyman W., and Lawrence E. McKibbin. 1988. *Management Education and Development: Drift or Thrust into the 21st Century.* New York: McGraw-Hill.

Porter, Michael. 1992. *Capital Choices: Changing the Way America Invests in Industry.* Washington, D.C.: Council on Competitiveness.

Post, James S., Edwin A. Murray, Jr., Robert D. Dickie, and John F. Mahon. 1983. "Managing Public Affairs: The Public Affairs Function." *California Management Review* 26: 135–150.

Pound, John. 1988. "Proxy Contests and Efficiency of Shareholder Oversight." *Journal of Financial Economics* 20: 237–265.

——— 1992. "Beyond Takeovers: Politics Comes to Corporate Control." *Harvard Business Review* (March–April): 83–93.

Powell, Thomas C. 1992. "Organizational Alignment as Competitive Advantage." *Strategic Management Journal* 13: 119–134.

Powell, Walter W., and Paul J. DiMaggio, eds. 1991. *The New Institutionalism in Organizational Analysis.* Chicago: University of Chicago Press.

Puffer, Sheila M., and Joseph B. Weintrop. 1991. "Corporate Performance and CEO Turnover: A Comparison of Performance Indicators." *Administrative Science Quarterly* 36: 1–19.

Rappaport, Alfred. 1986. *Creating Shareholder Value: The New Standard for Business Performance.* New York: Free Press.

——— 1992. "CFOs and Strategists: Forging a Common Framework." *Harvard Business Review* (May–June): 84–91.

Regan, Edward V. 1992a. "A New Way to Discipline Badly Run Companies." *Wall Street Journal* (June 5): A10.

——— 1992b. Quoted in Treece, 1992 (below).

Reimann, Bernard C. 1990. *Managing for Value: A Guide to Value-Based Strategic Management.* Cambridge, Mass.: Basil Blackwell.

Reinganum, Marc R. 1985. "The Effect of Executive Succession on Stockholder Wealth." *Administrative Science Quarterly* 30: 46–60.

Riesman, David. 1950. *The Lonely Crowd: A Study of the Changing American Character.* New Haven, Conn.: Yale University Press.

Robinson, James D., John F. Akers, Edwin L. Artzt, Harold A. Poling, Robert W. Galvin, and Paul Allaire. 1991. "An Open Letter: TQM on the Campus." *Harvard Business Review* (November–December): 94–95.

Rock, Milton L., and Lance A. Berger. 1991. *The Compensation Handbook.* 3rd ed. New York: McGraw-Hill.

Roe, Mark J. 1992. "That Menace, the Small Shareholder." *Wall Street Journal* (May 21): A12.

Roman, Paul M., and Terry C. Blum. 1987. "The Relation of Employee Assistance Programs to Corporate Social Responsibility Attitudes: An Empirical Study." In William C. Frederick and Lee E. Preston, eds., *Research in Corporate Social Performance and Policy,* vol. 9. Greenwich, Conn.: JAI Press.

Rosenbaum, Virginia K. 1986. *Takeover Defenses: Profiles of the Fortune 500.* Washington, D.C.: Investor Responsibility Research Center.

——— 1987. *Takeover Defenses: Profiles of the Fortune 500, 1987 Update.* Washington, D.C.: Investor Responsibility Research Center.

——— 1989. *Corporate Takeover Defenses, 1989.* Washington, D.C.: Investor Responsibility Research Center.

——— 1990a. *Corporate Takeover Defenses, 1990.* Washington, D.C.: Investor Responsibility Research Center.

——— 1990b. Special reanalysis of corporate takeover defense data base. Washington, D.C.: Investor Responsibility Research Center.

Rosenstein, Stuart, and Jeffrey G. Wyatt. 1990. "Outside Directors, Board Independence, and Shareholder Wealth." *Journal of Financial Economics* 26: 175–191.

Ryngaert, Michael. 1988. "The Effect of Poison Pill Securities on Shareholder Wealth." *Journal of Financial Economics* 20: 377–418.

Scherer, F. M. 1988. "Corporate Ownership and Control." In John R. Meyer and James M. Gustafson, eds., *The U.S. Business Corporation: An Institution in Transition.* Cambridge, Mass.: Ballinger.

Schrader, Stephan. 1992. "Informal Information Trading between Firms." In Thomas Kochan and Michael Useem, eds., *Transforming Organizations.* New York: Oxford University Press.

Scott Morton, Michael S., ed. 1991. *The Corporation of the 1990s: Information Technology and Organizational Transformation.* New York: Oxford University Press.

Securities Industry Association. 1990. Analysis of statistics provided by the Federal Reserve Bank. Washington, D.C: Securities Industry Association.

——— 1991. Analysis of statistics provided by the Federal Reserve Bank. Washington, D.C: Securities Industry Association.

Seely, Michael. 1991. "A Vision of Value-Based Governance." *Directors and Boards* 15 (Spring): 35–36.

Shapiro, Eben. 1991. "NCR Establishes an Employee Stock Plan." *New York Times* (February 22): D1.

Sherman, Howard D. 1989. "The Institutional Shareholder Perspective on Director Pay." *Directors and Boards* 13 (Spring): 45–46

Shiller, Robert J. 1991. "Discussion on 'Why Are Prices Sticky?' " *American Economic Review* 81 (2): 97–98.

Shleifer, Andrei, and Robert W. Vishny. 1986. "Large Shareholders and Corporate Control." *Journal of Political Economy* 95: 461–488.

Sikora, Martin, ed. 1990. *Capturing the Untapped Value in Your Company.* Philadelphia: MLR Publishing Company.

Silk, Leonard, and David Vogel. 1976. *Ethics and Profits: The Crisis of Confidence in American Business.* New York: Simon and Schuster.

Simon, Jane. 1988. "Polaroid's Booth Talks Back." *Boston Globe* (October 4): 27, 46.

——— 1990. "Same Managers, Same Problems: Polaroid One Year after Shamrock. *Boston Globe* (March 11): 33, 38–39.

Singh, Harbir, and Farid Harianto. 1989. "Management-Board Relationships, Takeover Risk, and the Adoption of Golden Parachutes." *Academy of Management Journal* 32: 7–24.

Skowronski, Walter E. 1991. Quoted in William F. Mahoney, "Bargaining in Proxy Contests Advancing Governance Agenda." *Investor Relations Update* (August): 12–15.

Slater, Robert. 1988. *This . . . Is CBS: A Chronicle of 60 Years.* Englewood Cliffs, N.J.: Prentice-Hall.

Smith, Randall. 1991. "AT&T's Bid to Buy NCR Is Hampered by the Recent Surge of Computer Stocks." *Wall Street Journal* (February 20): A4.

——— and Joseph B. White. 1992. "G.M. Shake-Up Adds Spring to Its Stock." *Wall Street Journal* (April 8): C1.

Smith, Vicki. 1990. *Managing in the Corporate Interest: Control and Resistance in an American Bank.* Berkeley, Calif.: University of California Press.

Sommer, A. A., Jr. 1991. "Corporate Governance in the Nineties: Managers vs. Institutions." *Cincinnati Law Review* 59: 357–383.

Standard and Poor's. 1989 (and other years). *Register of Corporations, Directors, and Executives, 1988.* New York: Standard and Poor's.

Stearns, Linda Brewster, and Mark S. Mizruchi. 1993. "Corporate Financing: Social and Economic Determinants." In Richard Swedberg, ed., *Explorations in Economic Sociology.* New York: Russell Sage Foundation.

Stewart, James B. 1991. *Den of Thieves.* New York: Simon and Schuster.

Swidler, Ann. 1986. "Culture in Action: Symbols and Strategies." *American Sociological Review* 51: 273–286.

Taylor, William. 1991. "The Logic of Global Business: An Interview with ABB's Percy Barnevik." *Harvard Business Review* (March–April): 91–105.

Tellep, Daniel M. 1991. "Be in Harmony with Stockholders." *Directors and Boards* 16 (1): 41–43.

Thomas, Alan Berkeley. 1988. "Does Leadership Make a Difference to Organizational Performance?" *Administrative Science Quarterly* 33: 388–400.

Thomas, Robert. 1993. *What Machines Can't Do: Politics and Technology in the Industrial Enterprise.* Berkeley, Calif.: University of California Press.

Thomas, Steven L., and Morris M. Kleiner. 1992. "The Effect of Two-Tier Collective Bargaining on Shareholder Equity." *Industrial and Labor Relations Review* 45: 339–351.

Thompson, Louis M. 1991. "Call for Action on SEC Proxy Reform Proposals." *Washington Alert* (September 11). Washington, D.C.: National Investor Relations Institute.

———— and Eugene F. Trumble. 1990. *The Battle for Corporate Control: The IR Role.* Washington, D.C.: National Investor Relations Institute.

Treece, James B. 1992. "The Board Revolt: Business as Usual Won't Cut It Anymore at a Humbled GM." *Business Week* (April 20): 30–36.

United Shareholders Association. 1990. Letter of March 20, 1990, to U.S. Securities and Exchange Commission. Washington, D.C.: United Shareholders Association.

———— 1991a. *1991 Shareholder 1,000: Rating Corporate America's Responsiveness to Shareholders.* Washington, D.C.: United Shareholders Association.

———— 1991b. *Executive Compensation in Corporate America, '91.* Washington, D.C.: United Shareholders Association.

U.S. Federal Election Commission. 1991. Information provided upon request. Washington, D.C.: Federal Election Commission.

U.S. General Accounting Office. 1987. *Plant Closing: Limited Advance Notice and Assistance Provided Dislocated Workers.* Washington, D.C.: U.S. General Accounting Office.

U.S. Securities and Exchange Commission. 1991. "Regulation of Securityholder Communications: Proposed Rules." Washington, D.C.: U.S. Securities and Exchange Commission.

Useem, Michael. 1984. *The Inner Circle: Large Corporations and the Rise of Business Political Activity in the U.S. and U.K.* New York: Oxford University Press.

———— 1987. "Corporate Philanthropy." In Walter W. Powell, ed., *The Nonprofit Sector: A Research Handbook.* New Haven, Conn.: Yale University Press.

———— 1989. *Liberal Education and the Corporation: The Hiring and Advancement of College Graduates.* Hawthorne, N.Y.: Aldine de Gruyter.

———— 1991. "Organizational and Managerial Factors in the Shaping of Corporate Social and Political Action." In James E. Post, ed., *Research in Corporate Social Performance and Policy,* vol. 12. Greenwich, Conn.: JAI Press.

———— 1993. "Company Policies on Education and Training." In Philip Mirvis, ed., *Building a Competitive Workforce: Investing in Human Capital for Competitive Success.* New York: John Wiley.

Vickers Stock Research Corporation. 1991. *Who Really Owns Your Company?* Huntington, N.Y.: Vickers Stock Research Corporation.

Vogel, David. 1978. *Lobbying the Corporation.* New York: Basic Books.

———— 1989. *Fluctuating Fortunes: The Political Power of Business in America.* New York: Basic Books.

von Hippel, Eric. 1987. "Cooperation between Rivals: Information Know-How Trading." *Research Policy* 16: 291–302.

Wade, James, Charles A. O'Reilly, III, and Ike Chandratat. 1990. "Golden Parachutes: CEOs and the Exercise of Social Influence." *Administrative Science Quarterly* 35: 587–603.

Walsh, James P., and James K. Seward. 1990. "On the Efficiency of Internal and External Corporate Control Mechanisms." *Academy of Management Review* 15: 421–458.

Wartzman, Rich. 1991. "A Raider Stalks It, but Leaner Lockheed Has Begun to Take Off." *Wall Street Journal* (February 14): A1, A6.

Weaver, Paul H. 1988. "After Social Responsibility." In John R. Meyer and James M. Gustafson, eds., *The U.S. Business Corporation: An Institution in Transition*. Cambridge, Mass.: Ballinger.

Weiner, Nan, and Thomas A. Mahoney. 1981. "A Model of Corporate Performance as a Function of Environmental, Organizational, and Leadership Influences." *Academy of Management Journal* 24: 453–470.

Weston, J. Fred, Kwang S. Chung, and Susan E. Hoag. 1990. *Mergers, Restructuring, and Corporate Control*. Englewood Cliffs, N.J.: Prentice-Hall.

Wharton, Clifton R. 1991. "Just Vote No." *Harvard Business Review* 69 (November–December): 137–139.

White, James A. 1991. "GM Bows to California Pension Fund by Adopting Bylaw on Board's Makeup." *Wall Street Journal* (January 31): A6.

White, Joseph B., and Paul Ingrassia. 1992. "Behind Revolt at GM, Lawyer Ira Millstein Helped Call the Shots." *Wall Street Journal* (April 13): 1.

Whyte, William Foote. 1955. *Street Corner Society: The Social Structure of an Italian Slum*. 2nd ed. Chicago: University of Chicago Press.

Whyte, William H. 1956. *The Organization Man*. New York: Simon and Schuster.

Wines, Richard A. 1990. "Who Owns Corporate America—13F Filings: How Reliable Are They?" *Boards and Directors* 15 (Fall): 52–53.

———— 1991. *Proxy Contest Study*. New York: Georgeson and Company.

Wohlstetter, Charles. 1990. Comments at conference sponsored by the National Investor Relations Institute, New York City (November 13).

Wolfe, Tom. 1987. *The Bonfire of the Vanities*. New York: Farrar, Straus and Giroux.

Woodridge, J. Randall, and Charles C. Snow. 1990. "Stock Market Reaction to Strategic Investment Decisions." *Strategic Management Journal* 11: 353–363.

Working Group on Corporate Governance. 1991. "A New Compact for Owners and Directors." *Harvard Business Review* 69 (July–August): 142–143.

Worrell, Dan L., Wallace N. Davidson III, and Varinder M. Sharma. 1991. "Layoff Announcements and Stockholder Wealth." *Academy of Management Journal* 34: 662–678.

Yago, Glenn. 1991. *Junk Bonds: How High Yield Securities Restructured Corporate America*. New York: Oxford University Press.

Yankelovich Group. 1988. *The Climate for Giving: The Outlook of Current and Future CEOs*. New York: Council on Foundations.

Yantek, Thom, and Kenneth D. Gartrell. 1988. "The Political Climate and Corporate Mergers: When Politics Affects Economics." *Western Political Quarterly* 41: 309–322.

Zald, Mayer N. 1969. "The Power and Functions of Boards of Directors: A Theoretical Synthesis." *American Journal of Sociology* 75: 97–111.

Zeitlin, Maurice. 1974. "Corporate Ownership and Control: The Large Corporation and the Capitalist Class." *American Journal of Sociology* 79: 1073–1119.

Ziegler, Bart. 1991. "Not All Job Cuts Recession-Related." *Philadelphia Inquirer* (December 21): 12-D.

Zuboff, Shoshana. 1988. *In the Age of the Smart Machine: The Future of Work and Power.* New York: Basic Books.

Index

ABB Aesa Brown Boveri Ltd., 240
Abnormal shareholder returns, 227–231
Abowd, John M., 127, 224, 229
Acquisitions. *See* Mergers and acquisitions
Advocacy advertising, 158
Akers, John F., 211–212
Albertson's Inc., 196
Alcar, 76
Aldrich, Howard, 35
Alignment, 1, 18, 56, 115, 234, 243–244;
    studying, 3–5, 247–254; defined, 5–10;
    task, 9; management of managers, 89–90,
    126–128; performance, 106–111, 126–
    127, 240–242; managerial diversity, 122;
    shareholders, 129–131, 155–156, 195–
    200; boards of directors, 191, 193, 200–
    209, 214–215; nonprofit organizations,
    210–213; leadership, 217–220; ideology,
    224; systemic change, 232–233
Allen, Michael Patrick, 237, 243
American Express Co., 208, 213
American Society of Corporate Secretaries,
    47, 202
American Stock Exchange, 230
American Telephone and Telegraph Co.
    (AT&T), 32, 40, 42–43, 49, 51, 256
Ameritech Corp., 256
Ammon, R. Theodore, 184
Amoco Corp., 32
Analysis Group, 40
Anderson, Roy A., 198
Anderson, William S., 184
Arista Co., 184
Armstrong World Industries, 178

Associated Press, 17
Atkinson, Lisa, 160
Atlantic Council, 184
Atlantic Richfield Co., 32, 198
Auerbach, Alan, 3
Autry, Ret, 82

Bacon, Jeremy, 51, 189, 200, 202, 204
Baker, G. P., 101
Barnard, Jayne, 203
Bartlett, Sarah, 34, 42
Beatrice Cos., 26
Becker, Brian E., 229
Beer, Michael, 9
Bell Atlantic Corp., 256
BellSouth Corp., 32, 183, 184
Bendix, Reinhard, 226–227
Berberian, Michael, 198
Berberian Bros., 198
Berenbeim, Ronald E., 239
Berg, Eric N., 200
Berger, Lance, 101, 107, 112
Berle, Adolph, Jr., 19, 34, 234, 236
Bettis, Richard A., 111
Bhagat, Sanjai, 231
Bhambri, Arvind, 11, 241
Bhopal (India), 231
Biersach, Jeffrey W., 27
Biggart, Nicole Woolsey, 9, 182
Black, Bernard S., 42, 44, 229
Blinder, Alan S., 252
Blum, Terry C., 124
Blumenthal, Karen, 27, 131
BMW (company), 206

Boards of directors: power, 19, 58, 191–195, 196–197, 214–215, 234; composition, 42–43, 183–189, 201, 203–206; management compensation, 106; meetings, 192–195; company change, 194; committees, 197; compensation, 201, 206–208; information, 201, 208–210; election, 202–203; chairman, 203; company performance, 204, 240–241
Boeing Co., 44
Boesky, Ivan F., 2
Bonfire of the Vanities, 250
Borg-Warner, 24, 26, 186
Boston, 253
Bounded rationality, 127
Bowditch, James L., 3
Bowers, Jack L., 198
Boyer, Peter, 2
Bradley, Michael, 229
Brancato, Carolyn, 29, 257
Brickley, James A., 53, 54, 148, 229, 231
Bristol-Myers Co., 32
Buono, Anthony F., 3
Burlington Industries, 186
Burris, Val, 162, 177, 181, 182
Burrough, Bryan, 35
Burt, Ronald S., 35
Business Roundtable, 47–48, 171, 174, 195, 201, 202, 235
Business Week, 32, 175
Butler, Albert L., 184
Buy-side analysts, 37, 114, 135, 141, 145
Byrne, John A., 253

California, 171
California Public Employees' Retirement System (Calpers): long-term investor, 28; market value, 29, 256; company pressure, 38–39, 52, 208; shareholder proposals, 39, 44, 53, 149–151, 259; regulatory reform, 47, 202; independent directors, 188
California State Teachers' Retirement System, 53, 256, 259
Campbell, John L., 6
Campeau Corp., 23
Carbonell, John L., 184
Carroll, Paul B., 211, 220
Cause-related marketing, 158
CBS, 2–3, 203–204
CDA Investment Technologies, 36
Celanese Corp., 183, 184

Chaganti, Rajeswararao, 53
Chamber of Commerce, 169, 174
Champion International Corp., 44
Chandler, Alfred D., Jr., 12, 20, 234
Chandratat, Ike, 48, 204
Charitable giving, 158, 159–161, 164–166, 167–168, 180–181, 185
Chase Manhattan Bank, 44
Chemical-products company, 4–5; decentralization, 61, 65–68; strategic planning, 64–65; contraction of central management, 79–80; managing managers, 97–98; management compensation, 105; managerial careers, 124–126; investor relations, 132; short-term pressures, 141–144; board of directors, 192–193, 195, 204; management power, 217–218
Chevron Corp., 32
Christensen, Kathleen, 249
Chrysler Corp., 113
Chung, Kae H., 230
Chung, Kwang S., 3, 49
Clark, Kim, 232
Classified directors, 43–46, 48–50, 147
Classwide political action, 181–189
Clawson, Dan, 162, 177, 181, 182, 185
Coca-Cola Co., 2, 32
Cochran, Philip L., 204
Coffee, John C., 3
Cohen, David K., 8
Cohen, Roger, 211
Coherence, organizational, 7
College Retirement Equities Fund (CREF), 28, 44, 53, 208, 259
Colleges, 212–213
Colodny, Mark M., 82
Combustion Engineering Inc., 184
Comment, Robert, 201, 230
Compact for owners and directors, 201
Compensation, 40; performance incentives, 98, 101–102, 224; contingent, 102–106, 116–119; shareholder value, 106–111, 221–223; asymmetry problems, 111–113; measurement problems, 111, 113–116; understanding, 116–119; ownership, 119–121, 221–223; boards of directors, 201, 206–208
Competitiveness Policy Council, 141, 241
Conference Board, 200, 204–205, 239
Confidential voting, 27, 43–46, 147, 198, 202

Congruence, organizational, 7
Conley, John M., 131, 145, 238, 251
Connecticut Retirement and Trust Funds, 259
Conte, Michael A., 232
Contel Corp., 155
Continental Illinois Corp., 198
Control share acquisition, 172–173, 179
Cook, Frederic W., 24
Coperland, Tom, 76
Corporate 300, 91–93
Council for Aid to Education, 161
Council of Economic Advisors, 171
Council of Institutional Investors, 39–40
Crawford, Edward K., 237
Crown Zellerbach Corp., 235
Crystal, Graef S., 112
Culture: shareholder value, 7, 71–75; management ideology, 8, 223–227; revitalization, 9; organizational, 89–90; contingent compensation, 116–119; ownership, 119–121
Cumulative voting, 44–46, 49–50, 202, 231
Cyert, Richard M., 7

Damanpour, Fariborz, 53
Dann, D. L., 231
Dart Group Corp., 167
Dauber, Kenneth, 6
Davidson, Wallace N., III, 229
Davis, E., 44
Davis, Gerald F., 26, 51, 54, 185, 204, 235
Davis, L. J., 131–132
Dayton Hudson Corp., 30, 167–168, 170
DeAngelo, Harry, 231
Decentralization, 75, 89, 119, 211, 220, 223–224, 243–244; authority, 57–62; acquisitions, 63–64; incomplete, 65–70; backfires, 70–71, 99–101; compensation, 105, 120; internal ownership, 221–223, 244
Defeo, Victor J., 228
Delaware antitakeover law, 27, 44
Democratic candidates, 177, 182
Den of Thieves, 131
Dertouzos, Michael, 212
Desai, Arnand, 229
Devolution. See Decentralization
Dickie, Robert D., 130
Digital Equipment Corp., 30
DiMaggio, Paul, 233, 234, 238
Directors: election, 27, 42–43, 196–200,

202–203; stock ownership, 44, 46, 147; outside, 52, 182–189, 197, 203–206, 228; power, 58, 191–195, 196–197, 214–215; state antitakeover laws, 172–173, 175, 179; networks, 181–189; classwide political action, 182–189; shareholders, 191–192; compensation, 201, 206–208; term limitations, 203; stock price reactions, 231
Disclosure Inc., 257
Diversification, 24
Diversity, 121–124
Dobrzynski, Judith H., 208
Doeringer, Peter B., 3, 249
Domhoff, G. William, 196
Donaldson, Gordon, 5, 94
Downer, Joseph P., 198
Dow Jones & Co., 186
Dow Jones Industrial Average, 228
Downsizing, 1–3, 21–22, 27, 68, 192, 239–240; central management, 57, 79–85; political giving, 164; nonprofit organizations, 211; stock price reactions, 229
Drexel Burnham Lambert Inc., 23
Drucker, Peter F., 6
Dual capitalization, 49–50
Du Pont and Co., 5, 16–17, 32, 256
Duracell Inc., 35, 119

Easterwood, John C., 13, 52
Education, 20, 212–213
Ehrenberg, Ronald G., 107, 127, 224
Eisenhardt, Kathleen M., 88, 196
Eisenstat, Russell A., 9
Electrical-products company, 4–5, 11, 33, 37, 250; shareholder value, 11, 74–75, 76–78; shareholding, 32–33, 38, 258; acquisitions, 63–64; strategic planning, 63–64, 219; measuring decisions and results, 76–78; contraction of central management, 82–87; managing managers, 95–97; compensation measurement problems, 113–114; ownership, 119–121; decentralization, 120, 221–222; managerial careers, 126; investor relations, 132; board directors, 205–206, 207–208, 209; preemptive change, 219–220; internal ownership, 221–223; ideology, 225–227
Electronic Data Systems, 78
Employee assistance plan (EAP), 124–125
Employee Retirement Income Security Act, 10

Employee stock ownership plan (ESOP), 159, 232
Etzioni, Amitai, 34
Exxon, 2, 32, 206

Fair price, 48, 50, 173, 175
Faludi, Susan C., 3
Fama, Eugene, 20, 88
Family capitalism, 235–236, 237
Faulk & Co., 204
Fidelity Investments, 178
Financial-services company, 4–5; knowledge of management and positions, 91–93; managerial misappointment, 98–99; investor relations, 132, 133; shareholder communications, 135, 140; shareholder retention, 138–139
Fiorito, J., 89
First Call Corporate Release, 41
First Interstate Bancorp, 198
First Wachovia Co., 184
Fligstein, Neil, 6, 19, 227, 233
Florida Board of Administration, 259
Florida State Teachers' Retirement System, 256
Flournoy, Houston I., 198
Fluor Corp., 186
Flynn, Patricia, 249
FMC Corp., 186
Ford Motor Co., 32, 113, 213, 256
Fort Howard Paper Co., 186
Fortsmann Little, 39
Fortune 500, 2, 4, 25–26, 49, 50, 83, 189, 235
Foulkes, Fred, 107, 112
Foundations, 28–29
Founders, 18, 243
Freeman, R. Edward, 11
Freeze out, 172–173, 175, 179
French, Kenneth, 28
Friedland, Roger, 233, 237
Friedman, Milton, 251
Friedman, Stewart D., 230
Fuhrman, Robert A., 198
Futatsugi, Yusako, 182

Galaskiewicz, Joseph, 160, 167, 181, 182
Galbraith, Craig S., 115
Garet, Michael S., 8
Garrison, Sharon H., 3
Gartrell, Kenneth D., 24

Gaughan, Patrick A., 29, 257
Geeraerts, Guy, 59
General Electric Co., 30, 32, 184, 206, 256
General Motors Corp. (GM): organizational change, 5, 17, 38, 52, 220; institutional shareholding, 32, 38; classes of stock, 78; executive compensation, 113; board of directors, 203, 228, 234; employee pension fund, 256
Georgeson & Co., 46–47, 53
Gerlach, Michael L., 182
Gerstner, Louis V., 194
Gibbons, James F., 198
Gibbons, Robert, 107
Gilberts, 44, 147
Gilson, Ronald J., 201
Ginsburg, Douglas H., 171
Glasberg, Davita Silfen, 12
Golbe, Devra L., 23–24
Golden, Brian R., 240
Golden parachutes, 44, 48, 54–55, 147, 198, 204
Goodman, Robert S., 231
Gorbachev, Mikhail, 223
Gordon, Robert Aaron, 20
Gordon, Robert J., 252
Governance, corporate, 43–48, 48–51, 52, 191–192, 200–209, 230–231, 240–241
Grace, J. Peter, 38–39
Granovetter, Mark, 180, 235
Grant, Linda, 28
Graves, Samuel B., 53
Greenmail, 49–50, 198
Greenwich Associates, 137
Greer, C. R., 89
Grenniaus, H. John, 184
Grierson, Ronald H., 184
Grimm, W. T., & Co., 25, 255, 256
Grundfest, Joseph A., 201
GTE Corp., 32

Hall, Bronwyn H., 26
Hall, Douglas T., 249
Hambrick, Donald C., 218
Hamilton, Gary G., 9, 182
Handler, Edward, 131
Hanley, John W., 184
Hannon, John M., 229
Hanson, Dale M., 38–39
Harianto, Farid, 55, 204
Hart-Scott-Rodino Act, 42

Hay Group, 110
Hay Management Consultants, 76
Hayes, Thomas C., 27
Helms, Jesse, 2, 166
Helyar, John, 35
Henderson, Rebecca M., 232
Henriques, Diana B., 178
Herman, Edward S., 19, 34, 236
Hewitt Associates, 76, 102–103, 109–110
Hicks, Jonathan P., 132, 147
Hill, Charles W. L., 53, 240
Himmelstein, Jerome L., 21, 129, 190
Hoag, Susan E., 3, 49
Hodges, Cheryl D., 203
Horrigan, Edward A., Jr., 184
Horton, Jack K., 198
Hoskisson, Robert E., 201
Hospital Corp. of America, 186
Howell, James Edwin, 20
Hugel, Charles E., 184
Hughes Aircraft and Delco Electronics, 78
Human-resource policies, 3, 79–85, 157,
    239–240; tracking managers and positions,
    90–94; selecting managers, 94–98; com-
    pensation, 101–111, 116–119; managerial
    careers, 124–126; education and training,
    212–213; stock price reactions, 229–230;
    technologies, 232
Hyman, Jeffrey S., 101

Icahn, Carl, 21, 132, 147, 154
Imitation, organizational, 233, 238
Indiana, 171
Information, 93, 100, 232, 233; shareholder
    value, 57, 71–75; managers and positions,
    90–94, 169; shareholder communications,
    133–136; boards of directors, 201, 208–
    210
Ingrassia, Paul, 228, 234
In Search of Excellence, 6
Institutional capitalism, 56, 235–236
Institutional Investor, 200, 256
Institutional investors, 53, 202, 238; influ-
    ence on companies, 22, 33–34, 51–55, 57,
    241–243; shareholding, 28–33, 138–139,
    257, 258; collective action, 38–43, 53–55,
    200, 224; recruitment, 136, 138–140; edu-
    cating, 144–146; state antitakeover laws,
    170–171; boards of directors, 193–194,
    204; director nominations, 200
Institutional Shareholder Partners, 40

Institutional Shareholder Services, 40, 200,
    250
Insurance companies, 28–29
Interco. Inc., 186
International Brotherhood of Electrical
    Workers, 259
International Business Machines Corp.
    (IBM), 5, 17, 32, 211–212, 220, 256
Investment trusts, 28–29
Investor capitalism, 234–238
Investor relations, 131–133, 133–136,
    138–140, 141–144, 145–146
Investor Relations Assoc., 250
Investor Responsibility Research Center
    (IRRC), 40–41, 44–46, 147, 178, 250, 259
Investors. See Institutional investors
Isomorphism, organizational, 238
ITT Corp., 2, 111, 195, 204

Jackall, Robert, 90
Jackson, D. L., 89
Jacobs, David, 36
Jacobs, Michael T., 141
Jahera, John S., Jr., 240
Japanese firms, 9, 182
Jarrell, Gregg A., 53, 229, 231
Jennings, P. Deveraux, 233, 237
Jensen, Michael C., 20, 34, 54, 88, 229, 231,
    234
Johnson, Elmer W., 201
Johnson, F. Ross, 184
Johnson, Roy B., 204
Johnson and Johnson, 30, 32, 124
Johnston, James W., 184
Joint ventures, 230
Jones, Thomas B., 204
Jordon, Vernon, 183, 184
Junk (high-yield) bonds, 22–23, 25, 148

Kahn, Lawrence M., 114
Kanter, Rosabeth Moss, 6, 114, 121, 223
Kaplan, Steven N., 25
Keefe, Jeffrey H., 249
Kennedy, Robert G., 167
Kentucky, 171
Kerr, Jeffrey, 106
Kerr, Steven, 111
Kesner, Idalene F., 204
Kidder, Robert, 35, 119
Kim, E. Han, 229
Kimberly, John R., 6

Kitchen, Lawrence O., 198
Kleiner, Morris M., 229
Knoke, David, 182
Kochan, Thomas A., 232
Koh, Jeongsuk, 230
Kohlberg Kravis Roberts & Co. (KKR), 26, 34–35, 39, 42, 119–120, 183–184, 207, 222
Koller, Tim, 76
Korean firms, 9
Korn/Ferry International, 189, 207
Kotter, John P., 94
Kotz, David M., 12, 19
Kraakman, Reinier, 201
Krafcik, John, 232
Kraft Inc., 119, 120
Krasnow, Lauren G., 44, 46
Kravis, Henry, 35
Kreiner, Peter, 11, 241
Kreps, Juanita M., 184
Kroger Co., 186

Large-block trading, 30–31
Larner, Robert J., 19
Laumann, Edward O., 182
Law of inverse uncertainty, 113–115
Lease, Ronald C., 54, 148
Leonard, Jonathan S., 127
Lester, Richard K., 212
Leveraged buy-ins, 207, 222
Leveraged buyouts (LBOs), 21–22, 157, 162, 186, 207; trends, 24–26, 256; ownership, 34–35; institutional investors, 42; political action, 162, 183, 187–188; boards of directors, 183–187
Levin, Doron P., 113, 228
Levine, David L., 223
Levine, David O., 20
Lichtenberg, Frank R., 164
Lieberson, Stanley, 217
Lincoln, James R., 182
Lindberg, Leon N., 6
Lipset, Seymour Martin, 158
Lipton, Michael, 170
Live for Life program, 124
Lobbying, 21, 129–131, 158
Lobbying the corporation, 131
Lockheed Corp., 26–27, 40, 44, 46, 197–200, 210
Lohr, Steve, 228
Long, Gerald H., 184

Long, William F., 157
Lorsch, Jay W., 5, 58, 94, 189, 191
Louisiana-Pacific Corp., 186
Lowenstein, Louis, 3, 32
Lubatkin, Michael H., 230

MacDuffie, John Paul, 232
Machold, Roland M., 178
Macke, Kenneth A., 167–168
Macomber, John D., 184
Mahon, John F., 130
Mahoney, Thomas A., 217
Mahoney, William F., 52, 131, 132, 155
Malatesta, Paul H., 231
Management: revolution, 1, 19–20, 34, 237, 243; professional, 19–20, 21, 34, 58; ownership, 20, 24, 34–35, 119–121; turnover, 34–35, 140, 228, 230; controlled firms, 58–59, 160, 236–237; knowledge, 90–94; careers, 94–98, 124–126; misappointment, 98–101; social similarity, 114, 121–124; performance, 121–124; networks, 168–170, 179–180; boards of directors, 191–195; power, 194–195, 216–219; ideology, 223–227, 242; short-term gain, 227–231. See also Compensation
Managerial capitalism, 55–56, 234–238
Marafino, Vincent N., 198
March, James G., 7
Marcus, Alfred A., 231
Markoff, John, 211
Markowitz, Linda, 227
Maryland, 171
Matasar, Ann B., 162
May Dept. Stores, 44
McGraw-Hill, 2
McGregor, Douglas M., 240
McGuire, Jean B., 159
McGurn, Patrick S., 171, 172
McKibbin, Lawrence E., 20, 213
McKinsey, 76
McMurray, Scott, 17
Means, Gardiner C., 19, 34, 234, 236
Meckling, William H., 20, 88
Medlin, John, 183, 184
Men and Women of the Corporation, 121
Merck & Co., 32
Mergers and acquisitions, 22–26, 63, 255, 256; boards of directors, 49–50; shareholder value, 77–78; stock price reactions, 229

Merrill, Gregory B., 115
Merrill Lynch, 25, 255, 256
Meyer, Marshall W., 35
Milkovich, George T., 229
Mills, C. Wright, 196
Minneapolis, 160
Minnesota, 167
Minow, Nell, 200, 201
Mintz, Beth, 11, 19, 235
Mintzberg, Henry, 35, 94, 167, 196
Missouri, 171
Mizruchi, Mark S., 11, 177, 187, 235
Mobil Oil Corp., 32
Money managers, 18
Monks, Robert A. G., 200, 201
Monsanto Co., 183, 184
Motorola Inc., 213
Mulkern, John R., 131
Murphy, Kevin J., 20, 107
Murray, Edwin A., Jr., 131
Murrin, Jack, 76
Mutual funds, 28–29

Nadler, David A., 7
Napier, Nancy K., 3, 13
National Academy of Engineering, 141
National Assoc. of Manufacturers, 174, 202
National Investor Relations Inst. (NIRI), 52, 133, 135, 141, 201, 202, 204, 250
National Planning Assoc., 247
NCR, 40, 42–43, 49, 51, 184
Neff, Thomas J., 207
Netter, Jeffrey M., 53, 229
Networks: pension investing, 154; management outreach, 168–170; political action, 179–180, 182–183, 238; boards of directors, 183–187; poison pill, 235
Neustadtl, Alan, 162, 177, 181, 182, 185
New Jersey, 178
New York, 2, 172, 250
New York City Employees' Retirement System (Nycers), 28, 44, 256, 259
New York City Fire Dept. Pension Fund, 259
New York City Police Dept. Pension Fund, 259
New York State and Local Retirement Systems, 228, 256
New York State Teachers' Retirement System, 256

New York Stock Exchange (NYSE), 29–31, 52, 133, 202, 230, 257
New York Times, 199
NL Industries, 26–27, 40, 46, 131, 197–199, 210
Nonprofit organizations, 28–29, 168–170, 210–213
Northern Ireland, 41
Nynex Corp., 256

O'Barr, William M., 131, 145, 238, 251
O'Bryne, Stephen F., 111
O'Connor, James F., 217
Office design, 61–62, 70, 80, 81–82, 216
Ohio, 171
Ohio Public Employees Retirement System, 256
Olson, Craig A., 229
Opt-out of state antitakeover laws, 177–180, 199, 214
O'Reilly, Charles A., III, 48, 204
Organizational change, 5–7, 13–14, 16–17, 54, 239–240, 241–242
Organizational logics: ownership-disciplined, 6–10, 11–14, 56, 115, 214, 234–238, 243; communitarian, 9; patrilineal, 9; patrimonial, 9; bank-disciplined, 12–13; management-disciplined, 12, 115, 235–237; financial, 227; manufacturing, 227; sales and marketing, 227; family, 235; institutional, 235–236. See also Alignment
Orru, Marco, 9, 182
Oswald, Sharon L., 240
Owens, James E., 230
Owens-Illinois Inc., 186
Ownership: influence and control, 14, 19–22, 24, 51–56, 236–238; change, 22–27, 34–35; research and development, 53; charitable giving, 159–160; political action, 181, 187–188; internal, 221–223, 240, 244
Ownership-disciplined alignment. See Alignment; Organizational logics

Pacific Gas & Electric Co., 44
Pacific Lighting Corp., 198
Palmer, Donald, 58, 233, 237
Pamepinto, Sharon, 171, 172
Paradox: executive power, 217–219; preemptive executive action, 219–220; internal ownership, 221–223

Partch, M. Megan, 231
Pearce, John A., II, 240–241
Pennings, Johannes S., 235
Pennsylvania, 178
Pension fund golden rule, 150
Pension funds, 6, 10, 28–29, 38, 39, 150–151, 152–153
PepsiCo Inc., 44
Performance share grants, 112
Performance units, 112
Perrow, Charles, 88
Peters, Thomas J., 6
Pettigrew, Andrew, 6
Pfeffer, Jeffrey, 35, 196, 216–217
Phantom stock, 78, 208
Pharmaceutical company, 4–5, 37–38; shareholding in, 37–38; decentralization, 61; strategic planning, 63, 65; contraction of central management, 85; managing managers, 94–95; investor relations, 132; recruiting and retaining investors, 139–140; political action, 166–167; nonprofit trusteeships, 168–169; board of directors, 193
Philip Morris Cos., 32, 183–187
Pickens, T. Boone, 39–40, 154, 156, 171
Pierson, Frank C., 20
Pinola, J. J., 198
Planning and development, company, 62–65
Poison pill (shareholder rights plan), 27, 53–54, 199; shareholder proposals, 43–46, 147; adoption, 48–51, 130, 234–235; board negotiations, 149; preservation, 149–155; state endorsement, 173, 179; outside directors, 204; corporate governance, 214; stock price reactions, 231
Polaroid Corp., 54
Political action, 20–21, 130–131, 190
Political action committee (PAC), 131, 158, 166, 182, 185; trends in, 161–164; impact of ownership, 162–164, 180–181, 187–188; state donations, 176–177
Porter, Lyman W., 20, 213
Porter, Michael, 201
Porth, R., 147
Post, James S., 130
Poterba, James M., 28
Pound, John, 47, 54, 201
Powell, Thomas C., 7

Powell, Walter W., 233, 234, 235, 238
Powers, Melanie, 233, 237
PPG Industries, 186
Principal-agent relations, 20, 85, 88, 127–128, 156, 195–196, 224
Procter & Gamble Co., 32, 213
Protestant ethic, 221
Proxy, 27, 130; contests, 26–27, 42–43, 45–48, 54, 55, 146–148; regulations, 47–48, 202–203; resolutions, 146–148, 249; solicitor, 148, 152, 155; director elections, 196–200
Proxy Working Group, 202
Public affairs, 6, 130–131, 158–159
Public opinion, 158
Puffer, Sheila M., 140

Quinn, Robert E., 6

Raether, Paul E., 184
Rappaport, Alfred, 76, 141
Ravenscraft, David J., 157
Reagan administration, 21, 181, 190
Reed, David L., 11
Regan, Edward V., 201, 228
Regulation: federal government, 20–21, 36, 41–42, 129–131, 190, 202–203; state government, 170–180, 190
Reimann, Bernard C., 76
Reinganum, Marc R., 230, 231
Relationship manager, 138–139
Rensch, Joseph R., 198
Republican candidates, 177, 181, 182
Research and development (R&D), 53, 115, 230
Restore preemptive rights, 46
Restricted stock grants, 112, 116–117, 208
Restructuring, 1–3, 3–5, 16–17, 243; studying, 3–5, 247–254
Retail-services company, 4–5; shareholding, 37, 42, 257; shareholder value, 72–73; managing managers, 97–98; management compensation, 105–106; investor relations, 132, 136, 138; shareholder communications, 134–135
Ridgway, Rozanne E., 184
Riesman, David, 89
R. J. Reynolds Industries, 34
RJR Nabisco, 34, 183–187
Robbins, Clifton S., 184

Robinson, James D., 208, 213
Robinson, John F., 171
Rock, Milton L., 107, 112
Roe, Mark J., 201
Rogers, Ronald C., 230
Roman, Paul M., 124
Rose-Ackerman, Susan, 3
Rosenbaum, Virginia K., 49, 50
Rosenstein, Stuart, 231
Rossi, C., 147
Rossi, E., 44, 147
Rossi, N., 147
Ruback, Richard S., 229
Ruhm, Christopher, 249
Ryngaert, Michael, 231

Safeway Stores, 3, 119, 186
Sage, Andrew G. C., II, 184
St. Paul (Minn.), 160
Salancik, Gerald, 35
Schaeberle, Robert M., 184
Schedule 13(d), 42
Schedule 13(f), 36
Scherer, F. M., 236
Schneeweis, Thomas, 159
Schneider, William, 158
Schrader, Stephan, 93
Schwartz, Michael, 11, 19, 235
Scott, Denise, 162
Scott Morton, Michael S., 232, 233
Sears, Roebuck and Co., 200, 203
Securities Industry Assoc., 30, 31, 174, 256, 257
Seely, Michael, 130
Sell-side analysts, 36–37, 114, 135, 140, 141, 145
Seth, Anju, 13, 52
Seward, James K., 201
Shapiro, Eben, 51
Shareholder: pressures, 33–43, 51–55, 129–131, 141–144; proposals, 43–48, 55, 146–148, 149–155, 259; advisory committee, 44, 203; privileged position, 129–131; communications, 133–136, 138; recruitment and retention, 136, 138–140; mobilization, 146–149; power, 17–18, 195–200; director nominations, 204–206
Shareholder value, 5–8, 10–13, 27, 72, 253; defined, 10–11, 75–76, 127; managerial actions, 57, 227–231; strategic planning,

62–65; acquisitions, 63–64; organizational culture, 71–75; measuring, 75–78; management compensation, 106–116, 126–127; political action, 164–168; internal ownership, 221–223; ideology, 224–227, 231; market reactions, 228
Sharma, Varinder M., 229
Shearson Lehman, 184
Sherer, Peter D., 114
Sherman, Howard D., 201
Shiller, Robert J., 252
Shleifer, Andrei, 20
Short-term market gains, 227–231
Short-term v. long-term, 37, 241; executive compensation, 101–103, 107–110; shareholder pressures, 141–144, 145; institutional investors, 151–152; political action, 159; organizational change, 219–220
Siegel, Donald, 164
Sikora, Martin, 76
Silk, Leonard, 21, 190
Simmons, Harold, 27, 40, 46
Simon, Jane, 54
Singer, Ronald F., 13, 52
Singh, Harbir, 55, 204, 230
Skowronski, Walter E., 27
Slater, Robert, 2
Smith, Clifford W., Jr., 54, 148
Smith, Randall, 3, 228
Smith, Vicki, 3
Snell, Scott A., 53, 240
Snow, Charles C., 230
Social similarity, 114, 121–124
Solow, Robert M., 212
Sommer, A. A., Jr., 10, 38, 42
South Africa, 41
Southern California Edison Co., 198
Southland Corp., 186
Soviet Union, 223
Special-machinery company, 4–5, 250; shareholding, 36–37, 42, 257; decentralization, 59–61; strategic planning, 65; shareholder value, 73; measuring decisions and results, 78–79; contraction of central management, 80–82; management compensation, 105, 117–119; managerial performance, 123–124; investor relations, 132; management power, 218; preemptive change, 220
Spector, Adam B., 171, 172

Spector, Bert, 9
Stakeholders, 11–14, 20, 130–131, 157, 158, 241, 242
Standard and Poor's, 4, 30, 41, 184, 186, 187
Standard and Poor's 500, 32, 107, 188, 226
Stanford University, 198
State antitakeover laws, 118, 170–180, 231, 244
State of Wisconsin Investment Board, 256, 259
State Teachers Retirement System of Ohio, 256
Stearns, Linda Brewster, 11
Stein, Jeremy C., 25
Stempel, Robert, 228
Stern Stewart and Co., 76
Stewart, James B., 131
Sticht, J. Paul, 184
Stock appreciation rights, 112
Stock market reactions to company actions, 227–231
Stock options, 111–112, 116–117, 206–208
Stout, Suzanne K., 26
Strategic business units: decentralization, 58–65, 84–85, 90, 240, 244; shareholder value, 75–80; compensation, 105, 114–115, 120–121, 221–223; managerial careers, 124–126; internal ownership, 221–223
Strategic planning, 62–65, 76–77
Strikes, 229
Stuart, Scott M., 184
Sum, Andrew, 249
Sundgren, Alison, 159
Supermajority vote to approve merger, 48–50
Supermarkets General Corp., 186
Svejnar, Jan, 232
Swearingen, E., 198
Swidler, Ann, 8

Taiwanese firms, 9
Takeover, 21, 26–27, 52, 249, 256; defenses, 48–51, 54; state laws, 118, 170–180; poison pills, 149; political giving, 162–163; charitable giving, 162–163, 167; stock price reactions, 229, 231
Target 50 program, 50
Taylor, William, 240
Teachers Retirement System of Texas, 256

Technimetrics, 36
Tellep, Daniel M., 27, 210
Texaco Inc., 52
Texas, 171
Theories of the firm, 36, 129–131, 195–196, 201, 234–235, 240
Theory X–Theory Y, 240
Thomas, Alan Berkeley, 217
Thomas, Robert, 6
Thomas, Steven L., 229
Thompson, Louis M., 201, 202
Tisch, Laurence A., 2
Total quality management, 213
Tower, John, 27
Towers, Perrin, Forster and Crosby, 76
Transportation company, 4–5; decentralization, 68–69; shareholder value, 71–72; management compensation, 107–109, 116–118; managerial performance, 122–123; investor relations, 132; charitable giving, 164–166; nonprofit trusteeships, 168–169; board of directors, 193–194, 208–209
Treece, James B., 228
Trumble, Eugene F., 201
Turk, Thomas A., 201
Turner, Ted, 2
Tushman, Michael L., 7
Two-tier wage agreements, 229
Tyson, Laura D'Andrea, 223

Union Carbide Corp., 231
Union pension funds, 259
United Brotherhood of Carpenters and Joiners of America, 259
United Brotherhood of Electrical Workers, 259
United Paperworkers, 259
United Shareholders Assoc. (USA), 39–40, 44–45, 47, 145, 146, 147, 171, 174, 202, 259
U.S. Federal Election Commission, 162, 163, 188
U.S. Federal Trade Commission, 42
U.S. General Accounting Office, 239
U.S. Justice Dept., 42
U.S. Securities and Exchange Commission (SEC), 36, 41, 47, 48, 202–203, 244, 253, 257
United Way, 159–160, 163, 210–212
Universities, 168, 212–213

University of Southern California, 198
Unseen Revolution, 6
Useem, Michael, 160, 181, 182, 202, 232, 235, 240, 249
USX Corp., 132, 147

Valuation Research Corp., 76
Venkatraman, N., 230
Viacom International Inc., 186
Vickers Stock Research Corp., 32, 36
Vishny, Robert W., 20
Visible Hand, 20
Vogel, David, 21, 39, 129, 190
von der Heyden, Karl, 184
von Hippel, Eric, 93

Wade, James, 48, 204
Walkling, Ralph A., 231
Wall Street Journal, 3, 131, 229, 234
Wall Street rule, 19, 28, 38
Wal-Mart Stores, 32
Walsh, James P., 201
Ward, Matthew P., 24
Warner, Jerold B., 54, 231
Warranted market value, 76–77
Wartzman, Rich, 27, 131
Waterman, Robert H., Jr., 6
Weaver, Paul H., 158
Weber, Max, 252
Weiner, Nan, 217
Weintrop, Joseph B., 140
Welch, James O., Jr., 184
Weston, J. Fred, 3, 49
Wharton, Clifton R., 201, 208
Whipp, Richard, 6, 7

White, James A., 23–24
White, Joseph B., 228, 234
White, Lawrence J., 23–24
White knight defense, 2
Whyte, William Foote, 253
Whyte, William H., 89
Wines, Richard A., 36, 47
Winn-Dixie Stores, 186
Wohlstetter, Charles, 155–156
Wolfe, Tom, 250
Wood, Robert A., 204
Woodridge, J. Randall, 230
Working Group on Corporate Governance, 201
Worrell, Dan L., 229
W. R. Grace & Co., 38–39
Wyatt, Jeffrey G., 231
Wyman, Thomas, 2

Xerox Corp., 5, 213

Yago, Glenn, 3, 12, 23
Yankelovich Group, 160
Yantek, Thom, 24

Zahra, Shaker A., 240–241
Zald, Mayer N., 234
Zeitlin, Maurice, 236
Zhou, Xueguang, 233, 237
Ziegler, Bart, 17
Zuboff, Shoshana, 71
Zucker, Lynne C., 35
Zumwalt, Elmo R., 27
Zurich, 240